History of Persia

An Enthralling Guide to the Rise and Fall of the Persian Empire and the Life of Cyrus the Great

© Copyright 2023 - All rights reserved.

The content contained within this book may not be reproduced, duplicated, or transmitted without direct written permission from the author or the publisher.

Under no circumstances will any blame or legal responsibility be held against the publisher, or author, for any damages, reparation, or monetary loss due to the information contained within this book, either directly or indirectly.

Legal Notice:

This book is copyright protected. It is only for personal use. You cannot amend, distribute, sell, use, quote, or paraphrase any part, or the content within this book, without the consent of the author or publisher.

Disclaimer Notice:

Please note the information contained within this document is for educational and entertainment purposes only. All effort has been executed to present accurate, up-to-date, reliable, and complete information. No warranties of any kind are declared or implied. Readers acknowledge that the author is not engaging in the rendering of legal, financial, medical, or professional advice. The content within this book has been derived from various sources. Please consult a licensed professional before attempting any techniques outlined in this book.

By reading this document, the reader agrees that under no circumstances is the author responsible for any losses, direct or indirect, that are incurred as a result of the use of the information contained within this document, including, but not limited to, errors, omissions, or inaccuracies.

Free limited time bonus

Stop for a moment. We have a free bonus set up for you. The problem is this: we forget 90% of everything that we read after 7 days. Crazy fact, right? Here's the solution: we've created a printable, 1-page pdf summary for this book that you're reading now. All you have to do to get your free pdf summary is to go to the following website:

https://livetolearn.lpages.co/enthrallinghistory/

Once you do, it will be intuitive. Enjoy, and thank you!

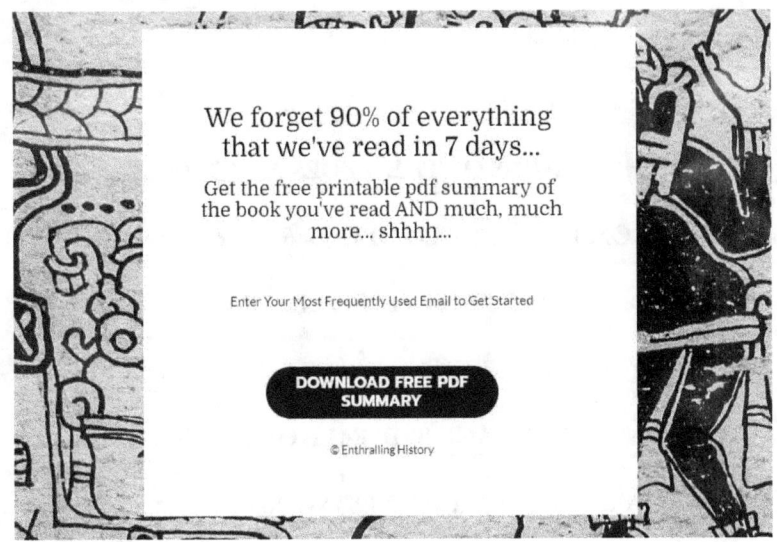

Table of Contents

PART 1: THE PERSIANS 1

    INTRODUCTION 2

    SECTION ONE: PERSIANS AND MEDES 4

    CHAPTER 1: THE ORIGINS OF THE MEDES AND THE PERSIANS 5

    CHAPTER 2: FROM DEIOCES TO ASTYAGES: THE MEDIAN EMPIRE .. 12

    SECTION TWO: THE PERSIANS – RISE AND PEAK 19

    CHAPTER 3: CYRUS THE GREAT 20

    CHAPTER 4: CAMBYSES II AND THE FALL OF EGYPT 27

    CHAPTER 5: DARIUS I: LOOKING WESTWARD 35

    CHAPTER 6: XERXES I: THE PERSIAN EMPIRE AT ITS PEAK 43

    CHAPTER 7: ARTAXERXES I AND THE EGYPTIAN REVOLT 50

    CHAPTER 8: DARIUS II AND THE PERSIAN INVOLVEMENT IN THE PELOPONNESIAN WAR 57

    SECTION THREE: THE PERSIANS – THE ROAD TO COLLAPSE 65

CHAPTER 9: ARTAXERXES II: A TROUBLED PERIOD 66

CHAPTER 10: ARTAXERXES III: THE INSTABILITY CONTINUES 74

CHAPTER 11: ARSES AND DARIUS III: THE LAST KINGS AND
THE DISSOLUTION OF THE EMPIRE 80

SECTION FOUR: ARTS, RELIGION, AND CULTURE 88

CHAPTER 12: ARTS AND ARCHITECTURE 89

CHAPTER 13: RELIGION 98

CHAPTER 14: MILITARY 106

CHAPTER 15: LANGUAGES AND THE TRUTH ISSUE 113

CHAPTER 16: GOVERNMENT OF THE EMPIRE 120

CONCLUSION 126

PART 2: CYRUS THE GREAT 129

INTRODUCTION 130

CHAPTER 1: THE PERSIANS BEFORE CYRUS 133

CHAPTER 2: CYRUS'S EARLY LIFE AND MYTHOLOGICAL
REFERENCES 144

CHAPTER 3: TAKING OVER THE MEDIAN EMPIRE 150

CHAPTER 4: THE CONQUEST OF THE LYDIAN EMPIRE 158

CHAPTER 5: THE FALL OF BABYLON 168

CHAPTER 6: RULING THE EMPIRE 175

CHAPTER 7: RELIGIOUS TOLERANCE 188

CHAPTER 8: THE CYRUS CYLINDER 200

CHAPTER 9: DEATH AND BURIAL 206

CHAPTER 10: THE LEGACY OF CYRUS THE GREAT 212

CONCLUSION 217

HERE'S ANOTHER BOOK BY ENTHRALLING HISTORY THAT YOU MIGHT LIKE 221

FREE LIMITED TIME BONUS 222

BIBLIOGRAPHY 223

Part 1: The Persians

An Enthralling Guide to the History of Persia and the Persian Empire

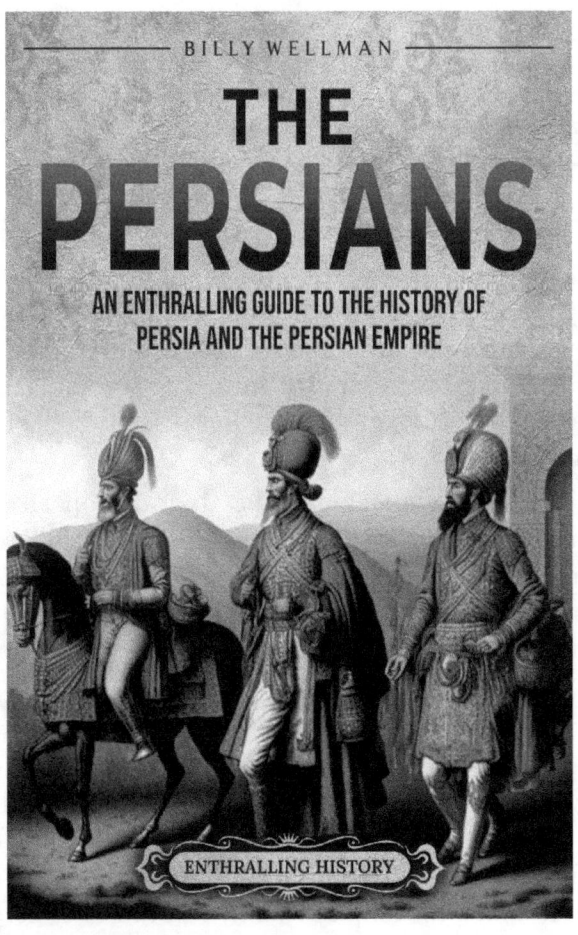

Introduction

Traditionally known as Persia, the Iranian Plateau boasts a rich and ancient history. In recorded written accounts, it goes as far back as the Assyrian Empire, which began in the late 10th century BCE. However, the history of the region goes back much further to the movements of many nomadic tribes to the Iranian Plateau that established empires in this fertile and strategic land.

The term Persia itself denotes the Indo-European peoples who migrated to the region and created their settlements under Assyrian and later Median rule. Later, this civilization would go on to establish its own dynasty. The Persian Empire refers to the kingdom that spanned over two centuries and is rightly believed to be the largest empire of ancient times.

The history of the Iranian Plateau is divided into three phases, given the extensive and rich succession of civilizations it was home to. The prehistoric period consists of the earliest evidence of civilization in the region, dating back to around 100,000 BCE. The protohistoric period, which started in the 1st millennium BCE, was next. The final period is based on the rule of the Achaemenid Empire, of which extensive written records can be found. This empire spanned from the 6th century to the 4th century BCE.

While the region was home to many different empires over the course of these three periods, the empires did not exist in isolation. In reality, these empires often coexisted and moved through the annals of history in various capacities, sometimes as the subjugated and later as the rulers. Since the region attracted the migration of many nomadic tribes, it consequently came to possess a rich and illustrious history, all of which have contributed to the culture, religion, and languages of the region today.

The recorded history of Iran begins with the Assyrian Empire, which ruled over Mesopotamia and the various ethnic groups found within it until its downfall. History then follows the rise of the Medes, a seemingly unsuspecting nomadic tribe that migrated to Iran and lived in relative peace until they one day rose to rule vast lands. The Median Empire saw a meteoric rise but also fell quickly to make way for the largest empire in ancient history.

This book elaborates on the rise of the Persian Empire and how it managed to expand its domain, covering much of Asia and Africa. As notable as this accomplishment was, this book also explores the downfall of one of the greatest empires to have ever existed. This text discusses the impact of the Persian Empire on the sociocultural landscape of Persia and its continued influence today. The Persian Empire is still remembered, long after its demise, for its art, religion, military, language, and governance.

SECTION ONE: PERSIANS AND MEDES

Chapter 1: The Origins of the Medes and the Persians

The beginning of the Iron Age in Iran was marked by a significant cultural and historical change that occurred in the region, which was experienced well before anywhere else in the Near East. While this shift began around 1250 BCE, iron artifacts did not appear in the Iranian Plateau until much later, during the 9th century BCE. Since no true written records existed in the region until the advent of the Assyrian Empire, much of the historical understanding of Iran during this time comes from archaeological excavations.

One of the most notable cultural movements in Iran during this time, as indicated by indirect historical references found among neighboring ancient civilizations, was the migration of the Median and Persian ethnic groups. The Medes and the Persians became the two dominant groups in Iran by the mid-9th century. The Medes occupied more widespread areas, and their importance increased significantly.

The Rise of the Medes

The large groups of migrants moving into Iran during the 2nd millennium are believed to be the ancestors of most modern-day Iranians. While these migrants were initially believed to be Aryans, recent archaeological evidence suggests the Aryans were descended from the tribes that originally migrated to Iran from the north.

Around the 7th century BCE, the Assyrian Empire sought to conquer Iran from the east through to the west and found most of eastern Iran occupied by the Medes as far as modern-day Hamadan. In western Iran, the Medes occupied regions mixed with indigenous non-Iranian people. The Medes had already infiltrated much of the eastern Zagros region and were steadily pushing into the west, reaching the borders of Mesopotamia in some spots.

The movement of the Medes and other Iranian peoples can be traced from the east to the west by the passage provided by the natural mountain topography of the region. The locals resisted the infiltration from this new and growing power and were often assisted by the Assyrians, the Elamites, and the Urartians from northwestern Iran. These powers were only too happy to help contain a growing threat and to further their own interests.

Origin of the Medes

Limited written and archaeological evidence has raised some questions as to the true origin of the Medes. They were an Indo-Aryan people who began moving in from the western end of the Iranian Plateau. One of their earliest mentions was among the Assyrian records in Mesopotamia. The Medes were subjects of the Assyrians until the Assyrian Empire was overthrown by the Medes in the 7th century BCE.

Media is often believed to be the first Iranian kingdom, which eventually took over the various tribes that populated the region, unifying them under a single banner. Much of this perception of the Medes' success came from their geographical position since they were located close to Mesopotamia. They were mentioned in the written records of the Mesopotamians, while other previous kingdoms were not. This suggests that the Medes may not have been the first Iranian kingdom but simply the first one that made it into the chronicles of neighboring empires.

Mythology

One version of where the name Media originates from states it came from the name of the sorceress Medea in Greek mythology. She is the daughter of King Aeëtes of Colchis and the granddaughter of the sun god, Helios. Medea is gifted with prophetic sight and agrees to help Jason, the leader of the Argonauts, to steal the Golden Fleece from her father. In exchange, he has to take Medea with him.

While Medea goes on to marry Jason, she later kills her two sons in a fit of rage to punish Jason when she finds him with another woman. She then escapes to Athens to start a new life. She later leaves Greece after failing to establish her son as king of Athens. The Medes are said to have taken their name from Medea since they deposed the Assyrians, just as

Medea deposed the king of Corinth, father to Jason's new bride.

The Persians

The Persians, along with the Medes, had migrated to Persis or modern-day Fars by the 10th century BCE. The Persian dynasty traced its ancestry back to Achaemenes, though there is no historical record of the existence of such a person. The earliest noted reference to the Persians appears in Assyrian records, where they denote a people living in the Sumerian region.

The Persians were composed of five major tribes, the most important one being Pasargadae, of which the Achaemenids were a clan. Following their entry into Iran, the Persians had, by the 1st millennium BCE, established themselves in southwestern Iran. The Persians were conquered by the Assyrians and later the Medes, who overthrew the former to establish their own kingdom. But under the rule of Cyrus the Great, the Persians revolted, overthrowing the Medes to establish the Achaemenid Empire.

Origin of the Persians

Many believe the Persians were horse-riding nomads who peacefully settled in Parsa for some five hundred years. Yet there is little record of how they ended up on the Iranian Plateau. Regardless, by the 7th century BCE, they had taken over Anshan, an Elamite territory, to establish their rule. Their leaders came to be known as kings of Anshan, although they remained subjects to the Assyrians and later the Medes.

The Persians played a role in the final downfall of Assyria. After the overthrow of the Neo-Assyrian Empire in the late 7th century BCE, the Median Empire was concentrated around Media, a region of political power and cultural influence. The Persians remained under the authority of the Medes until their revolt in 552 BCE. After that, the Persians extended their kingdom over the remainder of the Iranian Plateau, also assimilating the indigenous, non-Iranian peoples: the Elamites and the Mannaeans.

Basis in Mythology

The name Persia is believed to originate from Greek mythology with Perseus, the founder of the Perseid dynasty. Mythology paints him as the hero who slew the Gorgon Medusa and founded the city of Mycenae. He is believed to be one of the greatest Greek heroes.

Perseus was a demigod born to Zeus, the god of thunder. He went on to marry Andromeda, daughter of Cepheus and Cassiopeia, rulers of the mythical Aethiopia. Their descendants went on to rule Mycenae, the most powerful city of the Peloponnese. The Persians were believed to be familiar with the story since one of the Achaemenid kings, Xerxes I, tried to leverage it to turn Argos against Greece to aid in the Persian invasion of the region.

The Elamites and the Assyrians: Precursors to the Persians

Before the Medes and the Persians, Iran had played host to two other major dynasties that shaped its history and culture. First came the Elamites, a civilization that spanned thousands of years, from about the 3rd millennium to around the 6th century BCE. As the Elamite civilization began to decline, the Assyrian Empire began to grow, taking power around the 10th century BCE.

The Elamite Civilization

The Elamite civilization occupied the regions of the modern-day Iranian provinces of Ilam and Khuzestan. While the Elamites referred to their land as Haltami, the region is referenced several times in the Bible, referring to both a land and Noah's grandson. There is much debate as to the origin of the Elamites, though most historians believe they were indigenous to the Iranian Plateau.

Not much is known about the civilization since their language does not compare to any others around that time and is yet to be deciphered. Most of the references to the region are found in Akkadian, Assyrian, and Sumerian texts. At times, these texts contradict archaeological evidence, limiting the understanding of the true extent of the Elamite civilization.

Rather than a united region, the Elam civilization was composed of people spread out over a specific region and ruled under the separate leadership of various cities. These included Anshan, Awan, Susa, and Shimashki. Historians divide the civilization into four distinct periods:

- Proto-Elamite Period
- Old Elamite Period
- Middle Elamite Period
- Neo-Elamite Period

Artifacts and archaeological evidence suggest the Elamites had developed expansive trade relations with the subcontinent of India and also traded with Mesopotamia and regions to the east. The Elamite Empire was established by Shutruk-Nakhunte and took shape during the Middle Elamite period. The empire spanned over western Iran and much of Mesopotamia.

The downfall of the Elamites came after their alliance with the Medes in the takeover of the Neo-Assyrian Empire, which helped establish the Median Empire. The Elamite civilization did not disappear entirely until the Sasanian Empire rose up in the 3rd century CE. Until then, the Elamites continued to exist under various empires, although they were no longer rulers themselves.

The Assyrian Civilization

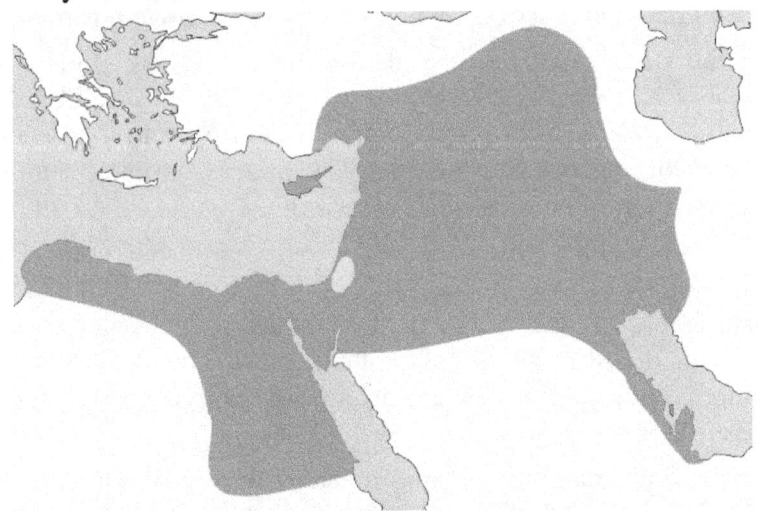

Neo-Assyrian Empire.
Puffoco, CC BY-SA 4.0 <https://creativecommons.org/licenses/by-sa/4.0>, via Wikimedia Commons; https://commons.wikimedia.org/wiki/File:Neo_Assyrian_Empire_671_B.C.gif

The Assyrian Empire occupied regions of modern-day northern Iraq, Asia Minor (modern-day southeastern Turkey), and parts of Egypt between the 10th and the 7th century BCE. The civilization was birthed in the Babylonian city of Ashur, where merchants became wealthy and influential through trade in the Anatolian Peninsula. The name is thought to originally derive from the Mesopotamian god of the same name.

Given the influence of the first ancient kingdom of Mesopotamia, the Assyrians spoke and maintained written records in Akkadian until they adopted Aramaic, which originated in Syria. Being one of the greatest Mesopotamian civilizations, the Assyrian Empire is marked by great economic and military growth. The Assyrian rule is divided by historians

into three periods:
- The Old Kingdom
- The Middle Empire
- The Late Empire or the Neo-Assyrian Empire

The Old Kingdom began with the city of Ashur, which had existed since the 3rd millennium BCE and was occupied by nomadic people. The date of the city's official formation is associated with the building of the temple of Ashur by Erishum I around 1900 BCE. It was an important commercial center, especially the port of Kanesh, which proved to be highly lucrative for the city. The port was home to much commercial activity, with merchants setting up and managing extensive businesses.

With the wealth earned through this trade and the trade relations established with Anatolia, Assyria was able to gain power and influence. Trade with Anatolia introduced the Assyrians to iron, and they went on to perfect ironworking, forging weapons like swords, javelins, and spears, which helped them achieve military superiority.

During the Middle Empire, Assyria temporarily fell under Mitanni rule. The Mitannis rose up around the 15th century BCE. After the Mitanni kingdom was taken over by the Hittites, the Assyrian king, Eriba-Adad I, gained influence in the Hittite court. The Assyrians saw an opportunity. They began planning to spread their kingdom outside of Ashur to areas previously occupied by the Mitanni.

Assyrian King Adad-nirari I, who defeated the vassal King Shattuara I of Mitanni and expanded Assyrian control, instated a deportation policy to prevent future uprisings. It was carefully devised to prevent inhumane treatment but was intended to drive the local population out of the region to be replaced with Assyrians. Deportees were carefully matched to a specific region based on their skills and where they would be most useful. Families were never separated.

This kind of leniency did not last in the Neo-Assyrian Empire. The empire underwent ruthless expansion. While the Assyrians used decisive military tactics, most notably siege warfare, they did not mistreat their prisoners. All were treated as citizens, regardless of if they were born Assyrian or acquired through conquest.

The Medes and the Persians

The Persians ultimately established their empire and developed one of the most influential and successful dynasties in the Middle East. The

Persian takeover of the Medes united the people of Iran under one rule. Before this, the Persians had existed in disparate groups, hailing from different regions and past empires and leading nomadic lifestyles.

The Persians and the Medes had existed independently, though their movements in Iran overlapped for much of history. Both people groups brought their own distinct cultures, traditions, and languages to the Iranian Plateau, and both held great influence over the region. While there is a lack of written sources prior to the Achaemenid Empire, making it difficult to map the true extent of the Median Empire, the available evidence suggests both civilizations contributed to the culture and growth of the Iranian Plateau. However, the power, influence, and identity of the Medes dissolved under the unifying banner of Persia.

Chapter 2: From Deioces to Astyages: The Median Empire

Northeastern Iran, present-day Iraq, and south and eastern Anatolia fell under the rule of the Median Empire. The lack of recovered records has made it difficult to discover much about the empire, and what little is known is based on the records of neighboring dynasties, such as the Mesopotamians. The Medes were believed to speak a language that most closely resembled Old Persian. Polytheism is believed to have been practiced, although it had Zoroastrian influences.

The empire is often credited with having been created by Deioces, who was able to unite various tribes in the region in the 7th century BCE. He is also believed to have founded its capital city, Ecbatana, which became the center of the Median kingdom. However, other historians believe it was his grandson, Cyaxares, who gathered together the Median tribes and defeated the Assyrians once and for all. While the empire was eventually overthrown by the Persians, it left a lasting legacy behind, which is still the subject of study and debate.

Overview of the Median Empire

The 1st millennium BCE saw the movement of nomadic cattle herders from central Asia to the Iranian Plateau. They spoke an unspecified Aryan language and infiltrated the northern side along the Zagros, settling among the locals. The Assyrian King Shalmaneser III first mentions the existence of such people in his kingdom, although they were perceived as hostile outsiders.

In truth, the Medes existed in scattered tribes, reaching from the Zagros to the edge of Mount Damavand. Since they were perceived as the enemy, Assyrian tribal leaders launched attacks against the Medes, managing to subdue many of them. However, they could not conquer all of the Median tribes, and historians believe this series of Assyrian attacks united the different Median tribes and ultimately resulted in the fall of Assyria.

The nomadic lifestyle of the Medes, which led them to the Iranian Plateau in the first place, shifted to permanent residence for another reason. The region occupied by the Medians offered direct access to trade routes with Babylonia.

Since Media controlled the east-west route, it gained many economic benefits. The Medians made trade one of their main occupations, along with agriculture, and began to gain influence in the region. It also led to the rise of Ecbatana as an important trade center.

In terms of agriculture, the Medes found immensely fertile land in the Zagros region. Its valleys and plains were well known for producing high-quality clover. The fruitful lands could support a wide variety of cattle, sheep, goats, and horses, as well as large populations. The Medes were located in an economically strategic region, which aided their subsequent rule of northern Iran.

The Median Tribes

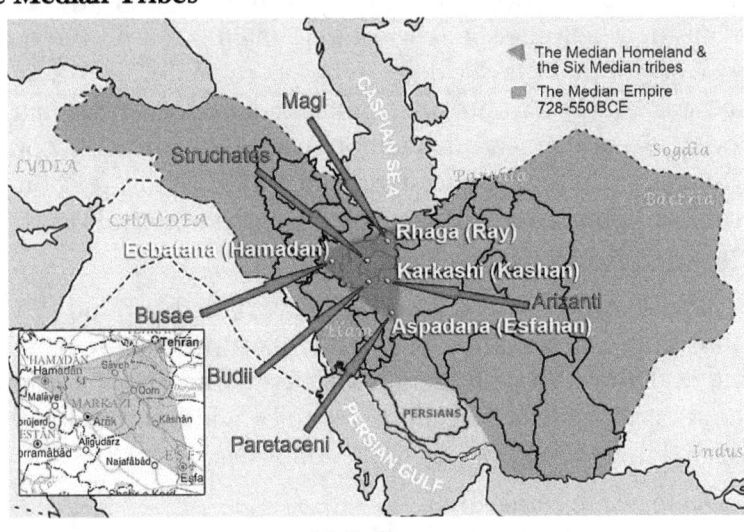

Media Proper

Key Mîrza, CC BY-SA 4.0 <https://creativecommons.org/licenses/by-sa/4.0>, via Wikimedia Commons; https://commons.wikimedia.org/wiki/File:Median_Empire_Map_2222.jpg

The Median civilization is believed to have consisted of six tribes, which were later unified as a single nation and ruled by Deioces. All six tribes resided in what was known as Media Proper, a triangular region that fell between Ecbatana, Aspadana, and Rhagae. Beyond their geographical location, little is known about the tribes besides some basic information.

The Busae tribe could be found in and near the capital of Ecbatana, close to what is today known as Hamadan. The Struchates tribe could also be found in Ecbatana. The Paretaceni tribe was found in and near Aspadana, which is today known as Isfahan.

The Arizanti tribe could be found in the province of Kashan, as well as on its outskirts. The Magi tribe resided in Rhagae, which is modern-day Tehran. Of the six tribes, only the Magi were known to be comprised of a sacred caste who looked out for the spiritual needs of the people.

The Median Language and Religion

The Medians are believed to have spoken an Old Persian language called Median. However, no written texts have been discovered in the Median language. Some later records do show examples of Median literature, as well as discoveries that some believe are written clauses on which Deioces based his rule. While the Median language itself has not been discovered, words of Median origin are found in Old Persian languages.

Regarding their religion, the Medians were paganistic. However, Zoroastrianism, a henotheistic religion (one main god with the possibility of the existence of other lesser deities), has its roots during this time. The Magi tribe was believed to provide spiritual advice to the Medians. They are believed to have practiced traditions common with the Zoroastrian religion, and as such, they are seen as being linked to this religion. By the 6th century, Zoroastrianism had begun spreading in western Iran.

The Rise and Fall of the Median Empire

The Median Empire is believed to have lasted around 130 years. During that time, four kings are believed to have ruled. However, there is conflicting evidence as to the identity of these kings and the duration of their rule. Regardless, historians have identified and estimated each of the four kings and their period of rule as the following:

- Deioces, 7th century BCE
- Phraortes, mid-7th century BCE (twenty-two years)

- Cyaxares, late 7th century BCE to early 6th century BCE (forty years)
- Astyages, early 6th century BCE to mid-6th century BCE (thirty-five years)

The Rule of Deioces

Deioces is credited with uniting the Medes, but it would be more accurate to say that the Medes united and then elected him as their leader. He was a renowned judge and regarded as just and infallible. As the Medes began to rebel against Assyrian incursions, Deioces took the opportunity to try and establish a justice system in his own village.

This undertaking soon spread to other Median villages, and he was often sought after to help resolve local issues. Overwhelmed with the fame he had accumulated as a judge and arbiter, he resigned. In response, the Medians chose to appoint him as their king, and he went on to rule for approximately fifty-three years.

Deioces appointed guards for his protection and set about constructing the Median capital, which was enclosed in seven concentric circles. Ecbatana was intended to be the uniting point for the Medes within Media Proper. Within the city, Deioces also built a fortified castle, from where he could manage the affairs of the empire. Deioces's brand of law and order involved appointing "watchers" and "listeners," which is similar to the term "the king's eyes and ears."

By establishing his own kingdom, Deioces became the first Median king to gain independence from the Assyrians. However, his activities also drew the attention of the Assyrian king, Sargon II. Deioces became a more prominent threat to Sargon when he offered his allegiance to the Urartian king, Rusa I, against the Mannaeans, who were Assyrian allies. His previous participation in an unsuccessful rebellion against the Mannaeans sealed his fate. Sargon entered Media, captured Deioces, and exiled him to modern-day Syria.

Deioces's Legacy: Phraortes

The second king of the Median Empire originally held the position of village chief of Kar Kashi. During his reign, he is believed to have continued fighting wars against the Assyrians, although he remained unsuccessful in overthrowing that empire. Phraortes developed an alliance with the Cimmerians, an eastern Iranian nomadic tribe, against the Assyrians.

During his twenty-two-year rule, Phraortes is believed to have conquered the Persians and other smaller Asian tribes of the time. However, little is actually known about his rule due to unreliable accounts and limited evidence. His subjugations came under the direction of the Assyrian Empire until he broke the temporary alliance and waged battle against them. The Assyrians took the offensive, and Phraortes was killed on the battlefield. The Assyrians then took over the lands he had conquered as part of their own empire.

The Legacy Continues: Cyaxares

Phraortes was succeeded by his son Cyaxares around 625 BCE. He allied with the Babylonians and took up the fight against the Assyrians, laying siege to their capital city, Nineveh, in Upper Mesopotamia.

The siege lasted three months before the invading army was able to break through the city's defenses. The city fell quickly, and it was burned and plundered by the Medes and the Babylonians. The Assyrian king, Sin-shar-ishkun, was killed in the battle, and Ashur-uballit II, possibly Sin-shar-ishkun's son, took the throne.

It is believed that the fall of Nineveh dealt a major blow to the Assyrian Empire. Over the following three years, the Neo-Assyrian Empire struggled but ultimately fell to the Medes and the Babylonians. In the decades to follow, the Assyrian Empire disappeared almost entirely.

Cyaxares was a successful military leader and launched campaigns against the Assyrians and Scythians. He focused on military efficiency, reorganizing the army based on the designations of bowmen, spearmen, and cavalry. He also instituted distinct uniforms.

During his forty-year rule, he subjugated the Kingdom of Mannaea, and the Urartians, the latter of which lived in what is today Armenia.

After the fall of Nineveh and Nimrud, the Medo-Babylonian alliance took over Assyrian lands, which were divided between the two to rule. The Medes took Harran, which became the Assyrian capital after the fall of Nineveh. Thus, Cyaxares was the one who ultimately defeated the Assyrians and established the Median Empire as a force to be reckoned with.

The Fall of the Scythians

The Scythians were an eastern Iranian people who migrated from central Asia to the Pontic Steppe. Their skill in mounted warfare gave them dominance over the Cimmerians in the region, allowing them to cross the Caucasus Mountains. This led to the Scythians frequently invading West Asia. After invading the Near East, they settled in the Mannaea region in northwestern Iran.

Initially, the Scythians used their martial skills to work as mercenaries, meeting much success in the Near East and Asia Minor. The Scythians also led an army against the Assyrians in Mannaea in the early 7th century BCE but were eventually defeated.

After losing Mannaea, the Scythians launched a series of attacks against the Assyrians, reaching as far as Egypt, which had been under Assyrian rule. The king of Egypt at the time, Psamtik I, bribed the invaders to retreat into Syria. At the same time, the Assyrians were facing a crisis in the form of civil wars and the Medo-Babylonian campaign.

The Assyrians forged an alliance with the Scythians, who helped them during the siege on Nineveh. This led to a battle between the Medes and the Scythians, which resulted in defeat for the Medians. This defeat led Cyaxares to seek revenge, and he invited a large number of Scythians to a banquet. There, they were inebriated and then murdered by the Medes.

The Last King of Media: Astyages

Astyages, son of Cyaxares, was the last of the Median kings. Before his death, Cyaxares had been fighting a five-year war with the Lydian Kingdom in western Anatolia. The Battle of Halys (also known as the Battle of the Eclipse) ended the war in favor of the Medes just before Astyages's succession to the throne. As a result, he inherited a vast empire, which included many Assyrian lands.

Existing accounts of Astyages's rule paint conflicting pictures, with some portraying him as cruel and others as a benevolent leader. A common belief, which many believe to be a myth, is that Cyrus the Great was the grandson of Astyages through his daughter. Astyages tried to kill Cyrus while he was still an infant based on a dream that indicated his downfall at the hands of Cyrus. However, there is no solid evidence of this ever occurring.

Astyages met his defeat at the hands of Cyrus the Great, who led a war against him around the mid-6th century BCE. The Medes fought back, ultimately leading to the siege and plunder of Ecbatana. Astyages was taken prisoner, and the fall of the empire's capital marked its end. The once-great Median Empire fell under Persian rule.

The Median Empire's Legacy

The Median Empire did not last long. Compared to the Persian Empire that followed, the Median Empire was a blip in Iranian history. However, the contributions made by the empire to the history, culture, and religion of the region cannot be underestimated. The fall of the Assyrian Empire at the hands of the Medes changed the course of Iran and paved the way for the next great empire.

The limited written evidence regarding the Median Empire makes it difficult to get a detailed idea of the events that occurred during its rule. What little is known about the empire based on recovered archaeological evidence and writing from neighboring civilizations shows that the Median monarchy experienced a successful rule. Its economy and military flourished. Just before its fall, it had amassed a large geographical area. But this region now fell under Persian rule.

SECTION TWO: THE PERSIANS – RISE AND PEAK

Chapter 3: Cyrus the Great

The Achaemenid dynasty was one of the most powerful empires in the world. The success of Cyrus II (better known as Cyrus the Great) can be seen in the Persian Empire's military and geographical expansion. The Achaemenid Empire grew to be the largest of its time, extending from Anatolia to the subcontinent of India and central Asia.

Cyrus the Great is also credited with introducing many innovative practices in his kingdom. While a popular myth believes Cyrus was descended from Astyages, as the grandson who was destined to overthrow the Median Empire, historical sources suggest he was descended from Teispes, the son of Achaemenes, who is credited as the founder of the Achaemenid clan.

The development of the Persian Empire began with the conquests of Cyrus the Great. While it continued to grow and advance after his rule, Cyrus's leadership created the foundation of the ancient world's largest empire.

The Early Life of Cyrus the Great

Cyrus the Great.
DiegoColle, CC BY-SA 4.0 <https://creativecommons.org/licenses/by-sa/4.0>, via Wikimedia Commons; https://commons.wikimedia.org/wiki/File:Cyrus_the_Great_of_Persia.jpg

Cyrus the Great was born to Cambyses I in the 6th century BCE. Before him, his father, grandfather (Cyrus I), and great-grandfather (Teispes) all held the throne in Anshan. Cyrus would later marry Cassandane, the daughter of Pharnaspes, who bore him two sons, Cambyses II and Bardiya, and three daughters, Atossa, Artystone, and Roxane. After the death of his wife, Cyrus declared public mourning, which lasted for six days.

Although many scholars believe that Cyrus was not related to Astyages, it is still a popular belief and is worth taking a look at. According to legend, Astyages had a dream about his grandson growing up to overthrow his kingdom and kill him. Fearful that this might come true, he ordered the assassination of his grandson, which ultimately failed. Instead of killing Cyrus, the infant was given to a shepherd family.

When Astyages discovered that Cyrus was still alive when the boy was ten years old, he decided against killing him. Cyrus was returned to his true family and apparently spent much time in Astyages's court. If the legend is to be believed, Astyages's dream ultimately came to be true since Cyrus grew up to overthrow the Median Empire. The truth of Cyrus's ancestry is still much debated, and it is likely that the tale of Astyages attempting to kill Cyrus in infancy is only legend.

The Rise of Cyrus II

When Cyrus became king of the Achaemenids in the mid-6th century, the throne was a vassal of the Median king, Astyages. It is unclear as to what ultimately led to the conflict between the Medians and the Persians, who still observed allegiance to the Medes. Regardless, Astyages sent an army, under the command of his general Harpagus, to attack Cyrus.

However, Harpagus held some enmity against Astyages. Instead of attacking Cyrus, he encouraged him to revolt. He defected to the Persians, bringing half the army under his command with him. The Persian revolt is believed to have lasted for around three years. It ended in the capture of the Median capital city, Ecbatana.

The Battle of Hyrba

The Battle of Hyrba was the first encounter between the Persians and the Medians. It was during this battle that Harpagus turned on Astyages. According to legend, Harpagus told Cyrus about the battle ahead of time, giving him time to prepare.

Cyrus allegedly wrote to his father, asking him to prepare the cavalry and infantry. He took these men to Hyrba, where they destroyed the Medians. Astyages realized he was no longer dealing with a revolt and sought to invade and destroy the Persians. Cyrus had proven himself and began expanding his empire.

Battle of the Persian Border

Following the Battle of Hyrba, the Persians moved to the Persian border to protect it against the Medians. Astyages marched to the border and engaged the Persians in combat.

This battle wasn't as intense or exciting as the one at Hyrba. It lasted for two days and saw Cambyses fight alongside his son. Although the Persians proved themselves, it wasn't a very convincing win. Even so, it was clear the Medians were outmatched.

It is unclear how many battles the Medians and the Persians fought, although it is believed the fighting lasted for three years. In the end, Cyrus emerged victorious when he captured the capital, Ecbatana. He also captured Astyages and brought him back to his homeland in Persia, where he remained until his death. Following this victory, Cyrus built the city of Pasargadae, which was to serve as the capital. The city consisted of several monumental buildings, two palaces, and the tombs of Cyrus and Cambyses II.

Major Conquests under Cyrus the Great

Cyrus was able to conquer two other major empires besides the Medes: the Anatolian Kingdom of Lydia and the Babylonian Empire in Mesopotamia. Under Cyrus's rule, the kingdoms of the Near East were united as a single nation, creating the largest empire of its time. His son, Cambyses II, was later able to acquire regions of northeastern Africa.

The skill and efficiency with which Cyrus expanded his kingdom speak to his capability as a ruler and military leader. He laid the foundation for an empire that lasted over two centuries.

Conquest of Lydia

Before the ascension of the Medes, Lydia had been an ally to the Assyrians. During the Median campaign against Assyria, the Medes forged an alliance with the Cimmerians. The Lydian Kingdom had suffered from constant Cimmerian invasions, so the Medes-Cimmerian alliance did not help matters, and the two nations remained at war during Median rule. When the Persians conquered the Medes, Lydians took notice of the rising power. Their king, Croesus, had doubts about Cyrus's rise to power.

Following a divine message from the Greek Oracle of Delphi, Croesus decided to lead a campaign against the Persians. He launched a surprise attack on the Persians across the Halys River in the mid-6th century, believing he was fated to destroy the rising empire. The Battle of Pteria led to an inconclusive result, with the Lydian army retreating toward their homeland.

In a strategic move, Cyrus pursued the Lydians, hoping to launch a surprise attack in their capital city of Sardis. The two armies met at Thymbrara. Although the Lydians were caught off-guard, they still heavily outnumbered the Persians. The ensuing Battle of Thymbrara marked the last confrontation between the Persians and the Lydians. Given the disadvantage of numbers, Cyrus resorted to a tactical approach. During the battle, the Persians placed their baggage camels, which were mounted by cavalrymen, at the forefront. The stench of the camels repelled the Lydians' horses, disrupting their charge.

The Persians successfully fought and laid a fourteen-day siege on Sardis, where the Lydians had retreated. The city eventually fell, and the Persians conquered Lydia, bringing its over six centuries of independence to an end.

Instead of destroying the newly conquered nation, Cyrus maintained his tolerant approach. Local cultures, laws, religions, and traditions were allowed to continue, and Croesus was admitted into Cyrus's court. Cyrus's accepting approach helped the Persian ruler attain the loyalty of the Lydian people.

The Fall of Babylon

The fall of Babylon is marked by the Battle of Opis, which took place around 539 BCE. Not much is known about the specific events of the battle, which was the final encounter between the Persians and the Babylonians. Written sources regarding this final standoff refer to Cyrus fighting the army of Akkad, which refers to the Babylonian Empire. But who the army was led by is not known and never appears to have been recorded. However, the popular belief is that the son of Babylonian King Nabonidus, Belshazzar, led the final assault against the Persians.

Little is known about the Babylonian army or its military capabilities. However, it is believed the Babylonians suffered a quick and sudden defeat. It may be that the Babylonians were unprepared for the onslaught levied by the Persians.

Babylonia was already suffering in the geopolitical sphere around the time of the Battle of Opis. It was surrounded by the Persians to the east and west and the Phoenicians to the north, making it more vulnerable to attack and at risk of being trapped. Severe social and economic problems within the Babylonian Empire had already taken root and were wreaking havoc. The region suffered plague and famine, and the unorthodox religious approach of their king had already turned the Babylonians against him. Cyrus used this unrest and turmoil in the region to his advantage. Cyrus is believed to have struck a deal with a Babylonian provincial governor to defect to the Persians, which brought the region of Gutium under Cyrus's control. Gutium was a strategically significant frontier that enabled a strong Persian offensive.

The battle led to a decisive Babylonian defeat. Following their victory, the Persians plundered and looted. Some historical sources suggest that massacres were carried out against the Babylonians; however, the basis and accuracy of such a belief are not set in stone.

Shortly thereafter, the Babylonian city of Sippar is said to have surrendered to the Persians, who marched on Babylon without further resistance. Babylonia was the last great power in West Asia not yet under Persian rule. Cyrus the Great was later declared king of Babylonia, bringing its independence to an end.

In 530 BCE, Cyrus the Great led a campaign into central Asia against the Massagetae. He was killed, although the sources differ on how. Most believe he died while fighting, although some believe he was killed by Tomyris, the queen of the Massagetae.

Regardless of how he died, Cyrus left a vast and successful empire to his son, Cambyses II, although his rule was short-lived and less successful than his father's.

The Persian Legacy: Cyrus the Great

Cyrus the Great is remembered as a leader with many achievements, the greatest of which is the empire he amassed within a span of just thirty years. He took over three great dynasties and brought them under the unified rule of the Persian Empire. During that time, he also gained a reputation as a benevolent and just ruler, examples of which are still cited today.

The Persian Empire's growth was unprecedented, bringing Persian culture into the global sphere. The rise and spread of Persian literature, philosophy, and religion were driven by the empire's growth and the geographical spread of its people. Cyrus's achievements form a very noticeable part of ancient history that continues to have a great impact on modern times.

As a ruler, Cyrus the Great was known by many titles, such as the Great, the Elder, the King of Kings, and the King of the Four Corners of the World, which all speak to his character as a ruler and conqueror. He was known for his exceptionally tolerant approach to different peoples, as he allowed the practice of local religions and cultures in any land he conquered. His system of governance was one that honored freedom, independence, and civil rights, rejecting any notion that rulers of his time needed to adopt a vicious, autocratic approach. Cyrus's military aptitude is exemplified by the size of his empire, which stretched from the Mediterranean Sea to the Indus River.

The Persian Empire went on to build the largest road network of its time. With the Royal Road, the Persians were able to establish trade connections across the Middle East. This road network, combined with the legacy of diplomacy and tolerance that Cyrus the Great left behind, marked the success of the empire.

Cyrus the Great is also referenced in the Bible. He appears as a liberator, as the Messiah who freed the Jews from Babylonian captivity.

Needless to say, Cyrus the Great's influence can be seen in his leadership style and in the success of the empire he built.

Chapter 4: Cambyses II and the Fall of Egypt

Following the death of Cyrus II in 530 BCE, his son took on the mantle of king. Cambyses II inherited what was, at the time, the largest empire to ever exist. Still, he continued in his father's footsteps and carried on campaigns to expand the empire. While many of his crusades were successful, Cambyses II did not possess his father's knack for strategy and planning, so he ended up losing some previously conquered lands.

Before his father's death, Cambyses II had already taken on many royal duties. During New Year festivals, he is known to have acted as king in his father's stead. Cambyses was largely responsible for managing Babylonian affairs and was appointed regent while Cyrus campaigned in the east. He officially served as vice-king of Babylonia until his ascension to the throne.

Cambyses II

Cambyses II.
https://commons.wikimedia.org/wiki/File:Cambyses_II_capturing_Psamtik_III.png

Cambyses II was the firstborn of Cyrus and Cassandane, making him heir to the throne. Historical reports suggest Cambyses had a younger brother, Bardiya (also known as Smerdis), with whom he had a rivalry when Cambyses became king. This same rivalry reportedly led to the death of the second king of the Achaemenid dynasty.

After the conquest of Babylon, Cambyses was appointed the crown prince of the region and later acted became vice-king. The Cyrus Cylinder, which is an important piece of evidence that talks about aspects of Cyrus's rule, also mentions Cambyses as being blessed by Marduk, the Babylonian patron god. Due to Cambyses's early involvement with Babylonian affairs, he was often referred to as the king of Babylonia long before he actually held the title.

Historical records differ on the subject of Cambyses's marriage. Some suggest he married Phaedymia, daughter of Otanes, the latter of whom is believed to be the brother of Cassandane. Other sources suggest that he may have married his two blood sisters, Atossa and Roxane. Such types of incestuous relationships were an accepted part of Zoroastrianism, so this possibly could have occurred. However, there is no definitive proof to suggest such a marriage ever existed.

Some reports also exist of Cambyses II being a "mad king." These mostly come from the accounts of Herodotus, a Greek historian who recorded the Greco-Persian Wars in great detail. While Herodotus offered many examples he believed indicated Cambyses's madness—such as his alleged marriage to his sisters—there is little other evidence supporting this. Such views are believed to be the product of oral tradition passed on among the Egyptians. Regardless, Cambyses is believed to have faced his fair share of problems during his rule as the king of the Achaemenid Empire.

Persia under Cambyses II

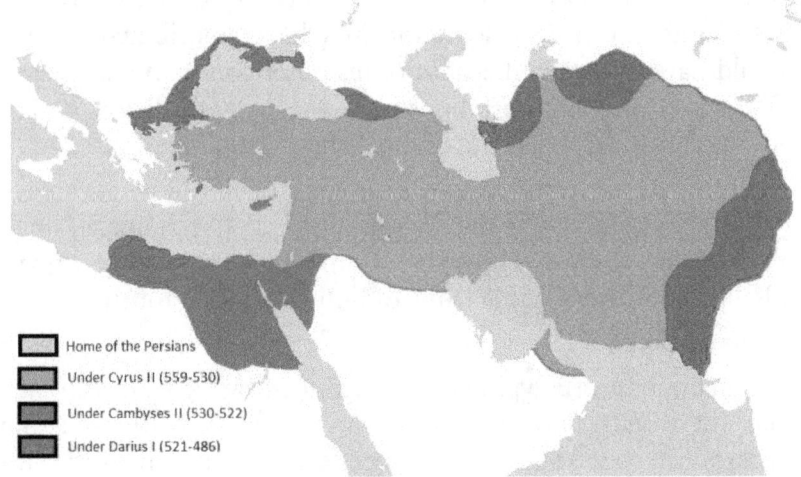

The Persian Empire.
Javierfv1212, CC BY-SA 3.0 <https://creativecommons.org/licenses/by-sa/3.0>, via Wikimedia Commons; https://commons.wikimedia.org/wiki/File:Achaemenid_empire_map_expansion.png

Since Cyrus had already appointed his eldest son as regent before his death, Cambyses was able to take the Persian throne without trouble. More specifically, Cambyses was given the title of king of Babylon and king of the lands, and he carried out these duties on behalf of his father until Cyrus's death. There is little to report of the early years of Cambyses's rule, as they remained rather uneventful. A short two-year famine in Babylon in that period did raise some concerns. Many believed that it was an indication of the god's disapproval of the new king.

The first event of notice that Cambyses was a part of as regent king was his inauguration as the king of Babylonia during the New Year ceremony. This celebration signified the divine approval for the new king and was an important tradition in Babylonian culture. Since Cyrus had created a reputation of religious tolerance and acceptance within his empire,

Cambyses's participation was crucial. However, little is known about the exact details of the rituals and customs involved in the ceremony.

What little is known is based largely on Herodotus's account and indicates the people's disapproval of the new king. Cambyses apparently showed up for the ceremony in the wrong clothing and was surrounded by armed guards. Babylonian tradition forbade the presence of arms during the procession and is believed to have earned him the displeasure of the priests present at the ceremony.

Cambyses eventually stepped away from his ruling duties in Babylonia. It is unclear what the reasons for the resignation were, but many believe the events of the New Year celebration may have contributed, at least in part. It could have happened because of his other commitments as king of Persia. Whatever the reason, this move led to speculation regarding Cambyses's ability to serve as king of the Achaemenid Empire.

Whether he was successful as king or not is a matter of perspective. His most notable achievement was the conquest of Egypt, a campaign that had been planned by Cyrus. However, Cambyses's rule over Egypt is surrounded by controversy and claims of him being unfit for the role.

Conquest of Egypt

Since the conquest of Egypt had been planned by Cyrus the Great, it is likely that he would have ventured into Africa following his failed campaign against the Massagetae. Since Cyrus died in battle there, Cambyses took on what would be the most important and significant conquest of his reign. Egypt was conquered in 525 BCE, five years after Cambyses became king.

The attack on Egypt was not a surprise, and the Egyptians were prepared to meet the Persian army. The Egyptians had forged an alliance with the Samians from the Greek island of Samos, who were able to provide naval support. This would have helped launch an attack along the route they were to take to reach Egypt. They also enlisted the help of mercenaries from Greece and Caria.

The Case of Egypt

The defeat of Egypt at the hands of the Persians came as a result of a strategic and effective move by Cambyses II. A particularly revered aspect of ancient Egyptian culture was the worship of cats. They were associated with the goddess Bastet, who often appears in Egyptian art as a woman who possesses the head of a cat.

Bastet was worshiped as the goddess of domesticity, childbirth, fertility, and cats. She acted as protection for households from diseases and evil spirits, particularly those that might affect the children and women of the house. As a venerated goddess, offending her would result in severe punishment.

Harming cats was one of the ways the goddess Bastet could be offended. Cats were sacred to the ancient Egyptians, so hurting one was a punishable offense. Killing a cat would result in a death sentence for the offender. And Egypt's defeat by the Persians came about because of their high regard for cats. Cambyses II knew the role cats played in their culture and used it to his advantage to conquer Egypt.

The Battle of Pelusium

Historical accounts of what transpired before the conquest of Egypt suggest that Pharoah Amasis II of Egypt offended Cambyses II, which led to the war. However, it is believed Cambyses had already been preparing for a campaign since it was something his father had planned to do before he passed. The Persian king had reportedly asked for Amasis's daughter's hand in marriage. Rather than refusing, Amasis reportedly sent his predecessor's daughter to Persia. Nitetis, the daughter who was sent, was also offended since it was against Egyptian custom to give away women to foreign rulers. She was adorned in clothes and gold and presented to Cambyses as Amasis's daughter.

When Cambyses discovered the deception, he accused Amasis of sending him the wrong wife and sought to get retribution for the insult. Preparations were made to launch a Persian assault. However, while many sources do suggest that Amasis had done something to earn the Persian king's wrath, they do not all support the story of a fake wife.

Whatever the reason may have been, it seems an attack on Egypt by Persia was inevitable. The Persian Empire had undergone rapid growth under Cyrus's leadership, and Cyrus was eyeing the region before his death. The Assyrian conquest of Egypt also left the impression of Egypt being a land that could be easily acquired. Egypt had been ill-equipped to take a stand against the Assyrian assault, so it did not seem likely that it could do any better against Persia's superior forces.

When the two armies met at Pelusium, the Egyptians were able to withstand the attack. Their help from Greece was undoubtedly of great assistance since the allied force was able to prevent the Persians from advancing farther. But Cambyses used his knowledge of the Egyptian religion to secure his victory. He ordered the image of Bastet to be painted on his soldiers' shields and had cats, dogs, sheep, and other animals sacred to the Egyptians lead the army into battle.

This move compelled the Egyptians to lay down their arms since they did not wish to shoot at either the image of their goddess or risk harming the animals. Those who did not surrender fled to seek refuge in Memphis. The Persians killed many on the battlefield of Pelusium that day and chased the others, with Memphis falling after a relatively short siege. Thus, Egypt came under Persian rule. Psamtik III, the son of the pharaoh, had led the charge. He was taken prisoner but was reportedly treated well until he attempted to revolt against the Persians.

The Conquest of Libya

The Persian conquest of Libya was more a matter of alliance. The king of Cyrene, a city in eastern Libya, likely did not want to go to war with a force like the Persian army, and he forged an alliance with the Persians following their conquest of Egypt. When the king was killed during unrest in the region, the Cyrene queen, Pheretima, extended an invitation to the Persians to enter the region, intending to avoid further fighting and hostilities. The Persian expedition into Libya ran for close to a year, resulting in the conquest of Libya.

The Persians were able to infiltrate as far west as modern-day Benghazi. A king loyal to the Persians was installed, and Cyrenaica became a Libyan region under Persian control. It remained so until the Egyptian rebellion and the defeat of the Achaemenid dynasty by Alexander the Great.

The Libyans of Cyrene and Barca in northeastern Libya did not resist Persian entry; in fact, they willingly accepted Cambyses's authority. They also sent him offerings as a show of submission and acceptance of his rule. To return the favor, Cambyses sent the widow of the Egyptian pharaoh back to Cyrene.

According to other historical accounts, Cambyses was unsuccessful in his campaigns in Ammon, east of the Jordan River, and Ethiopia. Some sources suggest the reason for the loss was Cambyses's failure to lead his men. According to Herodotus's accounts, Cambyses ordered his men to march to Ethiopia without sufficient provisions. However, this account is not supported by any other evidence, and it appears more likely that the challenges of the campaign, including the long distance, may have caused Cambyses to withdraw.

The Lost Army

The legend of the Lost Army is one of the great enigmas surrounding Cambyses II. Historical accounts narrate an army of some fifty thousand men who marched to Ammon to attack the oracle who would not legitimize Cambyses's rule of Egypt. This army is last reported to have reached the "Island of the Blessed," though it is not known where this was located. The next report is of a sandstorm that blew over the troops, burying them forever. That was the last this army was seen or heard from.

Since then, many historians and explorers have attempted to recover archaeological evidence proving the existence and the subsequent loss of this army. No definitive proof has been found, although the discovery of human bones in 2009 in the Sahara Desert raised speculation that they may belong to the lost army of Cambyses.

The Madness of Cambyses

While the conquest of Egypt was considered Cambyses's greatest achievement, some historical sources cite him as an unfit ruler. His actions as pharaoh mark him as unstable. The historian Herodotus said he was mad. Whether such accounts are true cannot be said for certain, but they certainly paint a picture of Cambyses II as a man who did not deserve the responsibilities and duties of a kingdom as vast as the Persian Empire.

There are many faults attributed to Cambyses during his reign as pharaoh of Egypt. While he kept with tradition and took on the titles of "King of Upper and Lower Egypt" and "descendant of Ra, Horus, and Osiris," he is believed to have gone too far. Some sources report that he engaged in extensive propaganda to portray himself as the rightful ruler of Egypt and to show the legitimacy of his ascension to the throne. Reportedly, he attempted to portray himself as having Egyptian heritage. He had himself crowned in the temple of Neith, the goddess who created the universe, as a religious ritual and even made sacrifices to the gods.

Cambyses is reported to have engaged in numerous examples of brutality during his rule over Egypt. Some sources claim he looted temples, scorned the local religion and gods, and did not hesitate to defile royal tombs and other places of religious significance. Many of these reports come from Herodotus; there are no other sources or recovered archaeological evidence that supports these claims about the Persian king.

Cambyses was also accused of killing a bull sacred to the Egyptians, Apis. The bull was believed to be the physical manifestation of the god Ptah and was therefore revered by the Egyptians. According to Herodotus,

Cambyses ordered the killing of Apis, which directly opposed his father's approach to religious tolerance. As with the other accusations, there is no evidence to be found in other sources or reported accounts of Cambyses's rule to support this claim. The closest evidence is Cambyses's order to have an Apis buried in a sarcophagus, yet there are no reports of an order to kill one.

Finally, Cambyses was also accused of killing his brother, Bardiya. Bardiya had a claim to the throne. According to some reports, Cambyses was worried Bardiya might contest his ascension to the throne and chose to deal with this potential threat by having it eliminated. There are also many other outlandish claims, such as Cambyses assassinating the son of one of his courtiers. He may have ordered the premature burial of twelve Persian nobles and the execution of several courtiers. Such examples are used to justify the claim that Cambyses was out of his mind and unfit to serve as ruler.

The Fall and Legacy of Cambyses II

Other than his conquest of Egypt, Cambyses II could not hold any great achievements to his name. While he was initially believed to have been blessed by the gods when he became king, this notion was later questioned as his rule progressed. In many ways, he was seen as a man who failed to fill the shoes of his father.

Others hold a different view of his leadership and credit him for introducing many improvements to the Persian army. He did manage to expand the Persian Empire, most notably with the conquest of Egypt, and the Persian military came to be known as one of the best of its time.

Cambyses II likely died from a wound to the thigh that became infected. He died in Syria in 522 BCE. His rule was relatively short and did not end on the best of terms. Following his death, a rather bloody succession crisis began, which would mark the future progress and later decline of the Persian Empire.

Chapter 5: Darius I: Looking Westward

Darius I eventually succeeded Cambyses II as the new king of Persia. His initial rule was punctuated by revolts and rebellions, which were spurred by the events that led to his rule. During this time, the Persian Empire expanded to the east into the Indian subcontinent and to the west, including Thrace-Macedonia in the Balkans and the Caucasus. The empire's growth brought increased wealth and power to the Persian king. However, it also brought him greater challenges, with Darius rarely stumbling upon a moment of relief due to a seemingly unending series of wars and revolts.

Early Life

Darius I was part of the Achaemenid nobility. He was the son of Hystaspes, who was a provincial governor, or satrap, of Bactria and Persis. Although Darius played a role in the Persian Empire before his rule, he had no legitimate hereditary claim to the throne. Based on historical records, he was a spearman during the Persian conquest of Egypt, and his father had been an officer in Cyrus's army. Darius held a special role in Cambyses II's army, serving as his spear carrier, and was tied to the royal family by marriage.

Darius was married to two of Cyrus's daughters, Atossa and Artystone, with whom he had six sons. Atossa gave birth to Xerxes, who would go on to succeed Darius as the ruler of Persia. Darius was also reportedly married to Parmys, the daughter of Bardiya, who bore him one son. He is also believed to have married two other noble women, with whom he had several children.

A popular story of unverified origin states that while Cyrus was on his final campaign, he saw a dream that he believed showed Darius taking over his kingdom. He had already installed Cambyses as regent, so Cyrus suspected Darius of treason. He ordered Hystaspes to return to Persis and watch over Darius until his return. Any plans Cyrus had regarding Darius never came to light since he perished during the campaign.

Becoming King

Reported accounts from Darius I and historians narrate variations of the circumstances under which Darius came to the throne. The common thread that follows these accounts is the assassination of Bardiya, the younger son of Cyrus the Great, at the hands of his brother, Cambyses II. Reportedly, Cambyses did so to suppress any idea of a fight for the throne, which he believed he had a right to.

Bardiya's death was not well known, and a usurper by the name of Guamata was believed to have taken the throne pretending to be Bardiya. During a revolt that broke out among the Iranian people, Guamata, as Bardiya, was installed as the new king. Darius and six other nobles killed Guamata, and Darius took the throne for himself in 522 BCE.

Darius the Deceiver

The Darius Seal.
Osama Shukir Muhammed Amin FRCP(Glasg), CC BY-SA 4.0
<https://creativecommons.org/licenses/by-sa/4.0>, via Wikimedia Commons;
https://commons.wikimedia.org/wiki/File:The_Darius_seal._Darius_stands_in_a_royal_chariot_bel ow_Ahura_Mazda_and_shoots_arrows_at_a_rampant_lion._From_Thebes,_Egypt._6th-5th_century_BCE._British_Museum.jpg

Since Darius was accompanied by six nobles on his mission to depose the fake king, it is unclear how he was chosen to take the throne. Sources, which are not wholly verified, report that the seven men discussed the future of the kingdom. Some wanted to establish a democracy, while others wanted an oligarchy. Darius wished to continue the monarchy and convinced the others that a republic would lead to corruption in the region.

Reportedly, six of the seven men decided on a test that would determine who the next monarch would be, with one of the men abstaining. The test required the men to mount their horses outside the palace. The man whose horse was the first to neigh with the rising sun would become king. It is believed that Darius I did not wish to leave his rule to chance and engaged in trickery to ensure his horse would be the first to neigh.

Darius's plan was carried out by his slave, who put the scent of a mare favored by Darius's horse on his hand. As the sun rose, he allowed the horse to sniff his hand. Darius's horse caught the mare's scent and neighed. As fate would have it, lightning and thunder followed the horse's call, and the other men immediately knelt before Darius, accepting him as monarch. The thunder and lightning were largely interpreted as divine acceptance, and Darius was believed to have been chosen by the gods to rule Persia.

Other accounts suggest this report of Darius's rise to power may be false. It is believed by some to be a fabrication created by Darius to legitimize his murder of Bardiya and his own ascension to the throne. It is true that Darius attempted to gain further support for his rule by claiming to be descended from Achaemenes, the ancestor of Cyrus the Great, who is credited with founding the Achaemenid dynasty. In truth, Darius had no relation to Achaemenes and did not belong to the same family as Cyrus.

The New Monarchy Begins

The beginning of Darius's rule was not smooth. While the six noblemen may have accepted him as the king of Persia and blessed by divine will, the rest of the kingdom did not. Whether the man Darius killed was a usurper or the son of Cyrus did not matter. That man was believed to be Bardiya, so Darius, therefore, was believed to be the killer of the rightful king of Persia.

Darius found himself facing revolts across the Persian Empire that were propelled by his assassination of "Bardiya." The eastern provinces, in particular, including Media and Babylonia, saw widespread disruptions, with men claiming to be the true Bardiya and setting up independent governments. These were not coordinated uprisings; they were scattered rebellions headed by different individuals and motivated by various purposes.

The dispersed rebellions were no march for Darius's army, which suppressed and defeated at least nine rebel leaders. By 519 BCE, he had put an end to most of the uprisings. In the following year, he visited Egypt, which he had declared to be a rebel state for the insubordination of its satrap, Aryandes. The satrap was sentenced to death, and Darius was, at last, able to establish his authority as the king of the Persian Empire.

Expanding the Empire: Indus Valley Conquest

The Persian Empire's conquest of the Indus Valley began with Cyrus the Great, who invaded the regions west of the Indus River. The Achaemenid Empire was able to expand its control to regions of modern-day Pakistan, and the Indus Valley campaign continued from the 6th century to the 4th century BCE. India's trade relations with the Near East are believed to have placed it in the sights of the Achaemenid dynasty. Starting in 535 BCE, Cyrus the Great is believed to have conquered regions as far as the Indus River. Other sources suggest he may have conquered regions up to Gandhara, located in northwest Pakistan.

Persian records of the campaign show that Darius I may have crossed the Himalayas around 518 BCE and progressed as far as the Jhelum River. Persian inscriptions during Darius's reign refer to the expansion of Persian rule to a region called Hindus, which is believed to refer to the Indus Valley. Sources suggest this conquest was not intended to expand the Persian Empire. Frequent invasions from the north led Darius to seek secure regions for his wealth and holdings in the east. The promise of untold riches, including gold, ivory, peacocks, and apes, piqued his interest in what lay in the Indus Valley.

Darius is believed to have commissioned an expedition along the Indus River to discover regions and trade routes. The expedition began in the north, with his men traveling around the Iranian coast, and ended in Egypt. Based on reports, the Persian king occupied an unspecified region near Gandhara and established the Indian Ocean as a trade route along the coast of Iran. The Behistun Inscription, which was erected by Darius near Kermanshah in Iran, states that the regions of Gandhara and Hindus were part of his empire.

Again, what specific region Darius was referring to as Hindus remains disputed. Most historians agree it must have been somewhere along the Indus River since there is some evidence of Persian presence. Most believe the region of Hindus may include the modern-day province of Sindh in Pakistan, while a few hold the belief that Darius may have proceeded northeast of Gandhara, though there is little evidence to support the latter claim.

The Persians are believed to have built many forts along the Indus River, at least one of which housed the Persian governor in Hindus. The reported wealth of the region was true, as it is believed to have made massive contributions to the Persian treasury in gold and other precious metals.

Persian influence in the Indus Valley had the effect of establishing better communication channels between the regions beyond those of trade relations. The organized administration the Persians brought with them impacted the region's management greatly. Stamped coins were introduced in the valley, and the Persians are also believed to have brought the Aramaic language and texts with them into the region.

In return, Indian concepts of mysticism, religion, and reincarnation were introduced to Western thought. The influence of such teachings and beliefs can be found in the works of Near Eastern and Greek philosophers of the time. The most notable contribution of the Indus Valley remains its treasures. It is also believed Darius I brought back an Egyptian canal into use that may have served as a predecessor to the modern Suez Canal.

The Scythian War

The Scythian War was a campaign led by Darius I against the Scythians, an Iranian-speaking nomadic tribe. The Scythians had previously invaded Media during the rule of Deioces and been defeated yet remained a constant nuisance to the Persian Empire. Their revolt during the rule of Darius threatened the trade between central Asia and the regions near the Black Sea, as these areas were held by the Scythians.

Because the Scythians led a nomadic lifestyle, they were able to avoid a direct confrontation with the Persian army. The Persians, on the other hand, had been suffering significant losses from Scythian invasions, as the Scythians destroyed food in the regions they entered and poisoned the wells, the first recorded use of scorched-earth tactics.

Darius had a bridge of boats constructed to cross the Black Sea, conquering regions of eastern Europe on his way to the Scythians. His invasion of Scythia was frustrating, as the Scythians evaded the army and moved eastward, destroying the countryside behind them. They blocked wells, destroyed pastures, and only engaged in small scuffles with the Persian army but generally maintained a distance when retreating, causing the Persians to chase after them.

While the Scythians' tactics helped them evade a direct confrontation, bringing the Persians deeper into unfamiliar lands, it also led to the loss of many Scythian lands. The Persians moved deep into modern-day Ukraine with no lands to capture and no army to fight. Regardless, Darius still held the upper hand, as his army was able to survive off of cultivated Scythian lands. Meanwhile, the Scythians laid waste to much of their lands, damaging them and their allies in the process.

A month into the campaign, Darius halted at Oarus, an unidentified Scythian river, where he built eight forts as a frontline defense. His army was suffering from fatigue, limited supplies, and rampant sickness. Darius failed to bring the Scythians into a direct confrontation but managed to take over or destroy most of their lands. The Scythians, for their part, were not bested by the Persians but had lost significant territories to them. The campaign concluded with a stalemate, though it is reported the Scythians developed a newfound respect for the Persian army. Fearing a lost cause, Darius abandoned the Scythian chase and turned his armies toward Thrace.

Conquest of Thrace and Macedonia

After turning away from Scythia, Darius diverted his attention toward Thrace. Under the leadership of his general Megabyzus, the Persian army headed east. Thrace was known as a populous region, and following a successful campaign around 514 BCE, Megabyzus set up establishing Persian rule in the region. This included removing many of the Thracian tribes from the region and transporting them back to Persia, which was meant to weaken the locals in case of an uprising and for them to serve as slaves in Persia.

After Thrace, Megabyzus turned his attention to Macedonia. The Macedonian campaign did not involve force. The Persians demanded that the Macedonian king surrender to the authority of Darius I. Megabyzus demanded a tribute made by earth and water. The Macedonians initially surrendered peacefully, becoming a vassal state to Persia. After the Ionian

Revolt, Macedonia helped assert Persian authority in the Balkans.

Suppressing the Ionian Revolt

The conquest of the Greeks by the Persians began with an attempt to conquer Naxos, a Greek island, which ultimately failed. The Persians had already begun to occupy Greek regions following their unfruitful pursuit of the Scythians. At the beginning of the 5th century BCE, Aristagoras, the leader of Miletus, urged the Persian satrap, Artaphernes, to invade Naxos. With Darius's blessing, his cousin Megabates was named leader of the Persian army. A reported quarrel between Megabates and Aristagoras at the pivotal moment before the campaign led to the latter betraying the Persians.

Aristagoras did not want to lose his position as the leader of Miletus, so he encouraged the Ionian states to revolt. The Ionians, along with troops from Athens and Eretria, captured and burned Sardis in 498 BCE. As they made the return march to Ionia, they were followed by Persian forces. A confrontation led to the Battle of Ephesus, where the Ionians were defeated. In 497 BCE, the Persians launched a triple attack, attempting to capture regions lost to the rebellion. The resulting battles did not produce any conclusive wins for either side.

Seeking to put an end to the revolt, the Persian army set out to attack the heart of the rebellion at Miletus in 494 BCE. The Ionians tried to defeat the Persians with their naval force but lost to them during the Battle of Lade. Miletus was besieged by the Persians and captured. After the defection of the Samians, the Ionian revolt ended. The rebellion officially concluded with a peace treaty, which required Ionia to pay tribute to the Persians.

Battle of Marathon

Although the rebelling states had been brought back into the Persian fold, Darius decided that Eretria and Athens needed to be punished for their involvement in the revolt. Darius sent an army to deal with these two city-states. Eretria was sacked, and then the Persians moved to Marathon, a city about twenty miles northeast of Athens.

The Battle of Marathon took place in 490 BCE. The Athenians were aided by a small Plataean force, while the Spartans refused to send aid, citing the ongoing religious festival as the reason for refusal. The Athenian force was able to block the two exits from the city and chose a mountainous terrain for the battle. The unfamiliar and uneven territory made it difficult for the Persian cavalry and infantry to launch a joint attack.

While the Athenians prepared for war, they were outnumbered by the advancing Persians ten times. This battle required the use of wit over force, so the Greeks strategized a direct and sudden attack on the Persians. As the opposing army approached at a casual pace, the Greeks, under the leadership of Athenian general Miltiades, broke into a sudden sprint, forcing immediate hand-to-hand combat.

After a few hours of fighting, the Greeks were able to break through the Persian ranks. Records show the Persians lost some six thousand men that day compared to only about two hundred fallen Greek soldiers. The Persian army fell, and the Greeks celebrated by using the marble blocks the Persians had brought to celebrate their victory to build a monument in memory of their fallen soldiers. Darius I took the defeat as a personal insult and vowed revenge; however, he died before he could bring his plans to fruition.

Succession and Legacy

Darius had been preparing to lead a war against the Greeks when a revolt broke out in Egypt. The heavy taxation in the region, coupled with the forced migration of Egyptian craftsmen, led to rising unrest against Persian rule. This diverted Darius's attention from the Greek campaign and worsened his already failing health. Darius I died soon after, in 486 BCE. His body was embalmed and placed in the tomb he had prepared for himself at Naqsh-e Rostam.

Darius the Great's reign is considered one of the most important periods of the Persian Empire. As the Persian Empire expanded, the reforms introduced by the king improved the living conditions of the people. The laws that were introduced during this time laid the basis for the current laws of Iran.

Chapter 6: Xerxes I: The Persian Empire at Its Peak

When Xerxes inherited the throne, he also inherited a revolt by the Persian satrapy, including the satraps in Egypt and Babylon. The Persians were angry and humiliated by their defeat at the hands of the Greeks. Thus, Xerxes faced a huge responsibility from the outset. While the Persian Empire still held its might, things began to change following the death of Darius I.

Xerxes's most notable effort during his reign remains his campaign against the Greeks. However, it did not solidify the Persian Empire's rule there; instead, it dealt a heavy blow and brought the leadership of Xerxes I into question.

The Life of Xerxes I

Xerxes I was the son of Darius the Great and succeeded his father to the Persian throne. While the legitimacy of Darius's ascendence to the throne was in question, Xerxes was born to Atossa, Cyrus's daughter, and, therefore, came from the house of the rightful Persian dynasty. By historical accounts, Xerxes was raised every bit as the son of Darius and the grandson of Cyrus until he took the throne.

Persian princes are believed to have been raised by eunuchs until the age of seven. They were first taught riding and hunting and later began their education at the hands of aristocratic teachers. Since Zoroastrianism was the major religion practiced in the Persian Empire at the time, Xerxes was taught it. He also served in the Persian military, achieving honors and medals.

Most Persian princes of the time are believed to have been raised in a similar fashion. A note of contention remains on the question of their ability to read and write since the Persians preferred the spoken word over written history. Xerxes maintained his main residence in Babylon until the passing of Darius I.

Accession to the Throne

Before the revolt in Egypt, Darius I had been preparing to lead another expedition into Greece. He had already appointed his son, Xerxes I, as regent, although Darius was never able to set out for Greece before his death. Xerxes believed himself to be the rightful heir to the throne. However, he faced some opposition from his half-brother, Artobazan.

Artobazan was Darius's eldest son; thus, he believed he had the right to the crown. It is believed that Darius chose Xerxes as his successor due to the special privilege he enjoyed, being born to Atossa and being the grandson of Cyrus the Great. Xerxes was also born after Darius had become emperor of Persia, which elevated Xerxes's status as the son of a king. On the other hand, Artobazan was born while Darius was still a commoner.

Xerxes also received the support of Spartan king Demaratis of the Eurypontid line, who was in exile in Persia at the time. This support, along with the authority Atossa and the descendants of Cyrus the Great enjoyed, helped Xerxes take the crown without much opposition in 486 BCE.

The Egyptian Revolt

Xerxes's first concern as king was the rebellion in Egypt, which had pushed his father to his deathbed. It is believed the revolt reached as far as the city of Thebes in Upper Egypt, though not all Egyptians may have supported the Persian opposition. Little else is known about the nature of the rebellion, how far it spread, and what exact measures Xerxes took to deal with it.

However, the general consensus is that the new Persian king marched to the region with his army, suppressing the rebellion. Based on limited accounts, he instated a more severe system of slavery in the region and appointed his brother, Achaemenes II, as the satrap.

Invasion of Greece

After restoring peace to the empire, Xerxes was ready to take on Greece and seek vengeance for his father. Xerxes undertook one of the biggest campaigns in the history of the Achaemenid dynasty.

The preparations for the invasion of Greece are reported to have taken between three to four years. Troops from every satrap were called, and great naval efforts were also made. The resulting military force is believed to be the largest ever seen in the region at that time. Xerxes took the campaign seriously and left nothing to chance.

Battle of Thermopylae

Xerxes's march on Greece led to the Battle of Thermopylae, which was fought at the same time as the Battle of Artemisium. While Xerxes gathered his forces to produce a mighty military, the Greeks did not sit idle. The Greek alliance between the various city-states was led by Athens and Sparta. The Spartan king Leonidas led the army at Thermopylae. The Greeks planned to block the Persian advance in Thermopylae while simultaneously blocking them at sea in the Straits of Artemisium.

In 480 BCE, a Greek army comprising about seven thousand men marched under Leonidas to Thermopylae to block the pass. The Persian army vastly outnumbered the Greeks and was estimated to comprise between 70,000 to 300,000 men. The Greeks were able to hold off the far superior advancing army for seven days. As the battle progressed, the Greeks were able to block the only road leading through the pass.

The Greeks may have endured longer were it not for the actions of a local resident who showed the Persians another pass that ran behind the Greek lines. Leonidas realized defeat was imminent and told most of the army to leave. He remained behind, along with some Spartans, Thebans, Thespians, and helots. Around two thousand Greeks were left behind. They did not surrender to the Persians and fought to their deaths.

The Persian army had foiled the Greek plan to hold off the approach at Thermopylae. While the Greeks suffered defeat, the defense of their home is still cited today as an example of the benefits of training, equipment, and tactical strategies.

Battle of Artemisium

The Greeks planned to block the Persians on land at Thermopylae and their naval force at Artemisium. The Greek allies were able to gather about 271 triremes to await the Persians at Artemisium under the leadership of Themistocles. Before the Persians even reached the Greeks, they were caught in a gale near Magnesia, losing about a third of their fleet. After reaching Artemisium, the Persians again attempted a strategic move and tried to maneuver around the Greeks from the coast of Euboea. They were caught in another storm, and about a third of their ships were destroyed.

For two days, the battle continued, with small skirmishes and engagements taking place. While this resulted in equal losses on both sides, the much smaller Greek fleet could not afford the losses. These skirmishes led to no decisive victory. Once the news of the Greek defeat at Thermopylae reached Artemisium, the Greeks realized their stand at the strait was pointless since it was supposed to be a combined attack.

The Greeks decided to retreat to Salamis, allowing the Persians to take over Artemisium. The Persians also entered Phocis, Boeotia, and Attica. They were even able to take Athens, which had already been evacuated. The Persians then headed to Salamis, seeking a definitive victory over the Greeks.

Battle of Salamis

After the Persians' takeover of Athens, Xerxes was unsure of his next steps. He consulted a war council, the majority of which recommended that he chase after the Greeks in Salamis and come back with a decisive victory. Only Artemisia I of Caria, a Greek ally to the Persians, recommended that Xerxes wait for the Greeks' supplies to run out and then secure a peaceful victory. Xerxes chose to go with the majority opinion and marched to Salamis.

The naval battle that followed in September 480 BCE proved to be a decisive victory—for the Greeks. When the much larger Persian army moved into the Straits of Salamis, their large size became a disadvantage. The Persian fleet struggled to maneuver and organize itself, thus falling into chaos. Seizing the opportunity, the Greeks, led by Themistocles, launched an offensive.

The Persians were defeated, and Xerxes chose to return to Persia. However, he left his military commander Mardonius behind to continue the Greek campaign. Mardonius would go on to lead the Persians in a confrontation at Plataea. By the time Xerxes I returned home, he was humiliated and defeated, and little was left of his army. They were greatly reduced due to a shortage of supplies on their return journey and rampant illness among the ranks.

Battle of Plataea

In 479 BCE, the Persian army led by Mardonius met the Greeks for a final confrontation at Plataea. While the Persians held control of Thessaly, Phocis, Attica, Athens, Boeotia, and Euboea due to their victories at

Thermopylae and Artemisium, their defeat at Salamis prevented them from taking over the Peloponnese, which would have connected the Persians to the central part of Greece. This time, the offensive was launched by the Greeks.

The Greek army marched out of the Peloponnese, forcing the Persians to retreat to Boeotia and fortify themselves near Plataea. The Greeks realized a further incursion into Persian-led territory would result in losses, so they refused to move forward, avoiding a direct confrontation for eleven days. As they gathered to retreat due to supply shortages, Mardonius saw an opportunity to attack.

However, the Persian general had misread the situation, as the Greeks were not fully retreating; rather than allowing the Persians to chase them, the Greeks halted and fought the Persians. The resulting battle brought about the defeat of the ill-prepared Persian army and the death of Mardonius. The Greeks trapped the Persians in their camps and slaughtered most of them. The Persians also suffered a naval defeat simultaneously with this land conflict.

Battle of Mycale

The Battle of Mycale in 479 BCE decisively ended the second Persian invasion in favor of the Greeks. The confrontation took place off the coast of Ionia along the slopes of Mount Mycale. As the Greeks mounted an attack on the Persians at Plataea, a fleet set sail to Samos, an island opposite Ionia. The Persians are believed to have encamped at the foot of Mount Mycale, hoping to avoid battle.

The Greeks decided to attack the fortified Persian camps. The Persian army could not withstand the attack and retreated to their camps. However, the Ionian members of the Persian army defected, leading to the Persians' defeat. Their camp was attacked, the Persians were slaughtered, and their ships were captured and burned. The huge losses sustained by the Persian navy and army suppressed the Persians, ending their invasion.

What followed the Persian defeat was the beginning of the Greek offensive against the Persians. In the larger Greco-Persian Wars, their victory against Xerxes's armies was a decisive factor that sealed Persia's fate. For Xerxes, it was a questionable facet of his rule since he lost his army and the people's respect in this humiliating defeat to Greece.

Battle of the Eurymedon

Between the years 469 to 466 BCE, the Persians began to gather forces to lead an attack against the Greeks. The combined army and naval force headed toward the Eurymedon. It is believed the force intended to move through Asia Minor, capturing cities along the way. The Persian plan was to obtain more naval bases and recapture areas that had been lost to the Greeks.

The news of Persian scheming reached the Greeks, who gathered around two hundred triremes to block off the Persian advance. Before the Persians could gather themselves, the Greeks attacked near the Eurymedon River. Many of the Persian sailors abandoned their ships and fled to land.

Greek naval and land forces attacked simultaneously, destroying the Persian camp and over two hundred Persian triremes. The Greeks were also able to take many prisoners. This decisive double victory prevented any further action on the part of the Persians until Artaxerxes's rule.

Xerxes after Greece

Historical reports suggest that Xerxes took the Persian failure in Greece hard. He withdrew, retiring to Persepolis. Any wealth he may have built up through excessive taxation schemes was rapidly depleted by extravagant construction plans. In Persepolis alone, he ordered the construction of a palace called Apadana, a treasury called the Hall of a Hundred Columns, and the Tripylon, or the "triple gate," which connected the palace and the treasury.

Few historical accounts note much about Xerxes I's reign following his defeat at the hands of the Greeks. He is reported to have removed himself from political affairs, retreating into his harem and remaining unbothered by matters of the state. His defeat, as well as his lack of involvement in the empire, has made him perhaps the most notorious ruler of the Achaemenid dynasty.

The King Assassinated

Xerxes I's unpopularity may have contributed to his untimely and violent death. He met his end in 465 BCE when he was assassinated, along with his son Darius II, by Artabanus. It is believed he was a powerful figure in the Persian court and was likely the commander of the royal bodyguard.

After Xerxes's assassination, his son, Artaxerxes I, sought revenge. He killed Artabanus and claimed the throne. The violent end to Xerxes's rule and a similar beginning to Artaxerxes's regime presented a slew of problems in the empire. The people of Persia had already been struggling under Xerxes I, and the change in emperors did not help matters. Widespread revolts broke out across the empire.

Chapter 7: Artaxerxes I and the Egyptian Revolt

Artaxerxes I's reign began in much the same way as that of his father. His succession to the throne was punctuated by violence. Egypt and Bactria, in particular, saw new revolts against Persian rule, and Artaxerxes was forced into clashes within his own regime to reestablish peace.

The rule of Xerxes I had been notorious, to say the least, and his reputation did not help his son. Artaxerxes remained involved in similar conflicts as his father. However, he showcased better military strategizing and ability and made use of cunning tactics rather than force against his enemies.

Artaxerxes I Becomes King

Artaxerxes I.
Diego Delso, CC BY-SA 4.0 <https://creativecommons.org/licenses/by-sa/4.0>, via Wikimedia Commons; https://commons.wikimedia.org/wiki/File:Artaxerxes_I_at_Naqsh-e_Rostam.jpg

Artaxerxes was reportedly raised by Artabanus, who was the commander of the king's guard. When Artaxerxes sought revenge for his father's assassination at the hands of Artabanus, he killed the culprit and his sons, the former in a hand-to-hand confrontation. After doing so, he became Emperor Artaxerxes I of Persia in 465 BCE.

Reigning a divisive Persia was no easy task, and these new hostilities added to the unrest within the empire. Another concerning revolt broke out in Egypt, presenting a considerable challenge to the new king. Before his death, Xerxes I had been planning another incursion into Greece, which did not come to fruition before his assassination. Artaxerxes I took on that new responsibility when he inherited the throne.

Artaxerxes I was often referred to as Longhand, reportedly due to a longer right hand. He was married to Damaspia, who gave birth to his son and heir, Darius II. Not much is known about Damaspia, but some reports suggest she may have died on the same day as Artaxerxes.

The Greek Problem

The second Persian invasion of Greece did not end much better than the first and left Persia at a considerable disadvantage. Following the Battle of Mycale, the Greeks took the offensive, continuing the Greco-Persian Wars. The Delian League, which was headed by Athens, continued attacking Persian-occupied regions in the Aegean, even after the Persian forces had withdrawn following their defeat at Mycale.

The Greek incursion Xerxes I had been planning before his death did not end well. He gathered forces to march against the Greeks to put an end to Greek hostilities. This led to the ill-fated Battle of the Eurymedon.

Themistocles Arrives

One of the defeats the Persians suffered in Greece under Xerxes I was dealt at the hands of the Greek general Themistocles. Therefore, it may have come as a surprise when he turned up in Artaxerxes's court. Themistocles had earned disfavor in Greece due to his general arrogance toward the Spartans and his demand to refortify Athens. He was ostracized and later made to stand trial on the charge of treason. He fled, making his way from Argos to Asia Minor, where he presented himself to Artaxerxes.

Artaxerxes accepted his offer of service and his help in defeating the Greeks. Historical records and recovered artifacts, including minted coins, show the Persian king made him satrap of at least three cities and also helped him smuggle his wife and children out of Athens. Themistocles's inside knowledge of Greek activities helped Artaxerxes plan his next move against the Greeks.

Manipulating Sparta

Much tension was caused in Greece due to the activities of the Delian League. It was led by Athens and had banded together for the express purpose of dealing with the Persian threat. The Delian League managed to stop the Persian invasion, and Athens grew powerful and wealthy by exploiting the other members, essentially creating an Athenian Empire. This caused strife with the Spartans, who wanted to be the dominant Greek power.

Artaxerxes used the increasing tensions in Greece to add fuel to the fire. He secretly funded the build-up of Sparta's military while offering gifts, symbolizing peace, to Athens. He then simply allowed the naturally festering unrest to take its course.

Soon enough, the Spartans and the Athenians clashed. Reportedly, the Spartans insulted the Athenians when the latter arrived to help deal with a helot rebellion. Sparta had been growing tired of what it saw as Athenian arrogance and aggression. When the Peloponnesian War broke out, Artaxerxes looked to Themistocles to help him destroy the Greeks.

Accounts vary as to what happened next. Some report that Themistocles had a change of heart at the last minute and was unable to betray his Greek brothers to the Persians, choosing to poison himself instead of helping Artaxerxes. Other accounts suggest Themistocles simply passed away from a natural death before the Persian king could call on him for aid. The Peloponnesian War caused both Athens and Sparta to seek an alliance with Persia; however, no treaty could be reached before Artaxerxes's death.

The Egyptians Revolt—Again

The Egyptian rebellion in 460 BCE came as a surprise for the Persians. Perhaps because Artaxerxes's attention had been focused on the Greeks, he did not foresee the unrest before an outright attack occurred. It was incited by Inaros II, a Libyan prince with connections to the Saite dynasty in Egypt. Inaros discovered the Athenians were planning to attack the Persians in Cyprus and forged an alliance.

The exact date of the rebellion is hard to pinpoint, as different sources suggest a slightly different timeline. However, some reports do suggest that Inaros may have already incited the rebellion before offering an alliance to the Athenians as they prepared to attack Cyprus. Some reports go as far as to suggest that the Persians were already struggling against Inaros's forces and had been pushed into a corner in Memphis by the time Athenian reinforcements arrived.

Regardless, it is agreed the rebels were able to deal heavy blows to the Persians. The Persian satrap of Egypt was killed during the Battle of Papremis, and the Athenian forces were able to take control of the Nile. They then laid siege to Memphis, taking control of most of the region with the exception of the citadels, where Persian soldiers had sought shelter.

The resulting conflict continued for six years, and Inaros, who was supported by the Athenians, proved to be a formidable force. The Persian army was led by Megabyzus, while Arsames, the satrap of Egypt, led the naval force. In 454 BCE, Megabyzus was able to defeat Inaros, just as Arsames defeated the Athenian fleet supporting the Egyptian revolt.

The Athenians made a final effort at the Battle of Prosopitis, which was surrounded by the Nile. The Athenians expected to be able to attack the Persians as their fleet passed by on the Nile. Instead, Megabyzus diverted the delta, leaving a dry and barren land behind, which his army used to march past the Athenian vessels that were now useless. Most of the Athenians died because of injuries, the harsh weather, and the lack of supplies. With the rebellion suppressed, the Persians were able to reestablish their rule and restore peace in the region.

Megabyzus Revolts

When Megabyzus brought forth captives from the rebellion, including Inaros II, Amestris, the queen-mother and wife of Xerxes, ordered their beheading. Megabyzus pleaded against this, as he had assured the prisoners they would not be harmed and that their lives would be spared. Artaxerxes initially chose to honor Megabyzus's word until he was pressured by his mother to have the prisoners executed.

Megabyzus saw this as a betrayal and revolted. He defeated the Persian generals sent against him in single hand-to-hand combat, not wanting to create a civil war in Persia. Finally, Amestris herself arrived as part of an embassy to make an offer of apology and restore peace. Believing his honor to be reinstated, Megabyzus accepted, ending his revolt.

Peace of Callias

Following the suppression of the Egyptian rebellion, Athens decided to continue with its initial planned attack on Cyprus while still fighting the Peloponnesian War with Sparta. Around 450 BCE, the Athenians gathered a large fleet from member states of the Delian League and charged Cyprus, which they found heavily fortified by Megabyzus's army.

Despite seeing an unbreachable island before them, Cimon, the leader of the fleet, still chose to attack. He was killed during the ensuing confrontation, and the remaining Athenians withdrew from Cyprus. Artaxerxes did not want any more interference from Athens, so he sent an embassy with a truce proposal. The Peace of Callias was negotiated, bringing an end to the hostilities initiated during the reign of Darius I. The Peace of Callias was enforced for about ten years and was broken by Athens in 439 BCE when it attacked Samos.

Artaxerxes in the Bible

Artaxerxes I giving his letter to Ezra.
From The New York Public Library https://digitalcollections.nypl.org/items/510d47e4-134f-a3d9-e040-e00a18064a99

Various historical accounts all report Artaxerxes to be a kind-hearted and gentle ruler. He is discussed in the Books of Ezra and Nehemiah. His treatment of the Jews granted them and other people of the Persian Empire a great deal of freedom and autonomy.

Ezra is believed to be a priest who was sent to Jerusalem by Artaxerxes to standardize the Law of Moses. He then went on to rework the Mosaic Law, which would revamp the lives of Jews in Jerusalem. Nehemiah, on the other hand, is thought to have been a member of Artaxerxes's court, where he served as a cupbearer. One day, the king saw him upset and asked him to state his issue. Nehemiah had been worried about Jerusalem's walls, which lay in ruins and left the city defenseless. He hoped for support in the restoration effort.

During Cyrus the Great's reign, Babylon was liberated, and the Jews, who had been held there by the Babylonians, were finally able to return home to Israel. Cyrus had also decreed that the Jews be offered lavish gifts as they left their Persian homes. The Jews who returned to Israel began to work on rebuilding their temple and walls; however, they continued to face opposition from surrounding lands.

Some of the people who objected to the return of the Jews wrote Artaxerxes, levying false accusations against the Jews and claiming that they refused to pay taxes. Based on this information, Artaxerxes ordered the rebuilding of the wall be ceased, allowing the opposers to march to Jerusalem to prevent the Jews from continuing construction. However, Artaxerxes continued Cyrus's policy of tolerance. Once he realized the true situation, he allowed Ezra to head to Jerusalem. Ezra was assured that the Jews would have as much silver, gold, and other amenities as they needed. Artaxerxes also removed tax obligations from those serving in the temple.

Artaxerxes funded the rebuilding of the walls and appointed Nehemiah as governor of Judea. Nehemiah was able to personally oversee the restoration effort, and both he and Ezra worked for the reconciliation of Jews with Persian rule. Artaxerxes also allowed the Jews to freely practice and develop their religion and culture. His efforts earned him a considerable section in the Bible.

The conflicting reports in historical accounts, which show Artaxerxes first deciding against the Jews before supporting them, have raised some questions. Many believe the first incidence, the narration of the rebuilding of the city walls and the construction of the beams for the temple being halted by "Artaxerxes," may not have referred to the Persian king but instead to a usurper, who may have manipulated his way to the throne before Artaxerxes. However, no historical records reflect either the rule or the existence of such a person, and it may simply be that Artaxerxes had not known the true situation in Jerusalem before ordering the temple construction to be stopped.

After Artaxerxes

During his reign, Artaxerxes focused his efforts on much besides war and strife. The city of Susa held most of his favor, as he introduced a lot of developments in the region. He ordered the restoration of the palace of Darius I, which was destroyed in a fire, along with the building of many other temples. He also took up his father's work and finished construction on the Hall of a Hundred Columns.

Artaxerxes had already appointed his son, Xerxes II, as his heir to the throne by the time he died of natural causes in 424 BCE. Xerxes II was not fated to rule long, for hardly a month later, he was assassinated by his half-brother, Sogdianus, Artaxerxes's illegitimate son.

Sogdianus managed to gain the support of some of the nobles of Artaxerxes's court and was able to establish his rule. However, six months later, he, too, was assassinated. Ochus, his half-brother, went on to take the name Darius II. What is considered to have been the rule of a peace-loving emperor came to a violent end.

Chapter 8: Darius II and the Persian Involvement in the Peloponnesian War

The Persian Empire had been rapidly declining since the failed Persian expedition into Greece, which resulted in a humiliating defeat and heavy losses. The succession to the Persian throne had continued to grow increasingly violent, and each instance brought about new problems; nearly every change on the throne resulted in revolts across the empire. While these revolts were never a united action and were always suppressed, they brought increasing instability to the Persian Empire.

While Darius II was the son of Artaxerxes, his status as an illegitimate son made him, in the eyes of many, unworthy of the throne. Darius II was an unpopular ruler before his reign even began. He also had many challenges to face. Once again, the Egyptian subjects had risen up in rebellion, and the Greek threat continued to be a cause for concern.

Early Life and Ascension to the Throne

Minted coins of Darius II.
dynamosquito, CC BY-SA 2.0 <https://creativecommons.org/licenses/by-sa/2.0>, via Wikimedia Commons; https://commons.wikimedia.org/wiki/File:Drachma_Darius_II.jpg

Darius II, whose original name was Ochus, was also often referred to as Nothus, meaning "bastard." His violent ascension to the throne did not bode well for the empire. Historians note that the Achaemenid court fell into rapid decline with his rule, as tensions, strife, and conflicts became commonplace. While he was the illegitimate son of Artaxerxes, his manner of obtaining the throne caused much unrest in the empire and became a hallmark of his reign.

After becoming king in 423 BCE, the focus of Darius II's life is reported to have been influenced by eunuchs and his harem. His wife, Parysatis, was believed to hold great sway over him. Darius II relied heavily on her counsel, and she held much sway over the Persian court, using a network of spies loyal to her.

Parysatis is believed to have ordered the execution of a number of dissenters or individuals she believed to be a threat to her power over the throne. She is also credited as the one who made Darius II's rule over Persia possible. She is believed to have held land in Media, Babylon, and Syria and extorted money in the form of taxation. Much of Darius II's rule was punctuated by unrest and claims of corruption.

The Peloponnesian War

While the Peace of Callias prevented any further fighting between the Persians and the Athenians, Darius II did not honor the treaty. In 413 BCE, Athens suffered a major defeat at the hands of the Spartans in Syracuse. Seeing an opportunity, Darius II decided to launch an attack on the Greeks. He believed it was time to take back control of the regions of Asia Minor that had fallen under Athenian command.

He ordered the satraps of Asia Minor, Tissaphernes and Pharnabazus, to begin collecting overdue taxes in the region and to forge an alliance with the Spartans to help him topple Athenian power.

Enter the Spartans

The beginning of the Peloponnesian War went mostly in the favor of Athens. The Spartans were unable to break the power of the Athenians or dismantle the Delian League. However, poor military decision-making on the part of Athens led to the Spartans gaining the upper hand. The Athenians had funded the Egyptian revolt, diverting considerable resources from their ongoing conflict with Sparta. When the revolt failed, they launched an attack on Cyprus, once again using up resources without seeing any results.

These moves resulted in a weakened Athenian force, and they were dealt a heavy blow at Syracuse. Using the mutual dislike of Athens as a weapon, Darius II created an alliance with Sparta, resulting in an official agreement in 412 BCE. Following Athens's losses at Sicily against Sparta, Syracuse, and Corinth, both the Spartans and Persians believed Athens could be easily defeated, once and for all, through the alliance.

Darius II and Tissaphernes dictated that the Spartans and Persians would jointly continue the war against Athens under the condition that no peace treaty could be reached with Athens without the consent of both parties. The treaty also stated that any enemy of one party would become an enemy of the other, effectively solidifying a joint defensive stance.

The treaty also laid out another common objective for the Spartans and the Persians. In addition to defeating the Athenians, the alliance was to prevent the Athenians from furthering their interests. This included but was not limited to preventing Athenians from obtaining wealth or resources from lands they had taken from either the Persians or the Spartans.

This first treaty was rejected by the Spartans. The treaty stated that the Spartans would surrender all regions outside of the Peloponnese, but the Spartans had begun the war to liberate Greece from Athenian influence, which had grown immensely because of its leadership role in the Delian League. Sparta still sought an agreement with the Persians and asked for a revision to the terms.

The second treaty that was presented before Darius II and the Spartans set out similar terms but with a few additions and revisions. It stated clearly that any lands under the dominion of Darius II were off-limits to the

Spartans. Similarly, any lands under Spartan rule were forbidden to the Persians.

Both parties were to provide assistance and aid to the other if and when such help was needed. The condition of war against the Athenians remained, including the condition of initiating peace with them. The treaty made a new addition that required the Spartans and the Persians to aid the other should one party face a rebellion or uprising from among their respective territories.

This second treaty was seen as simply clarifying the terms of the first one. To the Spartans, it was still not good enough. The promise laid out in the treaty of the Persian king rewarding the Spartans for their service seemed a moot point, as custom dictated Persian kings to do so for anyone who had done them a service. Moreover, the second treaty forbade the Spartans from creating a new empire following the Athenian defeat, which was unacceptable to the Spartans. They asked for another revision.

In late 411 BCE, the final treaty was presented to the two parties. This time, the treaty clarified that the lands under the rule of either party were their own, and each was free to do with them as they pleased. It also included payment for the material support the Spartans were providing, including ships, should they choose to receive it.

The treaty featured a significant negotiation. Darius II agreed to surrender the Greek regions of Macedonia, Thrace, Boeotia, Attica, and Thessaly once they had been recovered from the Athenians. He was also to send a fleet to the Spartans; in exchange, the Spartans promised that they would lay no claim to Greek regions in Asia Minor.

Once again, the treaty required the Spartans to give up the idea of liberating Greece. However, they were in a difficult position. The Athenian loss at Syracuse had presented a great opportunity; if they could deal a heavy blow with the might of the Persians, the Spartans could guarantee victory. On the other hand, the Persians had no strategic need for the Spartans since their greatest threat, Amorges, the leader of the Carian rebellion against Persia, had been suppressed.

The treaty held little meaning in the beginning and was not honored, for the most part, by the Persians, largely due to Tissaphernes, who did not offer the Spartans much assistance. Because of this, the Spartans felt they could attempt peace talks with Athens. However, once Darius II removed Tissaphernes as satrap and installed his son, Cyrus the Younger, in his place, the Spartans received much greater support from the Persians.

The Outcome of the Peloponnesian War

As the Peloponnesian War continued, the Athenians faced a much stronger foe in Sparta. While Athens's resources were rapidly depleting, Sparta had the support of the Persians and could engage in drawn-out battles. With the Persian fleet provided to the Spartans, they were able to gain some decisive victories. The Spartans built a fort in Attica, from where they could launch constant attacks on the Athenian countryside.

In 406 BCE, the Spartans were able to defeat Athens at the Battle of Notium in a naval confrontation. Despite an Athenian victory the same year, in 405 BCE, the Spartans defeated the Athenians, once and for all, at the Battle of Aegospotami. The Athenian fleet was captured, and Athens eventually surrendered, ending the Peloponnesian War in 404 BCE.

Following the war, Greece changed dramatically. It brought about the end of the once-powerful city-state of Athens and changed Greek warfare forever. The monetary and weaponry support provided by the Persians played a notable role in securing a Spartan victory, and it would go on to have a direct influence on dismantling the ruling influence of Athens. About sixty-six years later, Greece would be conquered by the Macedonian kingdom.

The Carian Rebellion

The rebellion that broke out in Caria in western Anatolia was led by Amorges in 413 BCE. When he rose up against Darius II, he was able to gain the sympathy and support of the Athenians. With this alliance, the Athenians hoped to weaken Persian rule, which, in turn, would hinder the support they were providing the Spartans, tipping the scales in favor of the Athenians. When the rebellion broke out, Tissaphernes was ordered to suppress the usurpers.

Since the Spartans were in a treaty with the Persians, they had to treat Amorges and the other rebels as their enemies. The Spartans set sail to Iasos, which had been occupied by the rebels between 412 to 411 BCE. The rebels celebrated their arrival, believing them to be the Athenian navy. However, they soon realized their mistake. The Spartans fought and defeated Amorges's army, arresting him and handing him over to Tissaphernes.

Background to the Egyptian Revolt

The previous Egyptian revolts had made the situation precarious in the region well before Darius II's violent ascension to the throne. Another rebellion began, this time with a more decisive outcome. After the Egyptian revolt during Artaxerxes I's reign, a new satrap, Arsames, was installed in Egypt. He chose to adopt a conciliatory approach with the hope of discouraging any new rebellion that might spring up. Part of his approach to managing Egypt was allowing Thannyras, Inaros's son, to maintain his lordship.

When Darius II obtained the throne, Arsames supported and pledged allegiance to him. Reportedly, between the years of 410 BCE and 407 BCE, Arsames was called out of Egypt to Susa. At the same time, a revolt broke out in Egypt.

The Egyptian Revolt

In 410 BCE, the region of Elephantine became the focal point of a revolt. Tensions between the Jewish community of Elephantine and the native Egyptians living there rose. Artaxerxes I had established a policy of religious tolerance across the Persian Empire, and various communities lived in relative harmony.

However, reports indicate that some strife was caused by the Jewish practice of sacrificing goats. The Egyptians saw this as an insult and took advantage of Arsames's absence to bribe a local military leader into destroying the Jewish temple. It is reported that Arsames punished the people responsible for the destruction, but to remain fair, he also banned the sacrifices, ignoring the pleas from the Jews.

The true cause and evolution of the revolt are not known for certain. Amyrtaeus, the pharaoh of the Twenty-eighth Egyptian dynasty, led a rebellion against the Persian Empire, with the rebellion reportedly starting as early as 411 BCE. The revolt led to guerilla attacks along the Nile Delta, which was taken out of Persian control by the rebels.

Amyrtaeus's grandfather may have participated in an earlier rebellion in Egypt. However, this time, Amyrtaeus sought help from the Spartans and forged an alliance. The Spartans were to engage the Persians in a conflict in Asia in exchange for Egyptian grain. This would turn Persian attention away from Egypt.

Reports vary on just how successful the revolt was. After the death of Darius II, Amyrtaeus was able to instate himself as the pharaoh of Egypt. Yet it appears Amyrtaeus may have only gained control of the Nile Delta at this point, with Upper Egypt remaining under Persian control. Darius II's successor, Artaxerxes II, was able to gather an army to lead a charge against the rebels soon after taking the throne. Political unrest at home and the threat of civil war prevented him from taking timely action, though. Eventually, the Egyptians were able to overthrow Achaemenid rule and declare independence.

The End of Darius II

Darius II died from an illness in 404 BCE. He was succeeded by his son, Artaxerxes II, who faced an increasingly struggling empire. He also faced internal struggles, as his younger brother, Cyrus the Younger, harbored ambitions for the Persian throne since his appointment as satrap of Persian-occupied regions of Greece. Cyrus had even reportedly hoped to enlist the help of the Spartans since he had been responsible for providing them aid during the Peloponnesian War.

The Legacy of Darius II

Darius II's role in the Peloponnesian War is considered a cunning example of military strategy. By identifying a true moment of opportunity, Darius was able to forge an alliance with the Spartans, which would go on to secure their victory against the Athenians. The Athenians, who had been defeated by the Persians at Cyprus, had already been weakened, and Darius II was able to make use of their weakened state and the Spartans' desire to overthrow them to ultimately destroy one of Persia's enemies. The continued fighting between the Greeks ensured they would be too occupied to launch attacks, at least any truly threatening attacks, on the Persians. The civil war could also pave the way for the Persians to take over Greece.

By using the alliance with the Spartans, Darius II was also able to overthrow Amorges, quashing the Carian rebellion and eliminating a true threat to the Persian Empire. However, regardless of his success, much of Darius II's rule was punctuated by rebellions, revolts, and general unrest. By the end of his rule, the Persians had to give up their regions in Greece and had lost many parts of Egypt, which were never regained again. The influence and corruption of Darius's wife caused unrest within the Persian court.

Aside from his campaigns, Darius II contributed to the religion, language, and culture of the Persian Empire. During his reign, he was able to bring back and mandate the use of three primary languages: Babylonian, Elamite, and Old Persian. Much of the writings recovered from this period were recorded in Elamite, which also served as the government's official language.

He continued to support and practice Zoroastrianism, paying tribute to Ahura Mazda, the creator deity in Zoroastrianism. Ancient records show Darius II was a great believer in spiritual and supernatural forces and maintained a collection of monuments with spiritual inscriptions on them. His tomb also showcases many such carvings.

SECTION THREE: THE PERSIANS – THE ROAD TO COLLAPSE

Chapter 9: Artaxerxes II: A Troubled Period

Following the death of Darius II, the Persian Empire came under the rule of his son, Artaxerxes II. By this point, the Persians had faced success in their funding of the Spartans during the Peloponnesian War, cultivating a strategic alliance with them as Athenian power was broken. With the threat of Athens vanquished, regions across the Aegean fell back under Persian rule, reestablishing, to some degree, the might of the Achaemenid Empire.

On the other hand, Artaxerxes II also inherited a revolt in Egypt, which had been stirring toward the end of his father's rule. The new king's reign would be marked with civil unrest and revolts, and the war waged on him by his brother in a bid for the throne would leave a lasting impression on the future of Persia.

About Artaxerxes II

Artaxerxes II.

Bruce Allardice, CC BY-SA 2.0 <https://creativecommons.org/licenses/by-sa/2.0>, via Wikimedia Commons; https://commons.wikimedia.org/wiki/File:Artaxerxes_II_relief_portrait_detail.jpg

Artaxerxes II, also known as Arsaces, was one of Darius II and Parysatis's thirteen children. He came to the throne in 424 BCE. His succession was contested by his younger brother, Cyrus, who may also have had the support of their mother, Parysatis. Cyrus had been appointed satrap of Lydia and other regions in Asia Minor under Persian control. When Tissaphernes failed to provide the promised amount of support to the Spartans during the Peloponnesian War, he was replaced with Cyrus the Younger. This position, along with his title of "Karanos," which denoted a higher rank than that of an ordinary satrap, greatly extended his military and political autonomy.

It was perhaps for this reason that Cyrus expected to be appointed heir to the throne. Many historians believe he was favored by his mother, who was known to hold great influence over her husband. However, Darius II appointed Arsaces as his heir on his deathbed. Upon Arsaces's acquisition of the throne, he adopted the royal title of Artaxerxes II.

Reports of hostilities between the brothers suggest that Cyrus may have attempted to assassinate his brother during his coronation. However, there is no real account of such an event occurring. Even if Artaxerxes II's coronation had gone smoothly, the remainder of his reign was marked with feuds, revolts, and unrest.

Blood Feud: Artaxerxes vs. Cyrus

As satrap, Cyrus managed to amass a large army and forge close alliances. His victory against the Cilicians and Syrians had given him great military prowess. He laid claim to the Persian throne immediately after hearing the news of his father's death. He believed he was the rightful heir. Although he was not the oldest, he was the firstborn after Darius II became king, whereas Artaxerxes had been born before his rule began.

Artaxerxes II's attempts at reaching a peaceful resolution did not come to any viable end. To aid his claim to the throne, Cyrus gathered his troops, composed of Lydian and Ionian soldiers and Greek mercenaries. Cyrus's plans were realized by Tissaphernes, who found flaws in the former's apparent excuse that he was gathering forces to launch an attack on the Pisidians in Asia Minor. His suspicion was solidified when Cyrus sought political support for his campaign from the Spartans and managed to receive funding from the Cilicians, whom he had conquered. Tissaphernes relayed his suspicions to the king, and Artaxerxes II began to prepare for a confrontation.

What occurred next was a bloody clash between the two brothers, with Cyrus leading a large army called the "Ten Thousand." This confrontation produced mixed results and led to more trouble.

Battle of Cunaxa

Cyrus the Younger's revolt came to a head in 401 BCE at Cunaxa near Babylon. Cyrus's army was led by a Spartan general named Clearchus. Artaxerxes II prepared an army four times the strength of Cyrus's, which was led by Ariaeus, his second-in-command. Accounts from one historian, who fought as a Greek soldier in the battle, report that Cyrus may not have had much control over his army. Reportedly, Cyrus wanted the Greeks, whom he deemed to be his best fighters, to take the center, where they would be in the best position to defeat the cavalry and kill the Persian king. The Greeks refused to do so, believing it would weaken their position.

When the battle began, the Spartans charged the left of Artaxerxes's army. They were heavily outnumbered and unable to break through, eventually breaking rank and fleeing. However, the Greek mercenaries were able to advance farther, forcing the Persians to fall back. By military standards, Cyrus's army was able to exact a defeat on the Persians, despite their fewer numbers. However, Cyrus was killed during the battle by a flying javelin, thus rendering the victory pointless.

The War with Sparta

The Spartan support of Cyrus during his rebellion went directly against the terms of the agreement the Spartans had signed with the Persians. Their betrayal angered Artaxerxes II, who wanted to act against them. The main conflict between the two powers began with the Corinthian War in 395 BCE. The Spartan invasion of Asia Minor, which was under Persian control, made the Persian king realize the Spartan threat needed to be neutralized immediately. To divert Sparta's attention from Persia, Artaxerxes began a mass political campaign, which involved heavy bribery, to encourage Sparta's enemies, including the Thebans, Corinthians, and Athenians, to begin a war with Sparta.

His strategy was successful, and Sparta became preoccupied with attacks on multiple fronts. It also led to an alliance, albeit a temporary one, between Persia and Athens. The two nations levied a joint attack on Sparta after failed peace negotiations. The ensuing Battle of Cnidus dealt a heavy blow to the Spartans, allowing Athens to make a comeback.

Battle of Cnidus

In 394 BCE, the Persians and the Athenians joined together to face off against the Spartan navy. Sparta's attempt to establish its newly built navy, which the Spartans began to build in 413 BCE, as a formidable force was led by King Agesilaus II of Sparta, who was recalled from Ionia to fight the Persian-Athenian threat. The combined navy of the latter was led by Athenian admiral Conon and Persian satrap Pharnabazus II.

The Spartan fleet met an advance guard of the Achaemenid fleet, against which the Spartans met relative success. But with the arrival of the remainder of the Persian fleet, the Spartans were hard put to resist. They were forced to abandon many ships and suffered massive casualties, with the Persians reportedly capturing at least fifty Spartan triremes. Although the Corinthian War continued, Sparta did not engage in naval conflicts after this defeat, which left the arena open for Athens to establish its naval power.

The allied forces of Persia and Athens raided the coast of the Peloponnese, which was under Spartan control, increasing the pressure on the Spartans. Persia was able to regain Ionia and its lost regions of the Aegean. This control was formally established with the Peace of Antalcidas, which began in 387 BCE.

The Resurgence of Athens

The Peloponnesian War had left Sparta as the reigning force in Greece, bringing Athenian supremacy in the region to an end. However, with Sparta's might breaking during the Corinthian War, especially with their defeat at Cnidus, Athens saw an opportunity to build itself back up. Athenian ambitions came to the attention of Artaxerxes, who feared that Athens would move against Asia Minor and strike up another war with the Persians.

As a result, Artaxerxes II sought a peace treaty with Sparta, which was, of course, seen as a betrayal to Athens. The Peace of Antalcidas was between the Greeks and the Persian king, and it restored peace and the Anatolian regions to the Persians. It also allowed Sparta to regain its dominance on the mainland.

The King's Peace

The Peace of Antalcidas is also known as the King's Peace since it was settled by Artaxerxes II. While it originated from the threat Athens posed to the Persian Empire, it ended the Corinthian War. The peace treaty allowed Athens to maintain its dominion in the regions of Lemnos,

Imbros, and Scyros and granted autonomy to other regions.

Since the Persians made the treaty possible and brought peace to the region, the Persians became arbitrators of future Greek conflicts. This status would go on to play a significant role in resolving conflicts between the Spartans and the Thebans.

Mediation between Sparta and Thebes

The King's Peace did not hold for long, and fighting resumed in Greece. Thebes, in particular, faced resentment from other Greek city-states on account of the level of influence it held within Greece. Between 367 and 365 BCE, further attempts were made to restore peace to the region, with Artaxerxes II acting as a neutral and fair arbiter. However, Theban attempts at organizing peace talks failed completely, especially when Thebes refused to return conquered Spartan land. The result was a continuation of fighting in Greece.

During the peace negotiations, Artaxerxes used an envoy, Philiscus, to act on his behalf. The failure of the peace talks led Philiscus to begin offering Persian funds to the Spartan military, offering them moral and monetary support. Records suggest he also funded the Athenian army and may have offered them services since he was named an Athenian citizen. With the Achaemenid Empire's backing, the war in Greece could continue.

The failure of negotiations was not well received by any of the Greek city-states. In 367 BCE, the Spartans and later the Athenians, as well as the Thebans and other city-states, sent envoys to the Achaemenid court, hoping to gain Artaxerxes's support to fund their war effort. Artaxerxes II proposed a new treaty that would theoretically end the war. However, it was perceived by all to be heavily in favor of Thebes, as it required the dismantling of other militaries. As a result, most city-states, aside from Thebes, rejected the proposal.

Artaxerxes II's apparent favoritism for the Thebans enraged the other states, who began to act against the Persian Empire in secret. Athens and Sparta began to offer military support to known enemies of Persia. As a result, both Athens and Sparta became involved in the Egyptian revolt, as well as the Revolt of the Satraps.

The Egyptian Attempt

With the Greek threat suppressed, Artaxerxes finally turned his attention to Egypt. Toward the end of his father's rule and the beginning of his own, Egypt had launched a successful revolt, taking delta regions out of Persian control and establishing a new pharaoh. While Upper Egypt remained under Persian control, the revolt was not satiated and required urgent action. Artaxerxes II's first attempt to subjugate the Egyptians in 385 BCE did not end well, so he turned to the Greeks for aid. He began recruiting Greek mercenaries and led an invasion into Egypt in 373 BCE.

Due to Pharnabazus's success against the Spartans, he was chosen to lead the attack on Egypt. After four years of preparation, Pharnabazus had a 200,000-strong military force backed by 12,000 Greeks and naval support, the latter of whom marched under Iphicrates, a Greek general, to face the Egyptian rebels in 373 BCE. The Egyptians were supported by an Athenian general named Chabrias, who brought many Greek mercenaries with him.

The Egyptians were prepared for the oncoming Persian force and placed the lands around Pelusium, to which the Persians were headed, underwater and blocked all available channels of the Nile by building embankments. Finding the heavily fortified Nile impassable, the Persian army had to move on from Pelusium without attempting an attack and look for an alternate way up the Nile.

The Persians then headed toward Memphis, finding a route through the sparsely guarded Mendesian channel of the Nile River. However, luck was against the Persians, as disagreements between Iphicrates and Pharnabazus, combined with the Nile flooding, created tensions. The fortifications and the attack put up by the Egyptians turned a certain victory into a sour defeat. Pharnabazus was later removed from his military duties due to his advanced age and was replaced by another general, Datames, who was to lead a second expedition into Egypt. Not only would this second campaign fail, but it also led to Datames leading the Revolt of the Satraps against the Achaemenid king.

Revolt of the Satraps

Repeated revolts and the utter defeat in Egypt led to increasing unrest in an already struggling empire. Starting in 372 BCE, the nobility of the Achaemenid dynasty revolted. They were led by Datames. While he was initially appointed to command the second expedition into Egypt, he changed his mind, instead turning against the Persian emperor. He and his troops withdrew from Egypt and headed to Cappadocia, where he was able to confer and ally himself with other displeased satraps.

This revolt within Persia, which would undoubtedly weaken it and render it unable to mount attacks or defenses against other enemies, offered a golden opportunity to the rebels in Egypt. Egyptian Pharaoh Nectanebo, who had been leading the assault against the Persians, lent support to the satraps in the form of financial aid and began cultivating ties with both Athens and Sparta.

The satraps planned to lead an assault against the Achaemenid king, starting with an attack from Syria, while an Egyptian-Greek alliance launched an attack from the southwest. While the satraps began their revolt as intended, the Egyptian army never came to their aid, as it was waylaid by the Egyptian revolt. Disagreements and infighting among the satraps led to an uncoordinated and messy attack against the Persian king, and he was able to defeat the rebels without much loss. However, to maintain peace within his empire, Artaxerxes II allowed many of the satraps to return to their governorship.

Persia Starts to Crumble

During his reign, Artaxerxes II spent a considerable portion of his wealth on several building projects. These included the restoration of the palace of Darius I and stronger fortifications in Susa. In Ecbatana, he funded the building of a new palace and several sculptures. A notable change in Persian culture during his reign was the growth of religion. While the Persian Empire was dominated by the Zoroastrian faith, which worshiped Ahura Mazda, the names of other gods were also recovered that date to Artaxerxes II's reign. These include Anahita and Mithra, who were lesser gods worshiped in conjunction with Ahura Mazda.

Artaxerxes II was the first of the Persian kings to recognize these two deities. Anahita was associated with healing, fertility, and wisdom. Artaxerxes erected temples, which were populated by statues of the goddesses across the empire, particularly in Babylon, Susa, and Ecbatana.

Despite such advances, the general view of Artaxerxes II is that of an inept ruler who reigned over an empire in constant conflict. He was unable to control the rising tensions, which finally erupted into war. Egypt was lost during his reign. His rule is highlighted not by the empire's expansion but by a constant struggle to maintain peace and control over the existing regions under Persian rule. The Achaemenid dynasty faced many complications during Artaxerxes II's reign, each with a lasting effect. The war Artaxerxes II waged against Cyrus the Younger is even believed to have laid the groundwork for future conflicts, particularly the Revolt of the Satraps.

Artaxerxes II died in 358 BCE and was succeeded by his son, Artaxerxes III. His successor did not inherit the region in any better condition than Artaxerxes II had, so he was destined to face similar challenges during his rule. Artaxerxes II was buried in his tomb in Persepolis.

Chapter 10: Artaxerxes III: The Instability Continues

During Artaxerxes II's reign, the Persian Empire struggled. It faced many challenges, and revolts broke out throughout the empire. Artaxerxes II's ineptitude in dealing with and suppressing these revolts left room for his successor to be perceived as weak if he could not restore peace. So, Artaxerxes III came to the throne with a clear ambition.

Under the new king, the Persian Empire saw a series of effective military operations designed to ensure that the empire would not fall apart. Artaxerxes III's ruthlessness and military strategy made him an effective emperor. While the foundation of the Achaemenid dynasty was shaky, it held on under the watchful and brutal eye of Artaxerxes III.

Taking the Throne

Artaxerxes III.
Bruce Allardice, CC BY-SA 2.0 <https://creativecommons.org/licenses/by-sa/2.0>, via Wikimedia Commons; https://commons.wikimedia.org/wiki/File:Artaxerxes_III_tomb_detail.jpg

Despite not being the next in line for the throne, Ochus, otherwise known as Artaxerxes III, ascended to the throne following his father's death in 358 BCE. Before beginning his reign over the Persian Empire, he served as a satrap and a military commander in the Persian army. Of Ochus's three brothers, any of whom could have inherited the throne, one committed suicide, another was executed, and the third was murdered. This type of violent pattern was to follow the entirety of Artaxerxes III's reign.

Artaxerxes II's oldest son, Darius, had been in line for the throne, and he was favored by the king. However, to quicken his succession, he began plotting against his father, hoping to gain the support of his half-brothers, his father's illegitimate children, rumored to be around 150 in number. The treachery was discovered, and Darius was executed. Next in line was Ariaspes, who, through clever manipulation from Ochus, was pushed into committing suicide. Artaxerxes II's other choice was his favorite illegitimate son Arsames, as he disliked Ochus and did not wish him to accede to the throne. However, Ochus had Arsames killed. Artaxerxes II died soon after finally appointing Ochus as the next king of Persia.

Artaxerxes III began his rule with major bloodshed within the royal family. To quash the potential of any other contender for the throne or anyone challenging the legitimacy of his rule, he murdered all the members of the royal family, including women and children, to secure the throne. He came to be known as one of the cruelest Persian kings. Through cunning, manipulation, and extreme violence, he conducted multiple campaigns in Egypt. He also led a defensive charge against the Greeks, who rose up against Achaemenid rule, and dealt with multiple other rebellions during his rule.

Artabazus Revolts

The Revolt of the Satraps during Artaxerxes II's reign made his son, Artaxerxes III, realize the threat the nobility presented to the throne. It wasn't all that long ago that Cyrus the Younger had engaged in a civil war to win the throne instead of Artaxerxes II. Artaxerxes III was adamant about avoiding such a situation. For this reason, after becoming king, he required all satraps to disassemble their personal mercenary forces.

Initially, the satraps complied with this order. However, two years later, Artaxerxes III's attempt to remove Artabazus II from his governorship of Hellespontine Phrygia in western Anatolia did not go as planned. Artabazus did not appreciate the dismissal and chose to revolt against the

Persian king instead. He also happened to be the son of the king's sister, which may have made him particularly hostile toward Artaxerxes III since he would have seen the discharge as an insult. During the Revolt of the Satraps during Artaxerxes II's reign, Artabazus led the resistance for the king and had been ultimately victorious in suppressing the rebellion. He is believed to have joined forces with his two brothers to lead this new revolt.

To counter the force Artaxerxes III sent against him, which included all the other satraps of Anatolia, Artabazus reached out to the Athenians for help. He was able to forge an alliance with the Athenian commander, Chares, who obtained the mercenaries Artabazus was forced to dismiss two years prior. This combined force was able to defeat the satrap force sent by Artaxerxes III. The king saw the greater danger posed by the Athenians and bribed them to remove themselves from the Persian conflict.

In response, Artabazus formed an alliance with the Thebans in 354 BCE, who supplied him with a military force to face off against the Persian king. For a while, it seemed the former satrap had the upper hand, as he was able to inflict defeat on the Achaemenid king multiple times. Artabazus's downfall came from within, as he had a falling out with the Theban general. Artabazus was defeated in battle and taken prisoner. His supporters were able to free him, and after a few half-hearted attempts to continue the revolt, he fled to Macedonia to the court of Philip II. His arrival in Macedonia proved to be significant, as this was where he met his future son-in-law, Alexander the Great.

Failure in Egypt

Artaxerxes II's defeat in Egypt and his failure to control the rebellion turned into a point of humiliation and contention within the empire, which later led to the Revolt of the Satraps. His son wanted to fix this situation and earn respect and the credit of bringing an unruly satrapy back under Persian dominion. Artaxerxes III is reported to have launched a new campaign against the Egyptians around 351 BCE, hoping to finally put an end to years of war.

Little is known about this campaign. Artaxerxes III is believed to have marched into Egypt with a huge army and directly engaged Pharoah Nectanebo II. The Egyptians had the support of both the Athenians and the Spartans. This allied force dealt a deceive defeat to the Persians after reportedly a year of fighting, at which point Artaxerxes III was forced to abandon the Egyptian campaign to address more urgent matters at hand—

another revolt.

The Cyprus Campaign

Cyprus, like Egypt, had a history of rebelling against the Persian Empire, though they had been repressed successfully in the past. During Artaxerxes II's reign, Evagoras, the king of Salamis, attempted a revolt, seeking to gain all of Cyprus.

With Artaxerxes II occupied by his brother Cyrus the Younger's attempt at seizing the throne, Evagoras secured the support of Athens and Egypt. Victory seemed inevitable for the rebels. However, the King's Peace with Athens meant Greek support was withdrawn, and the Cypriot revolt came to an end.

During Artaxerxes III's reign, Cyprus revolted again, seeking independence from Persia. Unfortunately for Cyprus, victory was still out of reach. With the help of its allies, the Persian Empire was able to, once again, suppress the uprising. Cyprus would eventually gain independence from the Persian Empire, but it remained part of the empire under the rule of Artaxerxes III.

The Defeat of Sidon

More rebellions sprang up. The Phoenicians in Sidon were tired of Persian rule as well. To handle the rebellion of Sidon, Artaxerxes III reached out to the satraps of Syria and Cilicia, Belesys and Mazaeus, respectively. The Persian forces might have been something to reckon with were it not for the support of Egypt, which sent four thousand Greek mercenaries to help Phoenicia gain independence from the Persian Empire. The satraps' army failed to deal with the rebellion and was driven out of Phoenicia. The failure of the satraps in Phoenicia led Artaxerxes III to reconsider this decision.

Following this failure, Artaxerxes III decided to lead an army himself into Sidon. Both the Athenians and the Spartans refused to provide aid to the Persian army, but he was able to secure aid from the Thebans, who added another 10,000 men to the 330,000-strong army Artaxerxes III had gathered. The king hoped to cripple the revolt by sheer force since his army far outnumbered the Phoenicians.

The outcome of the campaign against Sidon provides a look into the viciousness and barbarity of which Artaxerxes III is often accused. The strength of the Persian force worried the king of Sidon, Tennes, who led the rebellion. He decided to seek the king's pardon by offering one hundred influential citizens of Sidon. Artaxerxes responded by having each citizen speared with javelins. An additional tribute of five hundred citizens met the same fate.

Artaxerxes III then set about burning the city to the ground, killing about forty thousand people in the process. He went on to make a fortune from his victory by selling the ruins of the city to those who believed there were vast treasures to be found buried underneath it, which they hoped to excavate from the ashes. Tennes was executed for instigating the uprising, and the Jews who had supported the rebellion were exiled to Hyrcania.

Reconquering Egypt

Artaxerxes III spent many years preparing for reentry into Egypt. Between 340 and 339 BCE, he assembled a large army consisting of mercenaries recruited from Argos, Thebes, and Asia Minor. The Persians' challenge was not the strength of their army; indeed, the Persian force had always greatly outnumbered the Egyptian forces. The treacherous terrain was the problem. The Persians' limited knowledge of Egyptian topography and their arrogant refusal to recruit a local guide exacerbated the problem.

The Egyptian climate did impact the Persians, who were bested by quicksand. Their hasty attempt to take Pelusium was also quickly vanquished. Artaxerxes III then changed strategies, dividing up his troops into three divisions. The Theban division was assigned Pelusium. The Mentor of Rhodes, a Greek mercenary, was tasked with the campaign against Bubastis in Egypt, and the final division, made up of Argive troops, was to establish themselves against the Egyptians on the opposite bank of the Nile River.

The Egyptian ruler, Nectanebo II, was unable to dismantle the forces gathered on the opposite bank of the Nile and chose to retreat to Memphis. Pelusium, which was under siege by the Thebans, also fell, and Bubastis followed suit. The Greek mercenaries fighting for the Egyptians chose to surrender rather than face a brutal death at the hands of the Persians. They struck a deal with the Persians and defected, leading to widespread surrenders and allowing Artaxerxes to cross the Nile and reconquer Egypt. Nectanebo fled the country rather than face the Persians.

Egypt's fate was little better than that of Sidon. A reign of terror began; the city walls were destroyed, and the region was thoroughly looted by the Persians. The stolen riches greatly contributed to the Persian treasury and helped Artaxerxes reward his mercenaries. The king then set about weakening Egypt's people and the economy to prevent the likelihood of another revolt. Taxes were raised astronomically, and sacred books were burned. Temples were looted, and local religions were persecuted.

The Fall of Artaxerxes III

Egypt was not the last rebellion the Persian Empire faced, but it certainly had a lasting effect. Artaxerxes III continued his policy of vicious attacks in response to revolts, and within a few years of reconquering Egypt, he managed to subdue rebellions across the empire, bringing lands firmly back under Achaemenid control. Generals, including Mentor of Rhodes, who had played prominent and successful roles in the Egyptian campaign, were given important positions within the empire and worked to maintain Persian authority and create a successful and efficient government.

The Persian Empire regained control of the Aegean, including many of the Athenian regions. While the Greeks suffered from the might of the Persians, none were able to take a stand against them. However, the rising power of Macedonia remained a concern for Artaxerxes III. Persia became a focal point for Philip II of Macedonia when Persian aid helped Thrace topple the Macedonian siege and maintain independence.

The final years of Artaxerxes III's reign were spent in relative peace. In 338 BCE, Artaxerxes III and his elder sons were poisoned by a court eunuch named Bagoas. Bagoas ensured that a more malleable heir, one of the king's sons, Arses, ascended the throne. Artaxerxes III's sudden death wreaked havoc on an otherwise stable empire.

During his reign, Artaxerxes III built the Hall of Thirty-Two Columns for some unknown purpose and his own palace. However, many of his construction projects remained unfinished, including the Army Road and the Unfinished Gate, which would have connected the Hall of a Hundred Columns with the Gate of All Nations. His tomb was built next to his father's.

Chapter 11: Arses and Darius III: The Last Kings and the Dissolution of the Empire

Artaxerxes III managed to consolidate the Persian Empire largely by sheer force and unbridled violence. The empire had gone through one too many periods of unrest and had suffered considerably from external wars and internal rebellions. However, his death would spark unrest greater than the empire had seen before, leading to the complete decimation of the Achaemenid dynasty.

The last two rulers of the Persian Empire, Artaxerxes IV and Darius III, were unable to handle the demands of this vast and unstable kingdom. Their inability to do so may be attributed to several reasons, but the manner of their ascension played a large role. When Artaxerxes IV's rule began, the Persian Empire slowly came to an end.

Arses Takes the Throne: Artaxerxes IV

Artaxerxes IV.
Classical Numismatic Group, Inc. http://www.cngcoins.com, CC BY-SA 3.0 <http://creativecommons.org/licenses/by-sa/3.0/>, via Wikimedia Commons; https://commons.wikimedia.org/wiki/File:Artaxerxes_IV_portrait.jpg

The youngest of Artaxerxes III's sons, Arses, was not first in line for the throne. The purposeful poisoning of Arses's father and his other siblings left him suddenly in charge of an empire he may not have been fit to rule. Arses was still young when he became king in 338 BCE, taking the throne name Artaxerxes IV. The general consensus behind Bagoas's acts is that by making young Arses king of an empire he could not manage alone, he could take charge behind the scenes by exerting influence on the new king. Artaxerxes IV would be more acceptable to the Persian court and the people rather than Bagoas directly attempting to take it.

The Rise of Macedonia

The political unrest in Persia gave its enemies a golden opportunity to make use of its weaknesses. Artaxerxes III vowed to keep a united empire and worked on subduing revolts and maintaining peace. During this time, he became aware of the rising threat of Philip II of Macedonia, particularly after the Persians aided Thrace against the Macedonians.

The Macedonian king had been gathering power and influence in Greece. Many Greek city-states had already joined Philip II in the League of Corinth, which was led by him. The Macedonian king, supported by his own influence and the faltering Persian Empire, chose the time of Artaxerxes IV's ascension to demand monetary compensation from the

Persians. According to Philip, this compensation was owed because of what the Persians had cost the Macedonians by helping Thrace.

Artaxerxes IV refused to give in to the Macedonian ruler's demands. Philip II did not take this slight well and began to prepare for war, building up an army to enter Persia. However, Artaxerxes IV did not live long enough to meet the Macedonian threat.

The Reign of Artaxerxes IV

Little is known about Artaxerxes IV's reign. The main source of knowledge regarding the Persian Empire is ancient Greek historians, who took little interest in Achaemenid affairs at this time. Since Artaxerxes IV had little involvement in Greek affairs, historians were more preoccupied with events happening closer at hand. Few records speak of Artaxerxes IV's reign.

What is known is that Artaxerxes IV's rule did not strengthen the Persian Empire much. The Persians were struggling, with Egypt and Babylon both attempting to establish their independence. Meanwhile, the king was too preoccupied to deal with the Macedonians or the unrest within his empire.

Realizing how much ambition Bagoas held, Artaxerxes IV attempted to rid himself of the nuisance and traitor. He tried poisoning Bagoas, but the latter got there first. Artaxerxes IV was poisoned just two years after claiming the throne, bringing his rule to an end in 336 BCE. Bagoas proceeded to place the former king's distant cousin, Artashata, on the Persian throne.

Darius III Becomes King

Coin of Darius III.
Classical Numismatic Group, Inc. http://www.cngcoins.com, CC BY-SA 2.5 <https://creativecommons.org/licenses/by-sa/2.5>, via Wikimedia Commons;
https://commons.wikimedia.org/wiki/File:Daric_coin_of_the_Achaemenid_Empire_(Darius_III).jpg

Artashata was part of the Persian royal family, being a distant cousin to the previous king. Upon his ascension to the throne, he took the name Darius III. At this point, the Persian Empire had been considerably weakened, not because of outside attacks but because of internal instability, political threats, and a crumbling administration. Due to Bagoas's actions, the empire's focus had turned toward matters of succession and away from the management and security of a vast and rapidly deteriorating empire.

Reports suggest that Darius III may not have succumbed to Bagoas's influence easily. Bagoas attempted to poison the newly appointed king of the Persian Empire because of this or perhaps because of some other conflict. Historical accounts suggest Darius III discovered this treachery before it occurred and summoned Bagoas to his court. There, the king forced him to drink to the former's health from his cup, which had already been poisoned. Bagoas was pushed to consume his own poison and was killed.

Little is known about Darius III besides his rather flimsy connection with the royal family. He may have gained some recognition from his military career. He had been part of the Persian military since the reign of Artaxerxes III and is reported to have shown bravery during one of his campaigns. This achievement lifted him from obscurity, with the king making him the satrap of Armenia. However, his ascension to the throne may be more aptly attributed to the power-hungry actions of Bagoas than to Darius III's military aptitude. His main claim to fame is being the last ruler of the Persian Empire.

The Persians were completely distracted and blindsided by outside threats, which was a problem since Artaxerxes IV's offense had led to the Macedonian king, Philip II, gearing up for war. The Greeks prepared for yet another attack on the Persians. The Persian Empire's previous might had thwarted many such attempts before through force, strategy, alliance, and/or bribery. However, this time, the Persians were not prepared to put up any resistance when the Macedonians marched against them.

The Macedonian Campaign

Whether the Macedonians had already been planning an attack on Persia, perceiving it as weak, or whether it only came as a result of Artaxerxes IV's refusal to offer compensation is not clear. The reported revolts or unrest in Egypt and Babylon during this time may have demonstrated that Persia was unable to maintain the peace that Artaxerxes

III had worked so hard to establish. However, it is true that the Egyptian and Babylonian uprisings were not very significant, as little is mentioned about them in the historical records.

Regardless of how or why, Macedonia turned its eye to the Persian Empire. This rising force had gained great influence in Greece, and the League of Corinth had received substantial support. The league was assembled by Philip II, and its express purpose was to unite the military forces of the various Greek city-states against the Achaemenid Empire.

The First Charge

By 336 BCE, Philip II had received the full support of the League of Corinth to lead a charge against the Persian Empire. The charge was supposed to be revenge for the acts of barbarianism the Persians had committed during the second Persian invasion of Greece when they desecrated many Athenian temples, even though the offense had occurred a century ago and under a different ruler.

Philip II sent an advance force to Asia Minor with the goal of liberating the Greeks from Persian rule. This first campaign was successful, and the Macedonians were able to reclaim cities stretching from Troy to the Malandros River. The campaign may have continued were it not for Philip's unexpected death. He was stabbed by one of his bodyguards as he entered the town of Aegae to celebrate his daughter's marriage. He had arrived unprotected to appear friendly and approachable to the citizens. It is not known for sure why he was stabbed, although there are many stories about why people might have been upset with him.

Alexander the Great Arrives

Alexander the Great was already a seasoned warrior in the Macedonian military when his father was assassinated in 336 BCE. When he ascended the throne, he also became the leader of the League of Corinth. Two years later, he led an invasion into Asia Minor with allied armies made up of Macedonian and Greek soldiers. The threat of Alexander was vastly underestimated by the Persians.

Battle of the Granicus

The reported Egyptian revolt had taken priority for the Persian emperor, who turned his attention away from the looming Macedonian threat. When Darius III turned back toward the approaching Macedonian army, he did not believe it to be any great danger. He appointed his satrap with the task of dealing with the Greeks and refused to personally engage in battle.

The Persian army was able to defeat the Macedonian forces twice, in Magnesia and again in Troad in Asia Minor. The advance guard that had been sent by Philip II the previous year, which had acquired various regions of Asia Minor, lost its command, and the lands were restored to Persian control.

The satraps' initial success made Darius III confident in their abilities to defeat Alexander the Great. The Persian army was led by the satraps of Hellespontine Phrygia, Lydia, and Cilicia. The Persian army took the western bank of the Granicus River, where they waited for the Macedonians, who took the opposing bank.

The Persians likely thought they were favored to win. The Persians were fighting from higher ground and outnumbered Alexander's army, being almost twice its size. However, the Macedonians soon gained the upper hand, which is largely attributed to their more effective weaponry, particularly their lances. During the battle, Alexander killed Darius III's son-in-law, Mithridates.

Alexander's army was able to push the Persian forces back, gaining a strong foothold on the riverbank. Much of the Persian cavalry abandoned the battle and fled, though Alexander did not pursue them. Those who remained behind were defeated and captured. Alexander erected the Granicus Monument to commemorate his first major victory over the Persians.

Battle of Issus

In the following year, 333 BCE, the two armies met again near the town of Issus. Darius III had been surprised at the Macedonians' prior victory. This time, he took command of his army rather than rely on his satraps. His plan was to launch a surprise attack on the Macedonians, marching behind them as they advanced to Hellespontine and cutting off their supplies.

The Persians captured the town of Issus and marched as far as the Pinarus River when they saw Alexander's army approaching, forcing the Persians to set up camp there. The beginning of the battle seemed to go in the Persians' favor since the Macedonian army was unable to cross the river without being besieged.

Alexander the Great was finally able to break through the Persian forces in the center, with his right flank breaking through the Persian left flank, forcing the Persians to fall back. Alexander then charged directly for Darius III and his guard, forcing them to flee. Alexander may have given chase had he not seen his troops struggling and gone to their aid. When the Persians saw their king had fled, they, too, abandoned the battle. The Macedonians gave chase, resulting in the widespread massacre of the Persian army. This battle was a victory for the Macedonians and the definitive end of the Persian Empire. It was the first time the Persian army had ever lost with the king present.

Battle of Gaugamela

The loss at Issus led to the capture of Darius III's family. Darius III fled, leaving behind his family, and Alexander captured his wife, two daughters, and mother. Various messages pleading for their release reached Alexander, which he refused to do until Darius accepted him as the ruler of the Persian Empire. Alexander took over nearly all of southern Asia Minor with his last victory, while Darius III was forced to flee to Babylon and regroup.

Before waging another battle, Darius III attempted peaceful negotiations. Three attempts were made, with the final one offering Alexander his daughter's hand in marriage and joint rule of the Persian Empire. Alexander refused these offers and demanded that Darius either accept him as king or meet him in battle. Darius III began gathering his forces, encamping near Gaugamela. This news reached Alexander through some of the captive men from a fleeing Persian cavalry, most of whom managed to escape when faced with the Macedonians. With the knowledge of the Persians' whereabouts, Alexander headed for a final and decisive confrontation against the Persians in 331 BCE.

The Persian army is reported to have far outnumbered the Macedonians, and Alexander is credited with the use of superior military strategies. Knowing Darius III would not wish to attack first, citing the failure of that strategy at Issus, Alexander forced his hand with an unusual move, leaving Darius III vulnerable to an attack and making Darius come out into the open to fight. To deal with the issue of a much larger Persian force, the Macedonians used careful planning and reservation, allowing them to endure longer.

Alexander charged and weakened the center of the Persian army, leaving Darius III unguarded. Reports suggest that Darius, once again, abandoned his army and fled, with his army following suit. Alexander would have given chase if not for a message he received of his army struggling at the left flank, choosing to help them instead. Although the Persians put up a fierce fight, they fell.

The Last of the Achaemenid Dynasty: Darius III Falls

Darius managed to escape on horseback with a number of his cavalry. As he escaped, he gave a resounding speech about gathering another army to face and ultimately defeat Alexander and sent off messages to his satraps to remain loyal and stout. However, he may have counted too much on the loyalty of his people. Perhaps frustrated by the continuous losses or Darius III's cowardice, Darius's satrap, Bessus, who had fought alongside him, killed the Persian king.

Alexander the Great may be greatly respected for his military command and the empire he built, but he is also celebrated for his ethical stance during battles. When he found Darius III dead, he gave him a burial ceremony at Persepolis, the Persian capital, and hunted down Bessus. After the death of Darius III, the remaining satraps accepted Alexander as king and surrendered without war. Bessus later attempted to take the throne, calling himself Artaxerxes V and claiming to be the king of Persia. He was eventually captured, tortured, and killed by Alexander.

Darius III is regarded by many as inefficient, unsuitable for the throne, and cowardly. While unrest in Persia had been growing due to political instability, the empire still held on as it had before. However, during Darius III's reign, the whole of the Achaemenid Empire came to an end and was lost to foreign invaders. What is more, Darius's attempts at fighting the invaders were lackluster at best, as he abandoned his army more than once instead of engaging in battle to win or die nobly. With his death in 330 BCE, the Achaemenid dynasty officially came to an end.

SECTION FOUR: ARTS, RELIGION, AND CULTURE

Chapter 12: Arts and Architecture

The Achaemenid Empire had much to boast about during its two-century rule. It grew to form the largest civilization of its time under the leadership of Cyrus the Great and his successors. The Achaemenid Empire added to its rapidly growing dynasty with its conquests, with various people groups and cultures assimilating under the Persian flag.

Their many conquests brought the Persian emperors untold riches, power, and influence that reached beyond the regions of their rule. As the empire grew, so did its art, design, architecture, and craftsmanship. In addition to leading conquests, many of the Persian emperors spent considerable wealth erecting beautiful examples of artistry and architecture that portray the skill and might of the Persians, some of which still exist to this day. While the Achaemenid Empire held great political influence, it also left behind a great cultural heritage.

History of Achaemenid Art

The Achaemenid Empire lasted a little over two centuries, from the mid-6th century to the mid-4th century BCE. In that time, it grew to become one of history's greatest empires, stretching from the Indus Valley in modern-day Pakistan to Egypt in the northeast corner of Africa. As the empire grew and expanded, it gained unsurmountable wealth, riches, and power. With that came the development of a unique culture, complete with its own language, history, and art.

Before the Persian Empire emerged, the region had been dominated by a number of other civilizations that brought their own culture, tradition, heritage, language, and art with them. A combination of influences ruled over ancient Persia, such as the Elamites, Assyrians, and Medes. When the Achaemenid Empire took control, it created a new culture derived from the influences of those who came before. Many of these dynasties had coexisted for some time in the Iranian Plateau, leading to a cultural mix that produced novel traditions.

The Achaemenid conquests also played a major role in the emerging art and architecture during this period. Some of the major influences came from the Greek, Babylonian, and Lydian cultures. Some Chinese influences can also be seen in Persian art; in particular, miniatures created as illustrations or independent artworks often featured Chinese characters. Roman, Mesopotamian, and Egyptian influences can also be seen in the Persian artwork produced during this time.

Persian architecture emerged as a synthesis of the various influences arising from the conquests and history of the empire. Its architectural prowess spanned from picturesque cities that served as centers of administration and governance and symbols of Achaemenid power to mausoleums and temples, which were designed to honor the fallen and worship the sacred gods revered by the people living in the Persian Empire. The previous Elamite, Assyrian, and Median civilizations, as well as the conquered lands of Egypt, Lydia, and Asia Minor, all contributed to the construction and design process adopted by the Persians. The result was something inherently unique and clearly identifiable as Persian craftsmanship.

Some of the most significant examples of Persian architecture that represent its style and influence are the royal tombs, such as those of Cyrus the Great and Artaxerxes IV. These tombs were a hallmark feature of the empire, as kings of the dynasty often built their own tombs. The city of Persepolis, which served as one of the empire's capitals, is another example of the Persian Empire's magnificence, as it served as the hub of governmental functions and ceremonial proceedings.

Two other important cities were Ecbatana and Susa, which remained the focus of many Persian emperors, with the rulers ordering the construction of various landmarks, which have stood the test of time and attest to the craft adopted by Persian builders and architects. The preserved structures in these cities offer a great insight into the development of Persian architecture, as it features construction carried out throughout the empire.

The Persians showed great skill in various facets of art and architecture. They are particularly known for their love and expertise in creating rock and frieze reliefs and their skill with precious metals. They used their reserves of gold and silver to create functional and decorative pieces. Columned halls are a distinctive feature of Persian architecture, appearing most significantly in the constructions of Xerxes I and Artaxerxes III.

Rock Reliefs

Carved rock reliefs could often be found on high points beside an important road or sources of water and were commonly used to mark a successful conquest. Rock reliefs first emerged in the Elamite civilization and were subsequently adopted by many later civilizations, including the Achaemenids, and were often carved in the same places. Under Persian emperors, such reliefs were typically used to boast of Persian power and illustrate the empire's might and extent. Some of the more significant examples include the Behistun Inscription and the Naqsh-e Rostam.

Behistun Inscription

Behistun Inscription.
PersianDutchNetwork, CC BY-SA 4.0 <https://creativecommons.org/licenses/by-sa/4.0>, via Wikimedia Commons; https://commons.wikimedia.org/wiki/File:Behistun_Inscription_in_Persia_ca._520_BC-_UNESCO_World_Heritage_Site.jpg

The Behistun Inscription, which was written for Darius the Great, is a multilingual rock relief proclaiming the power of the Achaemenid dynasty. It first relates a short autobiography of Darius and continues to relate, in great detail, the rebellions that arose as a result of his predecessor's actions and Darius's success in suppressing them. The events are written in the Babylonian, Elamite, and Old Persian languages, and the inscription was crucial in helping to decipher the cuneiform script. As a proclamation of the empire's might, it also relates all the territories under Persian rule.

Naqsh-e Rostam

Naqsh-e Rostam.
Maasaak, CC BY-SA 4.0 <https://creativecommons.org/licenses/by-sa/4.0>, via Wikimedia Commons; https://commons.wikimedia.org/wiki/File:Naqsh-e_Rustam_necropolis_in_Iran.jpg

The Naqsh-e Rostam serves as the tomb and final resting place for four Achaemenid kings near Persepolis. Various archaeological sites are carved into the face of the mountain besides the tombs, including the Ka'ba-ye Zartosht and the Sassanid reliefs, which date from the Elamite dynasty to the Sasanians. The tombs of the kings are cut into the cliff, as well as with various depictions, which include images of the kings being blessed by the gods and rows of other figures, presumably soldiers and the king's subjects, offering tribute.

The emperors' tombs are sometimes referred to as the Persian crosses based on the way they are structured. The entrance lies at the center of the cross, which leads into the chamber where the king lies in a sarcophagus. Of the four tombs found here, only the tomb of Darius I is explicitly labeled. The other three are believed to be those of Xerxes I, Artaxerxes I, and Darius II. A fifth unfinished tomb is also located here, which has been speculated to belong to either Artaxerxes IV or Darius III; the latter's tomb has never been discovered to date. After the fall of the Achaemenid Empire, Alexander the Great's armies looted the tombs, along with many other Persian structures.

Frieze Relief

Frieze of Griffon, Palace of Darius.
Following Hadrian, CC BY-SA 2.0 <https://creativecommons.org/licenses/by-sa/2.0>, via Wikimedia Commons; https://commons.wikimedia.org/wiki/File:Frieze_of_Griffins,_circa_510_BC,_Apadana,_west_courtyard_of_the_palace,_Susa,_Iran Susa,_Iran,_Louvre_Museum_(12251831946).jpg

Frieze reliefs could be found in abundance in Persian architecture reliefs. These reliefs are sculptured decorative single panels portraying various designs. They are often found along royal staircases or buildings or as part of furniture. Many of these Achaemenid friezes can be found in Persepolis, particularly in palace architecture, such as in the throne rooms of Darius and Xerxes.

Most commonly, friezes appear in Achaemenid architecture as slabs with low carvings along staircases that lead to important ceremonial structures. Many of them feature or attempt to represent the empire's wealth by depicting servants bearing richly laden platters of drink and food for royal feasts.

One of the more recognizable frieze reliefs is the depiction of a Median. This relief is located along a stairway on the side of the Palace of Darius; however, it dates to the reign of Artaxerxes II. It portrays the Median, who can be identified by his dress, the typical tunic with a belt and a rounded cap, being led by a Persian. The frieze shows them walking hand in hand, perhaps representing harmonious relations following the conquest of the Medians.

Friezes that showcase the power of the Persian king are referred to as Treasure Reliefs, which illustrate scenes from across the empire, similar to the one found on the palace stairway. The Apadana in Persepolis features such scenes, such as one showing leaders and noblemen from the various Persian provinces appearing beneath a male lamassus, a design of a celestial being adopted from the Mesopotamian culture.

Paradise Gardens

One of the best depictions of Persian art and style is the gardens, which depict a particular Achaemenid influence. Known as the paradise gardens, they were typically designed in an enclosed, symmetrical style. A common and unique feature of these gardens was the *chahar bagh*, which literally translates to "four gardens," indicating the four-quarter split in the garden surrounding a body of water, usually a pond. Water and scents were essential elements of these gardens. Ponds, canals, and fountains were common features and were surrounded by fragrant flora.

The royal paradise garden at Pasargadae, which was built by Cyrus the Great, features the first known use of the *chahar bagh* design. A garden portico offers an opening through the garden, allowing not only an open landscape but also creating a fourfold design. This characteristic design is believed to be symbolic of the title Cyrus the Great held ("King of the Four Quarters of the World"). The garden is believed to have remained in use throughout the entirety of the Achaemenid Empire and is today designated as a World Heritage Site. It is one of the oldest remains of a Persian garden.

Precious Metalwork

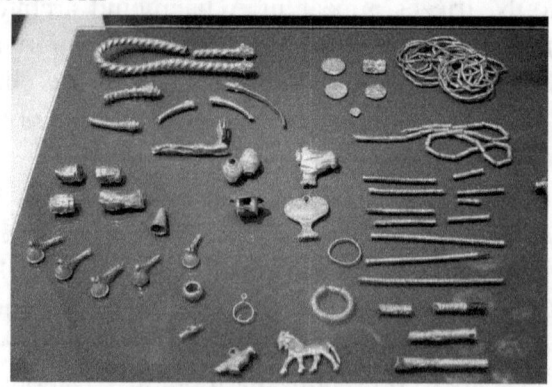

The Oxus Treasure.

British Museum, CC BY-SA 2.0 <https://creativecommons.org/licenses/by-sa/2.0>, via Wikimedia Commons; https://commons.wikimedia.org/wiki/File:The_Oxus_Treasure_by_Nickmard_Khoey_(BM)1.jpg

The discovery of the Oxus Treasure in the 19th century supplemented the modern understanding of Persian skill with metalwork. The discovered treasure held about 180 pieces of precious metalwork, including about 200 coins, from the Achaemenid period. The original treasure may have held many more pieces, as some historical reports suggest treasures may have been lost or melted down over time.

The metalworking skill of the Persians is greatly evidenced in the discovered treasure. Persian craft was exemplary and advanced for its time. Many of these pieces display highly intricate designs, which reflect a similar theme to that found in carpet weaving, pottery, and reliefs of the time. The metalwork would often be inlaid with beautiful stones. The pieces found within the recovered treasure feature bracelets and armlets, which were common gifts and often presented to the emperor as tribute.

The Statue of Darius I

The statue of Darius I.

National Museum of Iran, CC BY 3.0 <https://creativecommons.org/licenses/by/3.0>, via Wikimedia Commons; https://commons.wikimedia.org/wiki/File:National_Meusem_Darafsh_6_(42).JPG

Among the sculptures and statues the Persians created, the most notable and often-occurring feature is the Taurus—a two-headed bull commonly found at the head of columns. Another example of their statue craftsmanship is the statue of Darius I, which was discovered in Susa. It is believed to have been made in Egypt, given the grey granite from which it is made that can be found in Egypt.

The statue features Darius I enrobed and armed with a dagger on his belt. Within the pleats of his robe can be seen inscriptions in cuneiform text, with the other side featuring hieroglyphs. It is believed Darius I may have commissioned this statue after the conquest of Egypt.

Persepolitan Columns

Persian architecture notably used columns. Their type of column design has its own distinct categorization and commonly features a strong base topped with double-sided animal heads, which would usually be bulls. Apadanas were enormous halls within Persian palaces that often featured hundreds of giant columns, such as those featured in the Hall of a Hundred Columns.

The stonework skill this type of architecture required did not exist in Persia but was found in neighboring regions and in many of the empires brought under Persian rule. The Achaemenid emperors had many territories at their disposal and were able to obtain the services of craftsmen from around the empire. This resulted in a crossbred architectural style, which boasted Egyptian, Mesopotamian, Lydian, and Elamite influences.

Hall of a Hundred Columns

Hall of a Hundred Columns.
Carole Raddato, CC BY-SA 2.0 <https://creativecommons.org/licenses/by-sa/2.0>, via Wikimedia Commons; https://commons.wikimedia.org/wiki/File:Hall_of_Hundred_Columns_in_Persepolis,_Iran.jpg

The Hall of a Hundred Columns was started by Xerxes I but completed by his son and successor, Artaxerxes I. It features a northern entrance, with the portico decorated by two bulls—another hallmark of Persian architecture. Each of the one hundred columns features a wide base, which narrows as it proceeds to the top with a fluted shaft. The columns themselves are designed with floral patterns and topped by the signature two-headed bull. It functioned initially as a throne hall of Persepolis but may have become a storeroom later on to manage the vast treasures and wealth of the Achaemenid Empire.

The Royal Road

This ancient highway, which was refurbished by Darius I, served the purpose of improving communication links. It started in Sardis, crossing through Anatolia, Nineveh, and Babylonia, where it split; one end traveled through Ecbatana to what would become the Silk Road, and the other ran through Susa as far as Persepolis. Some parts of the road are believed to have been constructed during Assyrian rule, which Darius then improved and expanded.

It is believed the road was used up until the Roman period, with some parts of it, such as the bridge at Diyarbakir, still standing today. It stretched for over two thousand kilometers, and as a paved road, it could handle chariots and horse-drawn carts. Other than improving communication within the empire, the Royal Road also served to improve trade relations. As a military tool, it was particularly essential, enabling the Persian armies to cover great distances across the empire in comparatively shorter periods of time. It was a vastly important road to the empire and featured regular patrols and guard posts.

Chapter 13: Religion

Cyrus the Great's conquest of the Median Empire led to the establishment of the Achaemenid dynasty in 550 BCE. At the time of its formation, the empire was the largest ever seen and continues to be the largest empire in the history of the world based on the global population at the time. Forty-four percent of the world's population lived under the rule of the Achaemenid Empire.

Given such numbers, it stands to reason this was a diverse empire and included different nations, cultures, languages, and religions. To rule it successfully and for it to last as long as it did, an approach of acceptance and tolerance was needed, which was something its founder, Cyrus, championed.

Religious Policies of the Persian Empire

Religion played an important role within the Persian Empire. The Iranian Plateau had a rich religious history due to the many diverse groups of people that lived and conquered the land. By the time the Achaemenid Empire was born, many different religious traditions and affiliations already existed in Persia. Achaemenid conquests brought more religions under the rule of the empire.

The Cyrus Cylinder

The Cyrus Cylinder.
Prioryman, CC BY-SA 3.0 <https://creativecommons.org/licenses/by-sa/3.0>, via Wikimedia Commons; https://commons.wikimedia.org/wiki/File:Cyrus_Cylinder_front.jpg

After Cyrus the Great's conquest of Babylonia, he issued the Cyrus Cylinder, which narrates his conquest of Babylonia and the defeat of its king. It then goes on to detail his rules and policies for the regions under his rule. The Cyrus Cylinder promised religious freedom for members of all religious groups that were part of the Achaemenid Empire. Most notably, it granted Babylonian prisoners of war permission to return to their homelands. This act earned Cyrus praise for being a tolerant and just ruler.

Under his policies, Jewish prisoners of war who had been brought to Babylonia were able to return home to Jerusalem. Cyrus also granted them financial aid for their journey and political support, helping them rebuild their temple that had been destroyed in the war. Such acts of tolerance earned him great fame, and he set an example for his successors. Religious tolerance would become a hallmark of Achaemenid rule, at least until the years preceding its demise.

Magi

The Magi was the official designation of the priesthood that existed in the Median, Achaemenid, Parthian, and Sasanian Empires. During the latter two, the title Magi came to be referred to as Zoroastrian priests. The earliest designation of the Magi comes from among one of the six Median tribes, with one of them forming a priestly clan. Their position among the

Medians was that of great influence and repute, as they acted as interpreters of dreams and fortune-tellers.

During the Elamite period, other priests hailing from local cults practiced and preached their beliefs. However, during the Median rule over Persia, the Magi came to hold greater significance, performing priestly functions on a much grander scale. Some of this influence may have carried on even after the fall of the Medians since the Magi continued to hold power during the Persian Empire.

Records during Darius I's reign show that the Magi acted as the official priests for the Achaemenid royalty and enjoyed great influence in the royal court. Other than religious responsibilities, the Magi were also involved in the administrative and economic spheres. In return for their services, they were supplemented from the royal stocks with flour, wine, beer, grain, rams, and fruit.

During the Achaemenid period, the Magi appeared in Babylonia and Egypt. This appearance was probably due to the empire's rule in these regions, with the Magi traveling there to perform some administrative functions. They also appear in Greek texts and are referred to during the battles fought between the Persians and the Greeks.

Xerxes I was known to make no major decision without advice from the Magi, who would also act as prophets and accompany the Persian army on campaigns. No sacrifices could be made without the presence of the Magi. Historical accounts suggest that the Magi held great influence within the Achaemenid court, and some were even appointed as guardians of the tomb of Cyrus the Great.

Some accounts, such as those of Herodotus, suggest no temples existed for Persian gods. However, a clearly defined religious hierarchy existed, designating the chief priest and the lesser priests. Little is known about the Persian religion and practice before the adoption of Zoroastrianism, as any religion before it existed primarily as an oral tradition with no written scripture.

Before the advent of Zoroastrianism, the Magi enjoyed great privilege and were the strongest opponents of the rise of Zoroastrianism. The social system and status quo benefitted them greatly, giving them status and wealth. The teachings of Zoroaster threatened to endanger this lifestyle for the Magi. After Zoroastrianism entered the region and was widely practiced in Persia, priests within the religion began to be referred to as Magi.

Zoroastrianism

The rise of Zoroastrianism began with Zoroaster or Zarathustra, a prophet of the religion who may have preached sometime between 1500 to 1000 BCE. Little is known of him except that he came from nobility and was part of the priestly class. Around the age of thirty, he is said to have received a revelation from a being of light called Vohu Manah, a representative of Ahura Mazda, the one true god. This being represented the goodness of thought, words, and deeds.

The revelation Zoroaster received at this time told him the current religious practices of the Magi were incorrect. Thus, Ahura Mazda was introduced to him as the true god, and Zoroaster was appointed his prophet. Because a priestly class already existed, Zoroaster's teachings were not immediately accepted. A particular class of the clergy, the Karpans, were particularly against everything Zoroaster had to say. This new religious teaching was perceived to be a threat to the status quo by the priestly class, which forced Zoroaster to renounce or flee.

Zoroaster traveled to King Vishtaspa, who is known as the first righteous king who accepted the faith as preached by Zoroaster. In Vishtaspa's court, Zoroaster debated the nature of divine truth with Vishtaspa's priests. Initially, Vishtaspa was not pleased with this challenge to his faith and had Zoroaster imprisoned. When Zoroaster was able to heal his paralyzed horse, the king released him and accepted the faith. With his influence, the Zoroastrian faith began to spread, replacing the polytheistic beliefs of the time.

Until his death at the age of seventy-seven, Zoroaster is believed to have continued his teachings, living a life of quiet devotion. While some accounts relate that he passed away of old age, others suggest that he may have been assassinated for his beliefs.

The Basis of Zoroastrianism

The Zoroastrian faith, which is still around today, follows five basic principles. These reflect the teachings of other monotheistic religions in that it preaches the existence of one supreme god. In Zoroastrianism, that god is Ahura Mazda. Just as Ahura Mazda is the embodiment of all that is good, his eternal nemesis, Angra Mainyu, is the embodiment of all that is evil. A man's goodness can be seen through his thoughts, words, and deeds, and each has the free will to choose good or evil for themselves.

Earlier gods and entities that had existed were reassigned as spiritual manifestations of Ahura Mazda. Preexisting concepts became assimilated into this new faith, including that of Chinvat Bridge, which describes death as the crossing of a dark river via boat, the Crossing of the Separator. In Zoroastrianism, this bridge reflects the deeds of the person attempting to cross it, becoming narrow and razor-sharp for the condemned and becoming wider and easier to cross for the righteous. Two guards overseeing the bridge welcome the righteous while snarling at the condemned souls. The angel Suroosh guides and guards the souls as they cross, and the maiden of the bridge, Daena, comforts the souls as they come to the crossing.

Zoroastrianism largely operates on the principle of good and evil. There are both benevolent and malevolent spirits to be found roaming the world called the ahuras and the daevas, respectively. Since their influence exists all around the world and since humans have the free will to choose what they follow, it is an individual's responsibility to guard themselves against the evil and negative and accept the righteous and positive. In the same way, it is an individual's responsibility to lead a life of honesty, truthfulness, and honor, rejecting lies and deception. By doing so, one can enter paradise after death.

However, failure to lead a righteous life did not result in eternal punishment in the House of Lies. In Zoroastrianism, a savior-like figure, Saoshyant, will bring the End of Time when all souls will be forgiven and reunite with their creator. Angra Mainyu will be defeated once and for all, and everyone, whether righteous or condemned, will live in eternal bliss.

Ahura Mazda

Ahura Mazda.
A. Davey, CC BY 2.0 <https://creativecommons.org/licenses/by/2.0>, via Wikimedia Commons; https://commons.wikimedia.org/wiki/File:Ahura_Mazda.jpg

The all-good, all-powerful creator of life, Ahura Mazda, is believed to have birthed the other, lesser gods. He embodies all the positive, bright forces, which clash with the negative, dark forces intent on creating chaos through Angra Mainyu. The world, as created by Ahura Mazda, came to be in seven steps, beginning with the sky or, according to other traditions, water. This world would have brought about universal harmony were it not for the devious actions of Angra Mainyu.

The sky came to be in the form of an orb that held water, and the different bodies of water were separated by the earth, which was granted vegetation to sustain life. Ahura Mazda then went on to create the primordial bull, Gavaevodata, which was killed by Angra Mainyu. His corpse was carried to the moon, where it was purified. All other animals were born through Gavaevodata.

This concept of Ahura Mazda's creations, which were later destroyed or corrupted by Angra Mainyu, exists throughout the Zoroastrian faith. When the first human, Gayomart, was created, Angra Mainyu killed him because of his beauty. The man's seed was purified in the sun, birthing a rhubarb plant from which manifested the first couple on earth, Mashya and Mashyana. Ahura Mazda granted them souls, and they were to live in peace and harmony with one another. However, they were corrupted by Angra Mainyu, who convinced them of Ahura Mazda's treachery as a false god. The couple fell from grace and were banished to live in a world of chaos and strife.

Although the couple was forced into a world of conflict, they could still choose to live a life of truth and honesty, repenting to Ahura Mazda and rejecting the influence of Angra Mainyu. Thus, the essence of this faith was the battle between good and evil. All other entities within the faith, including supernatural beings, fall on either end of the spectrum, with humans also forced to make a choice between the two sides.

Zoroastrianism underwent many modifications, particularly after the death of Zoroaster. For example, the crossing of the bridge was altered to include a final judgment when a soul's deeds would be balanced against each other. The souls that led a life of truth would be admitted to the House of Song, their final paradise. Naysayers would go into the darkness and confusion, finding their ultimate end in the House of Lies, which was similar to the Christian hell.

Human Life under Zoroastrianism

The beginning of human life was intended as a gift, as the soul Ahura Mazda had given them was supposed to be cherished and cared for. Ahura Mazda took care of the humans' needs and only asked that they care for their souls by adhering to his teachings and acting as defenders of his values, namely truth, honesty, and righteousness. Human life gained its meaning from the protection of the gift it had been granted. However, the meaning was lost by rejecting that gift, instead following Angra Mainyu's vengeful purpose.

While humans had free will to choose the path they would take in life, Ahura Mazda intended to guide them to the right path. For this purpose, he created a legion of lesser beings who would aid people in making the right choices and protect them from the dark forces of Angra Mainyu. These included Mithra, the god of the rising sun, Hvar Ksata, the god of the full sun, and Ardvi Sura, the goddess of health and fertility.

Worship rituals in Zoroastrianism center around the four elements, as that is how Ahura Mazda created the world in the beginning. It begins with fire, which is lit on the outer altar, and ends with water, which celebrates the elements of life, as it stands on earth and is surrounded by air. Of these elements, fire is the most important, but all elements are respected and sacred.

The Persian religion did not feature temples or statues because of a basic Zoroastrian tenet that their god was everywhere. The idea of a single building that could contain their god was unacceptable, as it was believed impossible and inappropriate. The use of the four elements in their worship made other regions, like the Greeks, report that the Persians worshiped fire. This was inaccurate, as the Persians used the elements to symbolize their god and worshipped their divine power alone.

Zoroastrianism in the Achaemenid Empire

Zoroastrianism was one of the major religions practiced in the Iranian Plateau, and much evidence indicates that the Achaemenid Empire's rulers observed the religion. Following Cyrus the Great's many conquests that led to the establishment of the Achaemenid dynasty, he is known to have praised Ahura Mazda for his success. While this led to the assumption that he was a Zoroastrian, other sources suggest this may not be entirely true.

Historical records show Ahura Mazda as an entity that may have predated the advent of Zoroastrianism. He was considered the supreme deity, and Cyrus's worship of the god does not necessarily indicate affiliation with Zoroastrianism. Similarly, there is no concrete proof of the religious inclination of later emperors, although most sources suggest they practiced Zoroastrianism. Ahura Mazda, in particular, is praised in various artwork, decrees, and Darius I's Behistun Inscription.

The Achaemenid Empire's policy of religious tolerance meant that the religion practiced by the royal house was never imposed on its subjects. This is also the reason it is difficult to determine with absolute certainty which religion was practiced by the Persian nobility. However, this religious independence is believed to have birthed Zurvanism. This movement stemmed from Zoroastrianism. The supreme deity in Zurvanism was Zurvan, or Time, who created Ahura Mazda and Angra Mainyu. The two were created as equals and locked in a cosmic struggle, whose ultimate victor would be Ahura Mazda. Zurvanism thought is believed to have gained traction during the second half of the Achaemenid Empire but did not become relevant on a larger scale until much later during the Sasanian period.

Chapter 14: Military

The force of the Persian military is attested to by the might of the Achaemenid Empire. Since most of the empire's conquests were preceded by war, the Persian military can be credited with expanding the Persian Empire.

Whether the true credit of the military's victories can be attributed to the strength of the military, its skill, or its leadership is hard to say; however, its contribution to the empire is undeniable. Over the course of Achaemenid rule, the Persian military expanded and grew to include greater numbers and superior weaponry. Even at the time of the Persian military's final defeat at the hands of Alexander the Great, it greatly outnumbered its opponent.

Distribution of the Persian Military

The Persian military consisted of five main divisions, with tactics based on the movement of these groups. They included the archers, the cavalry, the infantry, the chariots, and later the war fleet.

Archers

Persian archers.
Pergamon Museum, CC BY 2.0 <https://creativecommons.org/licenses/by/2.0>, via Wikimedia Commons https://en.wikipedia.org/wiki/File:Persian_warriors_from_Berlin_Museum.jpg

The Persian archers were held in high regard since they were stationed on the front lines. The Persian tactic was to have the *sparabara*, or the shield-bearers, form a defensive line at the head of the army. The archers would then mount an attack on the opposing force, firing over the shield-bearers. This would pave the way for the infantry and cavalry to launch a more vicious attack against a now-exhausted opponent. The bow was also the national arm of the Achaemenid Empire, indicating the importance of archers in the military.

Scythian archers were hired by the Persians to train their archers since they had superior abilities. For this reason, the Scythians greatly influenced Persian archers, including their fighting style and weaponry. The Persians also adopted the Scythian bow and altered the bow to be recurved and made of wood rather than a chord, which granted greater flexibility when the arrow was released. Their arrows were also modified to be lighter and featured a bronze tip.

The altered bow and arrow proved so light and useful to carry that even infantrymen carried a bow and some arrows onto the battlefield. The

Persian innovations, combined with their military tactics, led to the archers being considered some of the most superior military fighters of their time, even more so than the elite Cretans, the Greek archers. Persian archers played a key role in the success of the Persian military during expansionist conquests.

Cavalry

Cyrus the Great first realized the importance of the cavalry after watching the Greek military, which utilized cavalry units to great advantage. Taking inspiration from the Khorasan horseman, Cyrus organized the Persian cavalry to form the world's greatest mounted army at the time. The light cavalry carried altered Scythian bows. The light cavalry was made up of diverse nationalities and instigated battles by drawing an opponent into the fight.

The heavy cavalry, on the other hand, featured mostly Persian men who were armed with the usual weaponry of the infantry: battle axes, shields, and bows. Later on, this weaponry was updated, and the cavalrymen would carry javelins, which had a feared reputation among Persian enemies. The cavalry also carried long wooden or metal lances, shields, and spears.

Chariots

Chariots were not limited to a military designation during the Achaemenid Empire; they also served a ceremonial purpose and were used as command vehicles. The Persian emperors, particularly Xerxes I, were known to ride into battle in chariots. A special, empty chariot would also make an appearance. It was dedicated to Ahura Mazda and was pulled by eight white horses, giving him a place to join the Persians in battle.

The Persian scythed chariots remained one of their most deadly and effective innovations. Cyrus the Great, who had never seen much utility in the chariot as a military weapon, commissioned the scythed chariot, which was a far more effective weapon. It operated like a regular chariot but had swords attached to the wheels, which stuck out on either side. The swords could sever or seriously damage the limbs of their victims.

The scythed chariot became a vicious weapon for the Persians, who inflicted great damage on their enemy without much danger to themselves. Its original purpose was to breach the Greek defensive lines. Their heavy infantry formation had proven too strong for the Persian cavalry, but the scythed chariots made it an easy task.

Persian Fleet

The Persian fleet was largely adopted from the Greek triremes and biremes. The fleet featured long, narrow ships. The triremes had three levels of rowers with a long oar in the back. In the front, an iron beam ram was set, which was designed to stab and attack opponent ships and potentially destroy them. The biremes supported only two levels of rowers and carried two hundred men rather than three hundred. It otherwise performed many of the same functions as the trireme.

The Persian navy did not exist at the beginning of the Achaemenid Empire; it was launched by Cambyses II for the Battle of Pelusium against Egypt. Darius I used the navy for the conquest of lands in Asia Minor to face the Greek navy. With their navy, the Persians were able to conquer Thrace and Samos and fought against the Scythians.

The Persian navy is believed to have been led by commanders chosen from the imperial aristocracy. Many of these commanders may have been non-Persian since the Persians did not originally hold a fleet and therefore had no experience in commanding one. These early commanders may have been Carians, although some were also reported to be Greek. Little is known about sailors of lower rank other than that Phoenician rowers and sailors were hired at some point. The marines were made up almost entirely of Medians, Persians, and Scythians.

The Persian navy had a profound impact on the future of naval warfare in the region. They formed what would be the first true imperial navy, as they established the first trireme navy in history. The navy also laid the basis for Iranian naval engineering that would come later. The naval bases enjoyed great benefits due to their position, and the regions they were located in enjoyed great wealth.

The Diversity of the Persian Military

The Persian Empire assimilated various regions under its rule, and with that came the recruitment of military personnel from a variety of regions. As a result, the Persian army was one of the most diverse at the time.

Historical records suggest that a nation's contribution of soldiers to the Persian army came from its proximity to Persia. In lieu of paying tribute to the empire, nations could contribute more soldiers to the army. As a result, the Medians contributed the largest number of soldiers and imperial generals. The remainder of the army was made up of Scythians, Egyptians, Ethiopians, Indians, Bactrians, and other groups.

The incorporation of these various groups into the Persian army also introduced different military techniques and weaponry. The archery bows from the Scythians, the triremes from the Greeks, and the war elephants from the Indians soon became a common sight on Persian battlefields. The Persians also came to rely heavily on mercenaries, particularly toward the end of Cyrus the Great's reign and during the rule of Cambyses II.

Greek mercenaries were very useful for the Persian army. For one, the Persian weaponry and armor were deemed to be inferior to that of the Greeks. Mercenaries were loyal to their employers and possessed skills and knowledge of tactics not known to the Persians. Since mercenaries were committed to war, they could fight with a zeal not found among other soldiers in the army. Mercenaries were sometimes even hired as generals and became part of the king's personal guard.

Division and Tactics of the Persian Army

The Persian army is believed to have amounted to roughly between 120,000 to 150,000 men, excluding the military support they gained from their allies. The *hazarabam*, which was made up of a thousand troops, was considered the best of the Persian regiments. Ten *hazarabams* made up the elite unit called the Immortals. They were the king's personal guards and were highly trained.

The default Persian war tactic was to use shields, through *sparabaras*, along the front lines and have archers launch the attack. The Persian army was also trained in shock tactics, which involved hand-to-hand combat, though this was not the Persians' preferred move, as they favored maintaining their distance from the opponent and defeating them through missile-style attacks.

The attack would typically begin with the actions of the light cavalry, who would seek to instigate the enemy. These were small attacks, with the soldiers using arrows and small javelins to goad their opponent to attack as the archers prepared an offensive. The cavalry would then move to attack the flanks, causing the opponent to gather together in a dense formation, which would make it difficult to maneuver. If the army chose to disperse instead, it would be subjected to shock attacks. In this way, Persian opponents, even the Greeks, suffered heavy casualties on the battlefield.

The Persian tactic was effective in theory but did not always work. For it to be effective, the Persians required large, open terrain that would not hinder the quick movements of the cavalry. It also required good timing and coordination between the cavalry, the archers, and the infantry and the inferiority of their opponent's weaponry and limited mobility. When the Persian army suffered a defeat, it was for the lack of one or more of these requirements.

For example, the Scythians engaged in scorched-earth tactics. They remained highly mobile and never engaged long enough with the Persian army to allow it to deploy its war tactics. This led to the Persians giving chase to the Scythians in a land wholly unfamiliar to them while the Scythians destroyed all possible resources, leaving nothing behind for the Persians to use.

The Battle of Marathon against the Greeks also resulted in failure for the Persians. The battle was conducted on a rocky slope, which was unfit for the Persians to scale and launch an attack. The Athenians returned to the plain when the Persians retreated to their ships, so the Athenians were able to avoid the hail of Persian arrows to engage them in close-quarters combat. The Athenians had no issues with mobility and did not have inferior weapons or skills the Persians could exploit. And although Alexander the Great's army was inferior in number, it was able to defeat the Persian forces due to superior tactical planning and the diverse divisions of Alexander's army. It comprised a variety of cavalry and infantry units that could launch attacks on all types of terrain with a variety of weaponry, forcing the Persians into close combat, where they were greatly outclassed.

The Greeks had far superior armor, which deflected the arrows and small javelins launched as part of the Persians' initial attack. Once the Persians had been forced into close combat, they stood little chance of victory since their inferior weaponry and lack of armor could not compete with the Greeks, though they did not possess any less valor or spirit than their opponents. The Persian army also relied heavily on their leader or king in battle. Although they remained coordinated under his guidance, they would immediately fall into disarray if the military leader was called or forced to flee, as was the case when Darius III faced off against the forces of Alexander the Great.

Preparing for Battle

While the Persian army had great strength in numbers, it was rarely sufficient for large expeditions. In such cases, the army needed to be recruited, and the process could take years. The Persian Empire held garrisons in important city centers, and the satraps had their own guard and local army. However, these were not called on to launch a campaign since it would leave the satrap vulnerable and defenseless in the face of a potential rebellion.

Mercenaries and tribal warriors were much easier to recruit and gather in times of need. They would be summoned to the *handaisa*, the recruiting stations, where they would be reviewed and recruited. The army would store provisions along the route it took for the campaign, although the men also carried supplies in baggage carts. Given the importance of religion in Persian culture, the Magi would accompany such campaigns, chanting hymns while circling the commander. They would carry an eagle standard and holy fire in portable holders.

Scouts would be sent ahead to watch for the enemy's movements. The military also established a great and reliable communication system while on the move. The Royal Road served as a way for couriers to convey messages quickly. The couriers would maintain their speed by changing horses frequently. The Persians also used fire signals to send news quickly.

The Persian army largely relied on day marches, as commanders disliked advancing or attacking at nighttime. The daytime procession was slow, owing to the baggage they often carried. In addition to provisions for the journey and the war, the procession would often include litters for the king's and commanders' wives and concubines. At nighttime, the army would make encampments on flat areas. If they feared an enemy approach, they would dig ditches, setting up sandbag defenses around them. Before the beginning of a battle, a council was held to discuss strategies and tactics.

Chapter 15: Languages and the Truth Issue

The Persian Empire adopted the Persian language, also known as Parsi, which remained the predominant language throughout the Achaemenid rule. Persian is part of the Indo-Iranian language group, and the spread and use of the language reached from Indian borders to Egypt and the Mediterranean and may have also influenced regions in the north. Old Persian, known locally as *ariya*, appears in the records and inscriptions from the Achaemenid period, most notably on Darius I's Behistun Inscription.

In modern times, the Parsi language has changed its form and is spoken and written beyond the regions of the Middle East. The Achaemenid Empire carried the Persian language with them into the subcontinent of India with their conquest of the Indus Valley. It remained a popular language in the royal courts until the arrival of the British, who banned many local languages.

Old Persian

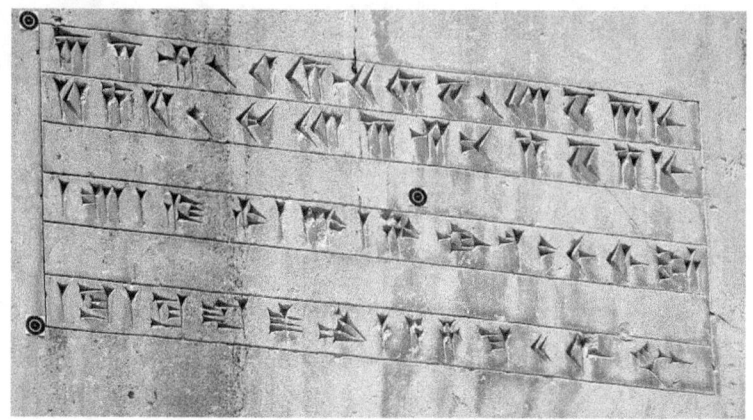

Old Persian inscription in Persepolis.
Truth Seeker (fawiki), CC BY-SA 3.0 <https://creativecommons.org/licenses/by-sa/3.0>, via Wikimedia Commons https://commons.wikimedia.org/wiki/File:I_am_Cyrus,_Achaemenid_King_-_Pasargadae.JPG

Old Persian is largely regarded as the language of the Achaemenid Empire. The language is used in administrative and legal texts and inscriptions celebrating the life and conquests of the Persian emperors. Its oldest recorded use is the Behistun Inscription, although the language dates back much further. A tribe by the name of Parsuwash is thought to have brought the language with them into the Iranian Plateau early in the 1st millennium BCE.

Later Assyrian records indicate the use of ancient Iranian languages, including the Persian and Median languages. Old Persian features many words from the Median language, which is now extinct, indicating its usage in the region long before the Achaemenid Empire came to be. The Behistun Inscription does not limit itself to one language. It repeats the same text in three cuneiform script languages: Old Persian, Elamite, and Babylonian. This indicates that, just as with religion, language diversity was welcome in the Persian Empire.

Even during the Achaemenid Empire, Old Persian did not retain its original form and developed and morphed into what is now known as the post-Old Persian language or pre-Middle Persian, as it lies in between the two distinct formations of the language. The language is evident in the 4th century BCE, where the inscriptions of Darius I differ greatly from the later inscriptions made during Artaxerxes II's and Artaxerxes III's reigns.

This form of Old Persian acted as a bridge to the Middle Persian language, which further evolved into New Persian. With each successive morphing, the language and syntax became more simplistic and straightforward than the one before it.

Middle Persian

The Middle Persian language gained traction after the Achaemenid Empire during the Sasanian period. Other than inscriptions and a few unearthed records during the Achaemenid Empire, few examples can be found of their writings, so we don't know the extent and diversity of the languages used during this time. However, many written texts, especially of the religious variety, have been unearthed from the Sasanian period that indicate the shift from Old Persian to Middle Persian.

The development of Middle Persian, like other Middle Iranian languages, began sometime in the mid-5th century BCE and continued until the 7th century CE. This period of development is marked by a change in the way the language was spoken, written, and used. The language was influenced by the empire's changes as well, taking on many features from the Greek language. Old Persian, as had been used by the Achaemenids, featured the Aramaic language, which began to lose its influence over time.

Modern Persian

Modern Persian, New Persian, or Farsi evolved from Middle Persian and is not wholly of Iranian origin. The language was slow to change, and the metamorphosis took until the 10th or 11th century CE and eventually formulated into the version known today. It took great influence from a variety of languages, including English, French, and German, but the most notable contribution comes from the Arabic language, which replaced many of the original Persian terms.

While European words exist in the Persian language, be it English or French, they exist largely out of necessity. Words for terms like "car" simply did not exist in the Persian language, and the solution was to import the word rather than invent a suitable term. Other words, like *merci*, which have suitable Persian counterparts, simply became enmeshed into the language to the degree that they sound natural rather than foreign to its speakers.

However, Arabic influence on the language was different. Not only did it replace the original Persian script, but many Arabic words and terms also outright replaced Persian words. This evolution of the Persian language is considered harmful since it completely annihilated many parts of the Persian language. These parts of the language are now extinct and sound more foreign to Persian speakers than the non-Persian words of their language.

The Use of Language in the Achaemenid Culture

Old Persian did not become one of the Achaemenid languages until much later. Starting with the reign of Cyrus the Great up until the rule of Darius I, the center of the Persian Empire was at Susa in Elam. Given this, the primary language of the administration remained Elamite since it made the most sense. The use of Elamite is attested in the tablets and fortifications found at Persepolis.

However, while Elamite remained the official language, it was not the only language used, even in the early days of the Achaemenid Empire. Any use of Elamite was always accompanied by text written in Old Persian, Babylonian, or Akkadian. This multilingual approach has led historians to believe that Elamite may have served as the central language in Susa. In other regions of the empire, other languages may have taken precedence. In any case, after the mid-5th century BCE, there is no recorded use of Elamite in Achaemenid-era records.

The Persians and Aramaic

Following Cyrus the Great's conquest of Mesopotamia, Aramaic was introduced to the Achaemenid Empire. Originating in Mesopotamia, it is believed to have been adopted by the Persians as their official language, which would help govern the diverse regions under Persian rule that otherwise hosted vastly different languages, peoples, and cultures. While many believe the Persians used Aramaic as an official language, there is no official document or inscription suggesting it was ever adopted as such. In fact, no such claim exists for any language used during the Achaemenid Empire. Aramaic was more pervasively used within the Persian Empire, and it continued to survive long after the demise of the Achaemenid.

The use of Old Persian was equally widespread; however, based on the recovered seals, artistic objects, and inscriptions, it may have been more commonly used in the western regions of Iran. The evolution of the language was rather drastic and differed greatly from its original form by the start of Artaxerxes II's reign. The reason behind this is believed to be that the language, in its original form, had largely been forgotten by that time in favor of other languages used within the empire. The scribes who wrote texts in Old Persian attempted to do so by recreating older inscriptions, obtaining imperfect and barely accurate results.

Greek Influence

The Achaemenids' entanglement with the Greeks meant that they did, at least occasionally, conduct some correspondence in the Greek language. The Persians had extensive, if usually hostile, relations with the Greeks, and they also conquered many Greek regions in Asia Minor. In addition, Greek mercenaries were a major part of the Persian army, and the Persians often forged alliances with the Greeks to aid in various campaigns. Artaxerxes II also acted as an arbiter to initiate the King's Peace between various Greek city-states. Therefore, the Greek language played an important role in the Persian bureaucracy.

However, there are no written records of Greek linguistic influences on the Achaemenid Empire. In addition to the Persians' frequent dealings with the Greeks, there is evidence to indicate that many Greeks also lived within the Achaemenid Empire, especially within Iran. Greek builders were involved in the construction of various Persian monuments, and some Greek inscriptions have been discovered at Persepolis. It seems inevitable that the Achaemenid Empire used, to some extent, the Greek language within its administrative circle.

Communication in the Persian Empire

One of the tenets of a successful empire is its communication channels. To run an empire as vast and diverse as the Achaemenid Empire, effective and quick communication was a prerequisite. Without it, not only would administrative processes come to a halt, but the empire would also be ill-equipped to respond to sudden threats. So, messages needed to be sent out quickly and reliably, but they also had to be relayed in a language that could be understood by all.

Hierarchy of Communication

Communication within the Achaemenid Empire followed a top-down route, starting at the royal court. Directives and orders were issued by the king, which were then passed to the satraps. These satraps would then carry out these directives in their respective regions of governance. The deployment of satraps to regional courts was intended to be an extension of the king's court, where his accepted practices were to be emulated.

This also established a more effective channel of communication. The Achaemenid Empire held a vast geographical region under its rule; attempting to disperse any message effectively throughout the kingdom would be a great challenge. Since the satraps were usually members of the royal family, they could be relied on to uphold royal tradition at regional courts and to maintain efficient and swift communication channels throughout their respective regions.

Correspondence

Since Aramaic had been adopted following the Mesopotamian conquest and established as the administrative language, it widely served as the major language of correspondence. The multilingual nature of the Achaemenid Empire necessitated this practice since there was no other way to ensure communication between the various satrapies. There is no record of the Achaemenid emperors themselves showing a preference for any particular language.

With a single administrative language, the work of scribes was made easier since they had only to learn Aramaic to fulfill their role in the royal court. Very few examples of royal correspondence survive, as much of it was inscribed on perishable items. The few surviving samples of communication between various satraps form the belief that Aramaic was largely relied on as the official language of communication.

The Truth Issue

One of the central tenets of Persian life, which is noted by various historians, is the focus on truthfulness. This is largely believed to have stemmed from a religious perspective. Zoroastrianism, one of the most commonly practiced religions in the Persian Empire, portrays Ahura Mazda as an all-powerful god, a being of light that values truth and honesty. Following his practices and upholding these principles was what gave meaning to life. It stands to reason then that the truth was very important in Persian life. Based on historical accounts, nothing was more disgraceful than telling a lie, and this would influence many Persian policies and practices.

However, it may be inaccurate to say that the importance of truth emerged from a religious basis. Even before the spread of Zoroastrianism, the Persian people followed a basic set of ethics that defined their lives. In the absence of orderly courts, laws, and enforcers of any such policies, a code of honor ruled supreme among the various Iranian tribes, among which was the basic tenet of truth-telling. Even those who had not grown up within the teachings of any religion followed and valued such ethical principles, forming a core part of Persian life.

Lying was considered the basis of every evil in Persian morality, within and outside the practice of Zoroastrianism. The Zoroastrian book, the Avesta, also mentions the fallacy of lying, stating that it led to the corruption of the righteous man. The concept of truth-telling was so deeply entrenched in Persian thought that Darius I used it to justify his actions to take the throne.

The Behistun Inscription narrates Darius I's ascension to the throne and the actions he then took to suppress rebellions in the Persian Empire. The inscription lists the names of a series of deceivers, including the imposter Bardiya, whose lies and deceit caused the nation to fall into rebellion, leading to unrest, chaos, and strife. Darius I emerged from this havoc as the bearer of light and truth, having quashed the rebellion and dealt with the challengers of Ahura Mazda.

Chapter 16: Government of the Empire

When Cyrus the Great founded the Achaemenid Empire, he established an organized regime. The empire boasted four capital cities during Cyrus's reign, which served as hubs for the administrative management of the vast, multi-regional empire. These four cities were Pasargadae, Susa, Ecbatana, and Babylon. These cities were also intended to show off the might and power of the Persian Empire.

The Achaemenid Empire also established a somewhat regional manner of governance. The satrapy system established administrative units across the empire, where governors or satraps were installed to oversee the region. In addition to the satrap, a general was also employed to manage military operations, and there was a state secretary for record-keeping. As the empire grew, so did the satrapies, and the Achaemenid form of governance influenced many later regimes.

The System of Governance

The satrapy system was not new to the Iranian Plateau, as it had been implemented by the Medians and the Assyrians before them. Cyrus drew inspiration for his own government from them, though he chose to make some vital changes. The Persian Empire is believed to have taken the greatest influence from foreign empires than any empire before it.

A common aspect of the Persian Empire and those that preceded it was that they all ruled over a diverse group of people. However, unlike the Persian Empire, the previous dynasties had neither been as large nor harmonious in their rule and so disintegrated. Cyrus the Great learned this lesson from the Assyrians and Medians, and it was a mistake he did not wish to repeat. One of the policies he wished to avoid was the Assyrian practice of the forced removal and deportation of large groups.

This forced relocation was not wholly insensitive; families were never separated, and people were transported based on where their skills may be needed most. Regardless, the forced move did not foster any goodwill for the ruling power. Previous empires also made no effort to preserve the cultures of their conquered lands. People belonging to regions were stripped of their identity instead of being embraced as new regions of the empire. Religious practices of the conquered lands were also ignored in favor of establishing the religious preference of the ruling empire.

While the official religion of the Achaemenid court is still debated, it is well known that no religion, cultural ideology, or tradition was imposed upon conquered subjects. People were free to practice whatever faith they chose, speak whichever languages they preferred, and continue living their lives as they had before. Cyrus the Great's liberation of the Jews from Babylonia is seen as another example of his commitment to this approach of acceptance and the mark of a true leader. The only obligation placed on newly acquired lands was that they pay their share of taxes and contribute men to the army.

While regional governments existed in the Achaemenid Empire, they were not entirely independent. In particular, during the rule of Cyrus the Great, officials were employed to keep an eye on the satraps. They would report regional affairs back to the king, acting as his "eyes and ears." This practice may have contributed, at least in part, to the peace the empire experienced during this time, for there is no record of any revolts during Cyrus's reign.

Achaemenid policies regarding tolerance for crime or treachery differed based on the emperors. Cyrus's successor, his son Cambyses, is often believed to have been harsher in the punishments he exacted as a ruler and thus seen as unfit for the throne. While he conquered Egypt, he also forged hostilities with the Egyptians and the Greeks, which might explain his more severe approach.

Ordinance of Good Regulations

Cambyses's successor, Darius I, took a more liberal approach, instituting what he called the Ordinance of Good Regulations. Given the lack of written records of the time, there is little known about the details of the ordinance. However, one of its essential principles related to the punishments for crimes, urging everyone, even the king, to reconsider harsh punishments for a crime. Rather, a person's good deeds should be taken into consideration when making any judgment.

Darius chose lenient punishments for first-time offenses, particularly when weighed against the individual's services. For instance, a judge who was caught taking a bribe would not be crucified, a punishment Cambyses would have thought just. Instead, Darius would have demoted the judge if that was his only offense.

The organization of the empire received further attention during this period, as Darius divided the kingdom into seven regions. These regions were further divided into twenty satrapies. Following Cyrus's policy of maintaining watch over the empire, Darius instituted a similar system. A royal treasurer was hired to ensure the satraps' spending and activities happened with the king's approval. In addition, inspectors were recruited whose job was to check up on various satraps. They would keep an eye on government officials, ensuring all jobs were being performed honestly. Another committee was tasked with reviewing revenue collection from each satrap, ensuring all citizens were registered, all taxes were being fairly imposed and paid, and that they were all being routed where they should. This may be considered a just and fair system designed to prevent corruption and protect the rights of all.

Chapar Khaneh

The postal system was not a new invention. The Neo-Assyrians and the Neo-Babylonians had already been using some type of mail delivery system. However, the Achaemenids' innovation created what can be referred to as the closest predecessor to the modern mailing system. The Royal Road played a pivotal role, as it connected various far-flung regions of the empire, cutting long journeys into a matter of days.

Messages would be delivered by horse-riding couriers through a relay system that allowed the speedy and consistent delivery of letters and messages. The Iranians, including during the Persian Empire, were particularly adept at horseback riding, and their delivery system involved changing horses at frequent intervals to ensure consistent speed. Since all administrative correspondence was done in Aramaic, it ensured a standardized language, which also aided the speed of delivery. The Chapar Khaneh, or postal service station, was located at intervals along the Royal Road.

The Taxation System

While an earlier taxation model was established by Cyrus, Darius I is believed to have improved on it, creating a just, fair, and well-distributed setup. Taxation was decided based on the economic capability of each satrapy, such as their productivity and how much each could realistically contribute. Based on their individual strengths—for instance, Egypt for its crops —each satrapy was required to pay that substance in taxation. Babylon is believed to have the greatest economic potential and consequently paid the greatest amount in taxes.

The Persians were not subject to the taxation system. It was reserved strictly for conquered lands, which could also contribute more soldiers to the empire's army in place of paying higher taxes.

Slavery was not a very common practice in the Persian Empire, but it did happen. Slavery had existed in the region before the Achaemenid Empire, and the term used to describe them, *bandaka*, referred to general dependence. The term slavery was often used to denote the kingly status of the emperor, marking the public as his subjects, making the degree of the practice of slavery during the Persian Empire unclear. Enslavement is also mentioned in regard to the conquest of neighboring lands that became part of the Persian Empire. Future empires that succeeded the Achaemenids would derive inspiration from this system to establish their own administrative policies.

Achaemenid Coinage

Achaemenid coinage.
Classical Numismatic Group, Inc. http://www.cngcoins.com, CC BY-SA 3.0
<http://creativecommons.org/licenses/by-sa/3.0/>, via Wikimedia Commons;
https://commons.wikimedia.org/wiki/File:Cyprus_and_Achaemenid_Archer_design.jpg

The use of coinage, in particular gold coin, was first attributed to the Lydians around the mid-6th century BCE. Lydia was conquered by Cyrus, and the coinage system was introduced on a much wider scale throughout the Persian Empire.

Before the conquest of Lydia, the coinage system was a foreign concept to the Persians. The barter system was the basis of economic activity, with some use of silver bullion. The coinage system brought about an economic revolution; Lydia had already been a leading power in trade through its invention.

Sardis became an important city center. The mint was located there, so Sardis acted as a capital city for the western Achaemenid region. Coinage coming out of Sardis supplied this region, becoming a vital force in making the Achaemenid Empire economically strong. When Darius I became king, he revolutionized the existing coinage system by minting it with images of Persepolis. The term for the gold coin, the daric, is even believed by some to have been derived from his name, Darius I, either because of his influence on the coinage system or the belief that he introduced the system in Persia.

The original Lydian coins were designed by a system of incuse punches on one side and some pictorial design on the other. Darius I simplified the Lydian model, which used two punches, replacing it with one. Earlier pictorial designs were adopted from the Lydians, which included animal designs and geometric shapes. Other than pictures of Persepolis, the Persians also used images of archers, which represented the might of the Achaemenid military.

Transportation

The trading system set up under the Achaemenid rule was supplemented by extensive infrastructure and a reliable coinage system. Tariffs earned from trade were a lucrative source of income for the empire, which also included agricultural and tribute taxes. The Persian economy, particularly after the introduction of Lydian coinage, was greatly boosted. However, its greatest support came from the infrastructure that the emperors, in particular Cyrus and Darius I, invested to boost trade efficiency and revenue.

The Royal Road provided various stations and caravanserais, or roadside inns, for merchants and couriers alike, helping to create a trading system that was like no other at the time. Trade along the Royal Road was also more reliable since it was less affected by changes in the weather and was built for speedy travel by horse. For the Achaemenid Empire, the Royal Road was a way to deliver messages quickly, supplement trade, and ensure the king had eyes all over his vast empire.

The Royal Road was not the only highway through which commerce was possible. The Great Khurasan Road connected Mesopotamia to the Iranian Plateau and then ran as far as the Indus Valley. It functioned as an unofficial alternate route for merchants and later became a route for cultural exchange after the conquest of Alexander the Great. During the Abbasid dynasty, the Khurasan Road became part of the Silk Road.

Conclusion

The Achaemenid Empire holds great significance even today, not only as the largest empire of its time to exist but also due to the lasting influence it had on the geopolitical makeup of the Iranian Plateau. Beginning with Cyrus the Great, the Persian Empire came to hold great importance. As the empire expanded, it gathered power and wealth.

With the diverse regions the Achaemenids were able to conquer, the Persian Empire assimilated many different cultures, religions, and languages. It also introduced the Persians to more efficient forms of governance, superior military techniques and weaponry, and laborers skilled in many crafts. The Achaemenid Empire's power can be seen by the monuments they left behind, which were inscribed with tales of their successes. In the empire's early years, it saw much success and remained a hallmark of diversity and tolerance.

Even after the empire fell to the Greeks, it continued to have a lasting effect on the region. Persian heritage and culture went on to hold great relevance in Asia and the Middle East, where it was assimilated by other empires and dynasties. Many of the Persian Empire's policies can be seen in later empires.

Alexander the Great's conquest of the Persian Empire brought him a vast land, which he was free to rule as he saw fit, yet the Greeks chose to continue with the Persian form of governance. Later, the Romans would adopt a similar method. The Persian governance model was adopted by the Abbasid dynasty in the mid-8th century CE during a period known as the Golden Age of Islam. The Abbasids followed the Achaemenid custom of setting up an empire center in Mesopotamia and were largely supported by the Persian aristocracy during their rise and expansion. The Persian language and architecture went to become heavily incorporated into the Islamic world.

While the Achaemenid Empire preached and practiced religious tolerance, it is difficult to determine the motive behind such a move. It may simply have been for the sake of acceptance and diversity, or it may be that it would have been practically impossible to enforce any single religion, culture, or language over such a vast empire; any attempt to do so likely would have disrupted the peace. Regardless, this approach set an example of religious tolerance and acceptance that is still hailed as a mark of a great ruler today. The impact of the religious policies of the Achaemenid emperors, in particular, their support of the Jews who were conquered and forced away from their homes by the Babylonians, earned them a mention in Judeo-Christian texts.

Since the Achaemenid emperors are believed to have practiced Zoroastrianism, or at least some of its teachings, they played a vital role in its spread. The empire was home to a large number of Zoroastrian followers, and with the expansion of the empire, the Persians were introduced to new cultures and religions. However, they also brought Zoroastrianism to the regions they conquered, along with neighboring territories. Due to the Persians, Zoroastrianism spread as far as China, where it thrived for close to a millennium until the Tang dynasty persecuted its practitioners.

The Persians are seen as the major instigators of the Greco-Persian Wars, and they greatly influenced the culture of Greek regions. The Athenians, for example, adopted many Persian customs and traditions into their daily lives. While the nature of the relationship between the two groups was often hostile, it did not prevent the two from engaging in a sort of cultural exchange, resulting in the development of new hybrid customs.

The Persian Empire's initial success seems just as inevitable as its later doom. The empire had begun with a clear vision and purpose, which Cyrus the Great and his successors put into action. The expansion of the empire was not simply a matter of waging wars; the emperors were also concerned with just and equal governance, tolerance, and kindness. Later rulers of the empire may be entirely responsible for the empire's fall, as the focus shifted from the empire's prosperity to fights for the throne, resulting in brothers waging wars and killing each other. Although the

Achaemenid Empire attempted to reestablish its dominance, it did so by picking fights it was ill-equipped to win, resulting in its disastrous but inescapable demise. However, its legacy will live on.

Part 2: Cyrus the Great

The Enthralling Life of the Father of the Persian Empire

Introduction

Writing was already common in the Middle East by the time of Cyrus the Great, creator of the Persian Empire in 550 BCE. And yet we have extraordinarily little factual and firsthand information about Cyrus the Great from contemporary Persian sources, except for the famous Cyrus Cylinder and a few inscriptions.

Most of the inscriptions are viewed as propaganda and are attributed to Darius the Great in the name of Cyrus, as he and later Persian rulers wanted to benefit from Cyrus's legacy. Scholars believe that Darius ordered the invention of the Old Persian cuneiform script in 521 BCE. He called it the Aryan script. These propaganda inscriptions are written in Old Persian, so they could not have been ordered by Cyrus. They are often inscribed in three languages—Old Persian, Elamite, and Akkadian—and simply state, "I am Cyrus, an Achaemenid king," to emphasize the Achaemenid family ties that Darius relied on to legitimize his rule.

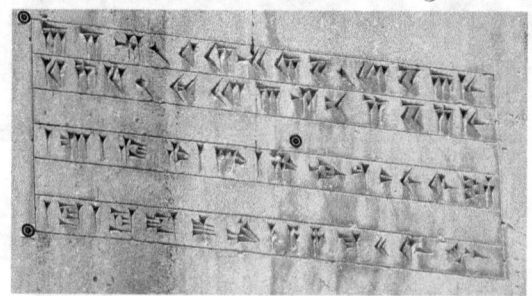

The inscription of "I am Cyrus, an Achaemenid king" in Old Persian, Elamite, and Akkadian.
Truth Seeker (fawiki), CC BY-SA 3.0 <https://creativecommons.org/licenses/by-sa/3.0>, via Wikimedia Commons; https://commons.wikimedia.org/wiki/File:I_am_Cyrus,_Achaemenid_King_-_Pasargadae.JPG

The most important and genuine Cyrus inscription is the Cyrus Cylinder. It was inscribed after the conquest of Babylon. It mentions the taking of Babylon, but its value lies in the proclamation of Cyrus's own values, intentions, vision, and actions. The cylinder talks about the liberation of the exiled peoples and slaves of the Babylonian Empire, which included the Jews. For this reason, Cyrus, or Koresh in the Jewish and Christian texts, is the only non-Jewish person to be called "Savior" in the sacred scrolls of the Jewish people.

A problem that crops up with the finer details of the Persian Empire's management is that Darius and his administration records and propaganda provide most of the information. The sum of it is that we use writings of ancient historians to extrapolate data for periods that are hazy or not described sufficiently in extant firsthand records. Those historians often did not really know much about the Persian Empire's methods of ruling. They often applied their contemporary observations and knowledge to previous times. That is especially the case for the Achaemenid Empire in regard to Cyrus II and Darius I.

It remains a monumental undertaking to sort fact from fiction, especially since Cyrus became a legend during his own lifetime. The embellishment of his life story started during his life and continued, with the first Greek historians recording tales of his ventures and achievements that had been passed down by his family, friends, and enemies. These later accounts are colored by the worldview of the cultured and learned Greek and later Roman historians and geographers. Admiration for Cyrus the Great from Persia's enemies, specifically the Greeks, must surely indicate he was a truly extraordinary figure who commanded respect and reverence as the father of the Persian Empire. He deserved to be called "Cyrus the Great."

In tracing the course of Cyrus's life, we are often left with choices between fact and fiction in the accounts passed on by ancient writers. Do we give the folk tales the benefit of the doubt because they could have happened? They were humanly possible and could have happened in real life. Cyrus was essentially a superhero but did not do superhuman things.

It often takes reading between the lines and an understanding of the historical context and contemporary environment of a historical figure to interpret their decisions and actions. For that reason, we have included various versions and viewpoints of the same events so you can see, feel, and understand the thrill of figuring out the people, culture, stories, and events of the past that have influenced humanity for generations.

At times, interwoven facts can be extracted from the tapestry of historical accounts and corroborated by annals and chronicles of contemporary rulers of nearby regions. Most of what we know of Cyrus the person comes from later accounts and extrapolations from records of contemporary nations. Some contemporary chronicles, like the Nabonidus Chronicle, roughly support the account of the conquest of Babylon, for example. This specific document, though, is fragmentary, with missing and unreadable pieces. The way in which both Cyrus and Nabonidus are portrayed indicates that it might have been written by priests of Marduk, the patron deity of Babylon, who hated Nabonidus and were glad to get rid of him. They also saw Cyrus as a liberator because he gave them their temple rights back, and they wanted to curry favor with him.

This book will serve partly as an overview of ancient life and times before, during, and after the life of Cyrus the Great. It is not limited to the accounts of the ancient historians about Cyrus the Great, as it includes brief histories of the worldviews, religions, and political and societal conditions of that time and the eras before and after it. Understanding these things will help you to understand how and why Cyrus the Great is still an icon today. His vision for a just, fair, and free society for all humanity echoes through the ages as an ideal that modern societies across the world should be striving to achieve.

Chapter 1: The Persians before Cyrus

Setting the Scene: The Ancient Near East in a Time of Turmoil

It was a time of great upheaval across the ancient Near East. Widespread, drawn-out droughts caused hunger, and hunger made people desperate. Desperate people who have nothing to lose steal, protest, and riot. They look for a culprit—someone or something to blame. Anarchy spreads, and governments fall. Crime and unrest roll like waves across the sea of humanity, recognizing no borders and no authority as they move on and on to find water and food.

This situation waxed and waned across the ancient Near East and farther afield for several centuries from around 1200 BCE until around 900 BCE. The period is known as the Bronze Age Collapse. The fallout lasted for several centuries in some areas, such as Egypt, where the Third Intermediate Period officially started in 1070 BCE and only came to an end in the 7th century BCE.

Deep and clear rivers flowed out of the pure mountain snow from which they sprang, collecting more water from tributary rivers on their journeys to the seas, such as the Mediterranean, the Black Sea, the Caspian Sea, Lake Van, and other lakes. These waters, which allowed human populations to flourish, their flocks of livestock to increase, and farmers to cultivate and irrigate their crops, dried up. They did not flow into the great life-sustaining and navigable rivers like the Nile, the Tigris, and the Euphrates any longer. Those great rivers slowed and shrank to mere streams or dried up in places. Nomads became raiders of the movable possessions of yesterday's friends, neighboring tribes, and farther afield into settled lands and urbanized cultures. During this time of scarcity and unrest, they settled with their families and livestock wherever there was a chance of bettering their lives—a trickle of water could sustain them for at least a while.

Large urban centers of once-mighty nations depopulated because there was no food left in the cities, and farmers could not supply enough even for themselves. Soldiers deserted and joined the raiders. Rulers lost their power. Great dynasties were ousted and replaced, at times by outside nations and at times by internal strife. When things settled down again, borders were redrawn. Underdogs and new nations were in charge. Those vast empires that had conquered states, which were obliged to contribute copious amounts to their ruling empire's income in goods and raw materials, lost control. The empires did not have the power to crush revolts in their own territories, let alone try to bring outside nations back into the fold.

In Egypt, the country went through a bleak intermediary period. In Mesopotamia, Assyria and Babylonia managed to hold on to a semblance of power, albeit under new dynasties. Egypt and the rest of the Middle East were invaded by nomads, semi-nomads, and the Sea Peoples. The invaders were held off in some cases, but many re-invaded, conquered, and settled the land. At the end of the tumultuous period, the old kingdoms were gone, and new ones had taken their place.

Origin of the Persian People

Around the end of the 2nd millennium BCE, nomadic tribes from Central Asia and the steppes migrated to the Iranian plateau and spread into the valleys and hills of the country we know as Iran today. The reason for the several waves of the southward drift of nomadic groups is not entirely clear. It could have been the extreme and long-lasting droughts, population growth, or strife between tribes and chiefdoms, although it is likely all three factors played a role. There had been several similar small and large migrations of Indo-Europeans, Semites, and other groups with still unidentified origins and heritage, like the Sumerians, in previous centuries and even millennia.

The nomadic tribes of migrants in previous eras were mainly cattle and sheep herders, but now they included horse breeders from the steppes. They included Indo-European tribes that originated from the steppes in the north from around the Danube River and up to the Ural Mountains. Scholars are still trying to figure out the exact people groups and their origins via linguistic and DNA leads, but efforts are complicated by the mixing, diffusion, and other types of blending of the settled residents and the newcomers from before, during, and after this period. The newcomers were often already a blend of various ethnic groups, including Indo-European, Indo-Iranian, and diverse Semitic tribes from several different places, with people coming from as far as the Mediterranean lands and islands, Anatolia, Central Asia, and East Asia.

An important link in the archaeological record is the tribes with a penchant for horses—for breeding, milking, riding, fighting, and pulling agricultural equipment and wheeled transport. The peoples of the Eurasian Steppe, east of the Ural Mountains, are believed to have domesticated and trained horses for riding as early as 3500 BCE. The similarity in domesticated livestock and etymology—roots of words, phraseology, the types and names of agricultural tools, and names of people and places—have often provided scholars with a definitive clue in a people group's origin and movement. Today, researchers are greatly assisted by innovations and cooperation between various fields of science in the analysis of ancient DNA, bioarchaeology, paleogenetics, and other related fields.

Tribes that became the large kingdom of the Medes were part of the migrations of this era. They settled in the northeastern part of modern-day Iran, where their first king, possibly Deioces, built his capital, Ecbatana (today's Hamadan). At the peak of their power, the Medians had many vassal states in Anatolia, northern Iraq, and Syria, including the lands of the loosely knitted Persian tribes to the south.

Cyrus II of Persia (better known as Cyrus the Great) overthrew King Astyages, the last king of the Medes, between 550 and 549 BCE (these dates come from the Nabonidus Chronicle and ancient historians) with the help of high officials and commanders of the Median court. The Medes did not lose their influence, though, as they remained by the Persians' side. The Persians and the Medes, in fact, became united in the empire. It is understandable if we remember that the Medes and Persians were of the same stock and language and cultural affiliations from the time before they entered Iran. One may also assume that the cooperation of high-level Median officials in Cyrus's victory over Astyages bound them together. It is obviously also the origin of the expression for an unbreakable law being referred to as "a law of the Medes and Persians."

The Persians

The tribes who would become the Persians moved farther south on the Iranian plateau than the Medes upon entering Iran. They began to take over some Elamite territory on the southern border of the Medes and other settled groups in the southwest of Iran and neighboring regions. It is generally accepted the Persians were Indo-Aryans from the Caucasus and the Caspian Sea areas. These tribes had spread as far eastward as South Asia (India). This latest wave of migrations moved into eastern Mesopotamia and the southwestern Iranian regions.

The Assyrian king, Shalmaneser III, mentions the Parsua around 825 BCE amongst tributary states in the southwest of today's Iran. It is generally assumed the people named Parsua on a black obelisk found in Nimrud and in other Assyrian and Babylonian cuneiform references refer to the Persian tribes. The Persian tribes were not united at this time. They were grouped into chiefdoms and later kingdoms. Shalmaneser III says that twenty-seven of their kings paid tribute to the Assyrians during his time.

After Cyrus succeeded his father Cambyses I as king of the city-state of Anshan, he set about uniting the Persian tribes, thus creating the Persian kingdom. According to Xenophon, another ancient Greek historian, there were twelve Persian tribes. He states the Persians raised their children from childhood to respect their elders and learn justice, discipline, and self-control above all other characteristics.

To the Persians, justice included fair and just laws against all the crimes that we view as crimes today, from stealing to assault and slander. But they also included ingratitude as well because they believed that trait to be shameless and at the root of many evil deeds. They were taught the traits of self-control, respect, and discipline by example, looking to their teachers, parents, officers, and elders as role models. Overindulgence and greed were unacceptable in their culture.

Cyrus was raised in Anshan by the Persians from the age of ten, according to Herodotus, and he was well versed in their culture and curriculum. As a teenager, he traveled with his mother to Ecbatana to visit Astyages, his grandfather. He charmed Astyages, his court, and the Median people to such an extent that he was begged to stay behind for a while when his mother returned home to Persia. This suited him because he was eager to learn horseback riding, which was not popular in Persia because of its hills. In addition, his grandfather, the king, promised that if he stayed, he could do and have anything he pleased.

Cyrus explained to his mother that he was better than anyone else when it came to Persian customs and that there was much to learn from the Medes. He stayed and learned the customs and skills of the Medes whilst bedecked in splendid robes and jewelry, as was their custom, which greatly differed from the more austere habits of the Persians.

Cyrus was a natural leader, and people wanted to please him and be close to him. It was thus easy for him to unite the Persians when he became king. Again, it is Xenophon who tells us that Cyrus grew up to be the most handsome and charming of all men.

The Beginning of the Achaemenid Dynasty

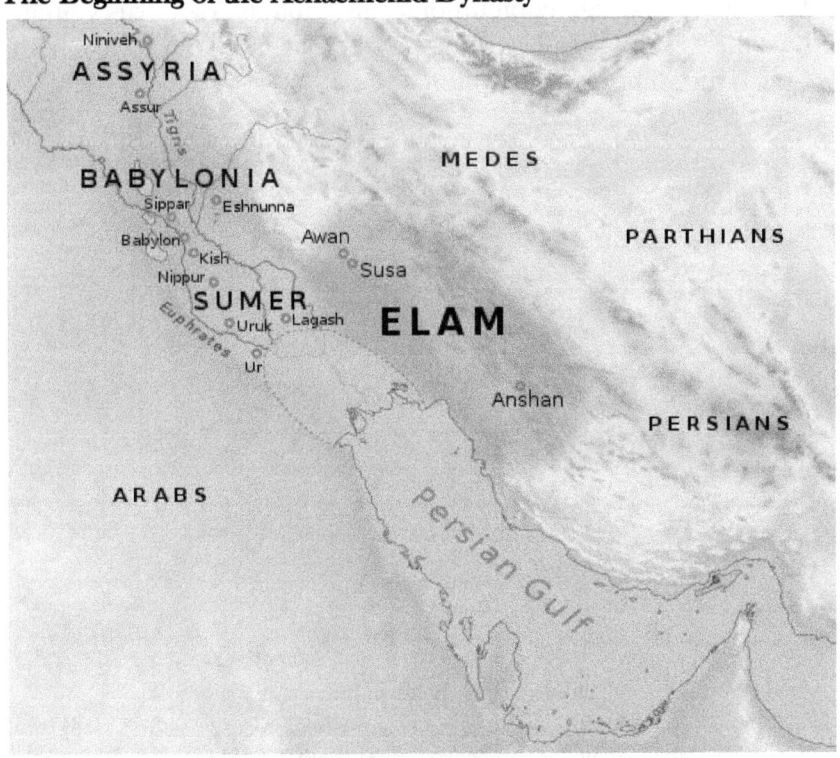

Anshan, the seat of the Achaemenid clan of the Pasargadae tribe, where Cyrus grew up
File: Near East topographic map-blank.svg: SémhurFile:Elam-map-PL.svg: Wkotwicaderivative work: Morningstar1814, CC BY-SA 3.0 <https://creativecommons.org/licenses/by-sa/3.0>, via Wikimedia Commons; https://commons.wikimedia.org/wiki/File:Elam_Map-en.svg

Anshan was one of the local cities taken over by one of several kindred Persian tribes when they settled in Iran. The Persians in Anshan were ruled by kings who traced their lineage to an ancestor named Achaemenes from the Pasargadae tribe. Scholars do not know whether this person was real or mythological, but the Persians derived the name of the Achaemenid Empire from his name.

It is generally accepted that Achaemenes was the father of Teispes, who was the father of Cyrus I, who was the father of Cambyses I, who was the father of Cyrus II or Cyrus the Great. Again, scholars have a problem with identifying and linking the names of the rulers in the various source materials. The name of the first Achaemenid king of the Pasargadae tribe was Phraortes I, according to Herodotus. According to the Behistun Inscription of Darius, who was the third king after Cyrus II, the first king of the Achaemenid tribe was Achaemenes. According to the Cyrus Cylinder, one of the few contemporary inscriptions of Cyrus's time, the dynasty started with Teispes, who was the second king of the dynasty according to the Behistun Inscription.

Close-up of the Behistun Inscription.
KendallKDown, CC BY-SA 3.0 <https://creativecommons.org/licenses/by-sa/3.0>, via Wikimedia Commons; https://commons.wikimedia.org/wiki/File:BehistunInscriptiondetail.jpg

Nevertheless, Cyrus II of the Achaemenid clan was the king of the Pasargadae tribe, and he eventually united the Persian tribes and built the Persian Empire. He first united the Persian tribes to throw off the Median yoke and then set out on a conquest across Anatolia, the Levant, and eastward through Central Asia and beyond. One by one, he conquered kingdoms and empires in all directions until his empire became the biggest the world had seen up to that time. Due to these widespread conquests north, south, east, and west, one of his titles in inscriptions was "King of the Four Corners of the World." His son and heir, Cambyses II, went on to conquer several more realms and carried forth that title, as did Darius I, another great Persian king.

The Achaemenid dynasty lasted until the Persians were conquered by Alexander the Great in 331 BCE.

Mythology and Religion

It is unclear what religion the ancient Persian tribes took with them to Iran, but it is presumed to be of a polytheistic nature, as that was common in the areas from and to which they migrated. In fact, polytheism was practiced around the world then and for millennia before that time, according to the plethora of myths that were eventually committed to writing. A mother goddess and several gods and goddesses for different natural and heavenly phenomena were prevalent across the Middle East and the rest of the ancient world.

Cyrus the Great depicted as a mythological being on a pillar in Pasargadae.
Nima Boroumand, CC BY-SA 4.0 <https://creativecommons.org/licenses/by-sa/4.0>, via Wikimedia Commons; https://commons.wikimedia.org/wiki/File:Cyrus_the_great.jpg

By the time of Cyrus's birth, a monotheistic religion, Zoroastrianism, was firmly rooted in the area, and Cyrus was ostensibly a follower of this religion. The dates mentioned for the beginning of Zoroastrianism are lost, although the religion began sometime between 1500 BCE and 700 BCE. The concepts of a struggle between good and evil, heaven and hell, angels and demons, a judgment day, and a final revelation, which can be found in the Abrahamic and many other faiths, stem from Zoroastrianism.

A man thought to have been part of the immigrating tribes into Iran had a vision while participating in an initiation ceremony. He was around thirty years old at the time, and his name was Zoroaster in Greek or Zarathustra in ancient Persian and Iranian. A supernatural being named Ahura Mazda appeared to Zoroaster during this vision.

Ahura Mazda, the supreme being of Zoroastrianism.
https://commons.wikimedia.org/wiki/File:Ahuramazda.jpg

He taught Zoroaster that he was the one and only god. He had created everything and was the only supreme being. Ahura Mazda explained to Zoroaster that the worship of many gods was wrong and that he alone, as Lord of Wisdom, was to be worshiped. Ahura Mazda is depicted as a male deity with wings or a winged vehicle.

Although Cyrus was devout in his religious pursuits, always making supplications and offerings before and after battles, he never tried to enforce his religion on conquered peoples. He incorporated and openly sacrificed to the local gods when in other countries. In fact, religious freedom is one of the basic characteristics for which he and his empire is remembered. Cyrus did not rely on priests to make sacrifices and supplications to his god, as was the common practice of rulers at the time; he was trained by his father and others to perform the ritualistic practices himself.

The legacy of Zoroastrianism, which was the religion of Cyrus's family, is still visible today in the fire temples, although after the long Muslim reign, there are very few practitioners left. Near the city of Yazd in Iran, there is a fire temple where a so-called eternal flame has been burning for centuries. Although it has been moved several times, it is believed to have been continuously burning since at least 470 CE.

The Persian Empire followed Cyrus's examples and doctrines and became known for its religious tolerance and freedom for all peoples to follow their own cultural practices. Cyrus practiced as he preached, ruling with truth and righteousness as his guiding light whilst respecting other people, their cultures, and their beliefs. He was, and still is in some places, called the father of the Persian people.

Key Figures

Astyages

The last king of the Medes was Astyages. His daughters were married in diplomatic unions to several other kings, linking royal houses in that part of the ancient Near East. One daughter, Mandane, was married to Cambyses, the king of Anshan. Astyages's brother-in-law was Croesus, the fabulously rich king of Lydia, who is remembered in the simile "as rich as Croesus."

The Medes had a tribe of wise men, the Magi, who interpreted dreams and signs. At the time, people were quite superstitious. Herodotus recounts a story verging on the edge of mythology about Mandane. When she was born, Astyages had a dream that the Magi interpreted as a warning that her offspring would rule the world, including Astyages's kingdom. A later dream was again interpreted as the same omen.

Astyages tried to prevent this by marrying Mandane off to Cambyses, the crown prince of an obscure far-away kingdom, and when she gave birth to a son, he arranged for the child to be killed. The child was saved and later became Cyrus the Great, who eventually ruled the known world. Luckily for Astyages, Cyrus was a magnanimous ruler who forgave his grandfather and looked after him until his death. Astyages was buried in the Persian capital of Pasargadae.

Cambyses I and Mandane

Cambyses was the son of the king of Anshan in Persia, a vassal state of the Medians. He was married to Mandane, daughter of Astyages. They became the parents of Cyrus the Great. According to Herodotus, Cambyses was known as a good man from a good family with quiet habits. This was why Astyages chose him as a husband for Mandane, as he assumed that his docile nature would rub off on his offspring and prevent a threat to Media.

Astyages obviously did not know about the strength of character that would be built in his grandson through the educational system of the austere Persians.

Harpagus

Harpagus was the Median nobleman who saved Cyrus's life when his grandfather Astyages wanted the baby killed. The cruel Astyages tricked Harpagus into eating the flesh of his only son at a feast after he discovered that Harpagus did not kill Cyrus as a baby when he had ordered him to do it.

The devasted Harpagus did not show his shock and grief but bided his time for revenge. When the time was right and Cyrus was grown up, he reminded Cyrus of his grandfather's plot to kill him and assured him that most of the Medians were ready to welcome him and join him in overthrowing Astyages.

Thus, if there was no Harpagus, or if Astyages had chosen a different courtier who was prepared to do his bidding to kill the newborn infant, there would be no Cyrus the Great!

Cassandane

Cyrus the Great's wife, Cassandane, was from the Achaemenid clan like him. She is said to have been the great love of his life. The Nabonidus Chronicle records that there was a six-day mourning period for everyone in the Persian Empire when she died in 538 BCE. She was buried in the royal garden at Pasargadae, close to the tomb of Cyrus.

One of her daughters, Atossa, was married to her son Cambyses (Cambyses II) and later to Darius the Great (Darius I). Atossa was the mother of Darius's son, Xerxes, who became king after Darius. Talk about keeping it in the family!

Cyrus Influencers

The most prominent figures of the Persian Empire that Cyrus created were his advisors. He surrounded himself with men from all social classes and nationalities whom he deemed fit and able in wisdom and decision-making. He even included his erstwhile enemies. These councilors were called together when serious decisions had to be made. Cyrus would lay the known facts before them, and those who had any suggestions for or against his suggested solution could then freely voice their thoughts and views on the matter. In this way, Cyrus was able to evaluate options from several different angles before deciding on the best course of action.

Of these men, a few proved to be outstanding councilors. If we believe Herodotus's and Xenophon's accounts, then Croesus of the Lydians became one of these councilors after Cyrus conquered his country. Some other accounts state that Croesus was killed in battle or put to death shortly after Cyrus conquered his capital, Sardis. Yet, according to Herodotus, Cyrus kept Croesus close and often, if not always, asked for his opinion before making hefty decisions.

Harpagus, the Mede who was instrumental in saving Cyrus as a baby from his grandfather, was another of Cyrus's loyal and trusted advisors and generals. In fact, Harpagus brought many erstwhile Mede vassal states that strived for independence after Cyrus's conquest of the Medes back into the new fold. Harpagus went on to conquer more Anatolian, Bactrian, and other independent kingdoms for the growing Persian Empire, while Cyrus marched on the eastern and southern kingdoms with visions of totally conquering Elam, Babylon, and eventually Egypt.

Cyrus's habit of gratitude, appreciation, and humble requests for advice from his men ensured that he was respected and protected by the most loyal of men. His own Persian friends and advisors were always willing to protect him with their own lives. Advisors were selected from conquered peoples to help with local regions, and they soon learned to respect and like Cyrus as much as his own people because he treated them with respect and diplomacy.

Chapter 2: Cyrus's Early Life and Mythological References

Timeline of Cyrus the Great's Life

Estimated Dates	Occasion	Place
c. 600 BCE (other sources 590–580 BCE)	Birth of Cyrus II	Anshan, Persia or Ecbatana, Media
c. 590 BCE	Cyrus sent back to his parents at age ten	Anshan, Persia
c. 559 BCE	Cyrus takes over from his father Cambyses I (abdication) as king of Anshan	Anshan, Persis (Fars Province, Iran)
c. 550 BCE	Cyrus unites Persian tribes and creates Achaemenid Empire	Persis (Fars Province of Iran)
c. 550–549 BCE	Cyrus invades Media and captures Astyages	Ecbatana

Estimated Dates	Occasion	Place
c. 547 BCE	Cyrus conquers Lydia and takes their capital and king Croesus	Sardis, Anatolia
c. 540 or 538 BCE	Cyrus conquers the Elamites	Susa, the capital of the Elamites
c. 547–530 BCE	Cyrus creates satrapies and establishes a successful administration system for a large empire	Iran, Mesopotamia, ancient Near East, Asia, Anatolia
c. 539 BCE	Cyrus conquers Babylon	Babylonian Empire
c. 530 BCE	Cyrus campaigns against Massagetae tribes	Central Asia and Zagros Mountains
530 BCE / 529 BCE	Death of Cyrus II	Asia or Persia

Cyrus Becomes king of Anshan

Scholars are not in agreement with the role of Anshan in Cyrus's life. The controversies are mainly around the prominence of Anshan in Cyrus's titles. Ancient sources always name him as king of Anshan as opposed to king of Persia, such as on one of the best-known artifacts of Cyrus's reign, the Cyrus Cylinder. Firm historical facts are scarce, as there are few contemporary written records from primary Persian sources.

Several ancient writers after the time of Cyrus ventured into the mire of myths and legends surrounding his birth and as a young man, similar to myths and legends about many other great figures of the ancient past. It seems the ancients were compelled to create at least some kind of miraculous or wonderous stories around such figures, as no mere ordinary mortals could achieve the success and greatness with which they are credited.

Herodotus's Account of Cyrus before the Empire

Herodotus (484 BCE-425 BCE) recounted tales of Cyrus the Great's birth and childhood in *Histories*, with his usual caveat that he was only repeating what he had been told. To Xenophon (431 BCE-354 BCE), Cyrus was obviously a hero and idealized ruler. Xenophon even devoted eight volumes, the *Cyropaedia*, subtitled "The Education of Cyrus," to Cyrus the Great.

What all the accounts have in common are the details of his parents. Cyrus was the son of the crown prince of Anshan, Cambyses I, and a Median princess, Mandane. Anshan was an old Elamite city that had been usurped by one of the Persian tribes, the Pasargadae. At this time, the disunited Persian tribes were tributary states of the Medes.

Mandane was the daughter of the Median king, Astyages, and her mother was Aryenis. Aryenis was the daughter of the king of Lydia and a sister of legendary King Croesus. Astyages was the last king of the Median Empire.

The Medes were civilized and educated people, although they also seemed to have been rather cruel and strict. They had skilled astronomers, mathematicians, and scribes, but they were also superstitious. They had a tribe or class of sages, the Magi, who interpreted signs and dreams. When Mandane was born, her father Astyages had a dream that she urinated to the extent that it covered the whole world. The Magi were called to interpret the dream. They conferred and said that Mandane would have a son who would grow up to take over the world, Astyages's empire included.

Astyages believed them and set about creating a plan that would stop this from happening. When Mandane reached marriageable age, he married her off to the crown prince of Anshan, an obscure and far-away kingdom to the southwest. Then he had yet another dream. This time, an olive tree grew out of Mandane's womb and covered the entire world. The Magi agreed that it predicted the same foreboding message. When Astyages received the news that Mandane was pregnant, he summoned her to his court when her child was about to be born so that he could make sure it would not live to threaten him and his empire one day.

He took Mandane's son as soon as it was born and gave it to his trusted vizier, Harpagus, with orders to kill the baby. Astyages did not tell him that it was Mandane's child. The astonished Harpagus saw the baby was dressed in royal funeral clothes, bedecked with gold. He could hear the wailing in the palace when he was summoned and gathered that it was Mandane's newborn son. He had to obey his king, not just out of loyalty but also because he would face death if he disobeyed. Harpagus discussed the matter with his wife, and they both agreed he could not kill the little prince.

Harpagus went in search of one of the cowherds of the royal cattle and gave the baby to him. He ordered the cowherd, Mitradates, to take the baby into the mountains so the wild animals could kill it. It so happened that the cowherd's wife was pregnant. She had delivered a stillborn infant that very day. Mitradates and his wife conspired to switch the babies. They quickly switched the clothes of the two infants, and the cowherd took his own stillborn boy into the mountains instead. After three days, he sent word to Harpagus that the deed had been done.

Harpagus sent a messenger to view the dead infant, who confirmed the baby was indeed dead. Harpagus confirmed to Astyages that the boy had been killed as requested. Meanwhile, the cowherd and his wife raised the boy as their own. We do not know what the boy's name was, but Strabo, another ancient Greek historian, says he was called Agradatus by his adoptive parents. Cambyses I renamed him Cyrus after he was returned to his parents. Cyrus (or, at this time, Agradatus) grew up in a little rural village where his adoptive parents lived, believing that his parents were Mitradates and his wife.

According to Herodotus, when the boy was ten years old, he was happily playing with the other village children. They decided to play a game where they would elect a king, and this king would then tell each of them what to do. Because Cyrus was popular, he was chosen as their king. He turned out to be a clever and capable king, appointing each of his more capable playmates to a leadership role. They would be responsible for gathering their own teams to perform their tasks with them.

One of the boys, whose father was a high official in Astyages's court, refused to obey him. Cyrus and his friends gave him a thrashing. This boy went running to his father, who was as angry as he was. How dare the son of a cowherd order him around and then have the audacity to beat him up for not obeying! The father took his son to the king to show him the lashes on his son's shoulders. The king summoned the cowherd and his son. Cyrus took over his adoptive father's explanation and clearly told the king what had happened.

The king was perplexed that a mere cowherd's son could be so unafraid and forthright in explaining the matter to him, the king! But he seemed to recognize traces of himself in the boy. He ordered everyone, including Cyrus, to leave the room. He demanded that the cowherd stay behind, though. Astyages intimidated the cowherd, who broke down and told him the whole truth. Hiding his anger, Astyages then separately questioned Harpagus.

Seeing the cowherd inside the palace, Harpagus realized the story was out and resolved to come clean. Astyages acted as though he was actually relieved because the matter of his grandson's death and subsequent estrangement from his daughter had been a heavy burden on him. The Magi confirmed that he did not have to fear his grandson any longer when Astyages consulted them about the whole saga. Astyages acted as though he had forgiven his vizier for the deception, but in his mind, he planned an act of hideous revenge for the deceit. On the advice of his Magi, Astyages sent Cyrus off to his parents in Anshan.

Xenophon's *Cyropaedia* does not include the story of Cyrus's birth and life as the son of a cowherd. He places Cyrus in Persia from birth until his early teens when he visits Astyages with his mother and then stays behind to learn Median customs. His grandfather, Astyages, is upset when Cyrus eventually concocts a story that his father, Cambyses I, is ill and has to go home to Persia. According to Xenophon, this lie kindles Astyages's wrath to the extent that he instigates war against the Persians.

Stepping toward Greatness

Herodotus says Astyages sent Cyrus to his parents in Anshan after he was assured by the Magi that Cyrus, now a ten-year-old, was no longer a threat to him. Cyrus learned about the whole story of his birth, the betrayal of his mother, and Astyages's attempt to have his own grandchild murdered by the Medians sent by Astyages to escort him.

Cyrus was reunited with his overjoyed parents in Persia. He effortlessly fell into the culture and was a keen student of all that he could absorb from their education programs. Xenophon later described this in great detail in his *Cyropaedia*. Despite Xenophon's biased admiration of Cyrus and his veering off into a treatise to describe an ideal ruler's qualities rather than a realistic one, he gives us a solid idea of the values and systems of the Persians, specifically the Achaemenid culture into which Cyrus was now fully entrenched.

Etymology and Mythology

Much has been made of the origin of Cyrus the Great's name. Both ancient and modern writers have analyzed, considered, and debated how and why Cyrus was named Cyrus II. However, this may be an exercise in futility. Firstly, Cyrus was named after his grandfather, King Cyrus I, so the name did not originate with him. All the insightful and graceful meanings that are read into the name when attaching the name specifically to Cyrus II could not have been thought out by his parents, as Cyrus developed these attributes later.

Secondly, we do not know what Cyrus's name was for the first ten years of his life spent as the son of a cowherd (if that was how he indeed spent his early childhood). The name Cyrus was probably already planned by his real parents for a future crown prince, just as Cyrus named his firstborn son Cambyses (II) after his father. When Cyrus was returned to his parents from the dead, so to speak, they automatically called him by the name given to him at birth.

As for the name of the Achaemenid clan to which he belonged, there are no records of the founder of this clan. This man was called Achaemenes on various inscriptions. He could have been a mythical figure or a prominent member of the Pasargadae tribe who was chosen as the chief or leader over the kings of all the tribes at a time when the clans were loosely knitted together. This could have applied during times of upheaval, especially during the migrations to Iran with the other Persian tribes.

The nomadic herders across the ancient world, to which the tribes of the later Persians belonged, left few permanent or extant artifacts and structures behind as far as is known. They seldom had permanent seasonal settlements in the vast open grazing lands or mountains and valleys to the north. And yet, with modern technology, many previously unknown structures have been discovered over the past fifty years or so. There may be many more unexpected Göbekli Tepes to come.

Chapter 3: Taking over the Median Empire

The Medes

Among the migrants to the lands of today's Iran after c. 1000 BCE were the Medes, who settled in the northwest of Iran. Although the tribes settled there around the turn of the millennium, the Medes only came to unite and expand their territory into a kingdom and later an empire beginning around the 8th century BCE. Most of what is known about the Median Kingdom is based on Neo-Assyrian and Babylonian records.

Since the beginning of the Median Empire (675-549 BCE), its kings seem to have followed a harsh pattern of despotic rule. Its first king, Deioces, tricked the Median tribes into believing they needed a judge, and the position soon became that of a king. Since Deioces had long ago proved himself to be a good judge, he knew they would naturally select him. Although he first came to attention as a wise judge within his own tribe and later the rest of the Medes, he became a power-hungry and arrogant tyrant.

Deioces had the people build him a magnificent palace on a hilltop in a new city known by the Greeks as Ecbatana, today's Hamadan in Iran. One of the ancient writers wrote that it was known as the most magnificent palace and city of its time. The city was surrounded by seven concentric walls, each painted in a different color. Deioces lived in splendid isolation and allowed only certain people near him, partly as a means of intimidation. In his mind, he was too important to be seen by just anybody. He expected those seeking his judgment to wait outside and hand their messages to his aides, who would then bring them to Deioces and return his replies to the petitioners.

The Medes were pestered by the Scythians to the north and paid tribute to the Neo-Assyrians, who helped to protect their territory against invaders. When the Neo-Assyrian Empire was in decline, the Medians were one of its tributaries that stopped paying tribute. In 612, the Medes, in alliance with a few other subject states, conquered Nineveh and brought about the end of the Neo-Assyrian Empire.

The language of the Medes, like that of the Persians, belonged to the western branch of the Indo-Iranian branch of the Indo-European language group. The Medes consisted of six tribes spread over an area of northwest Iran and neighboring territories. Their capital city was Ecbatana (modern Hamadan). Scholars do not agree if Media remained only a kingdom or whether it held the status of an empire.

Astyages, the last king of the Medes, was only the third Median king, as the line of kings had been broken by a period of Scythian rule. Herodotus's account of Astyages's cruel punishments includes the birth story of Cyrus and the cruel revenge on Harpagus, his vizier, to whom he slyly served his own son as a meal as punishment. These two, Harpagus and Cyrus, would unite when the time was right to exact their revenge on Astyages.

Harpagus and Cyrus: Double Revenge

Astyages was the master of his own demise through his harsh and, at times, exceedingly cruel treatment of his subjects and courtiers. Harpagus had never forgotten that he had unknowingly been served the fried and boiled flesh of his only son. And then, after he had indulged in the meal, the king presented him with the feet, hands, and head of his son. Harpagus bided his time and waited for his revenge, and in this case, revenge worked out for him, lest we forget the warning of Confucius that one should first dig two graves before setting out for revenge: one for oneself and one for the object of your revenge.

When Cyrus was grown up, Harpagus contacted him. He reminded Cyrus that his grandfather had set out to have him killed when he was born and that he, Harpagus, was instrumental in saving him. He suggested that Cyrus might want to take revenge, hinting that if Cyrus set out on this venture, the Medes would welcome and join him in overthrowing Astyages. Harpagus had already set about quietly convincing his Median colleagues that it was time to rid themselves of Astyages. They were ready to join Cyrus if he decided to attack.

Whether myth or fact, neither Xenophon nor any other ancient source confirms Herodotus's story of the conspiracy between Cyrus and the Medes to overthrow Astyages. Harpagus somehow managed to send Cyrus this very confidential message. The message was clearly treason, and Astyages was not a forgiving king. Herodotus's story says that Harpagus selected his most trusted servant for the task. He caught a hare, cut a slit in its stomach, and inserted the message. Then he sewed the slit up again. The servant was given the hare inside some nets so he could act like a hunter with his catch. The plan worked, and the servant got safely past the guards and delivered the message to Cyrus.

Growth of the Persian Empire

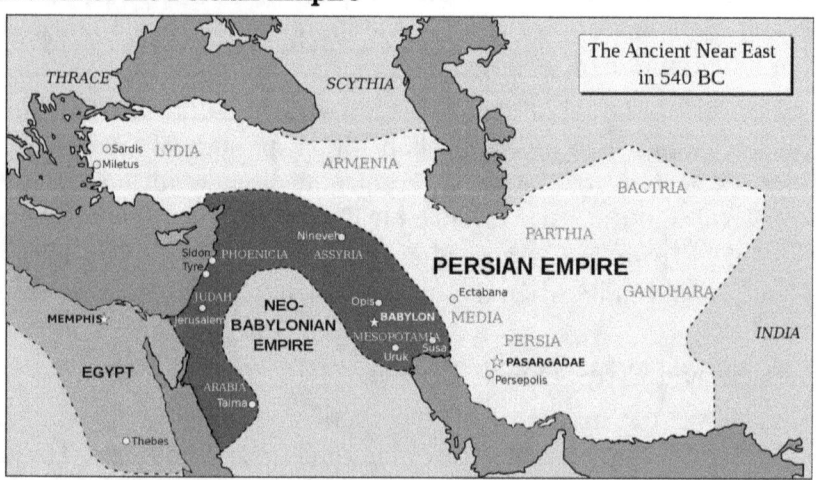

The ancient Near East in 540 BCE.
https://commons.wikimedia.org/w/index.php?curid=5061033

According to some sources, Xenophon included, Cyrus was still the crown prince of Anshan in Persis or Persia. Cambyses I, his father, was still the king and thus had the final say over any Persian troops. But Herodotus states he was king of the Pasargadae tribe by this point.

In any event, Cyrus received the message from Harpagus. He then had to decide how best to get the Persian tribes to unite and revolt. According to both Herodotus and Xenophon, Cyrus was extremely popular, but he was not in the habit of ordering his friends and others around, despite his position. He followed a more subtle approach, telling the Persians that Astyages, as overlord of the Persians, had made him leader of the troops. He then asked the tribal leaders to come to him the next day with their sickles. Cyrus set them to clear a difficult piece of land, and they toiled at it all day. He then sent them home and asked them to return the following day.

On the second day, Cyrus treated them to a lavish banquet. Afterward, he asked them which day they preferred. They naturally chose the second day. Cyrus promised them that if they followed him in revolting against the Medes, they would be treated like this often and be showered with many more blessings. If they did not want to follow him, they could be assured that challenging work lay in store for them. The Persians did not only promise to join Cyrus because of his tantalizing promises but also because they had been resenting paying tribute to the Medes for a long time.

The newly united Persians under Cyrus marched on the Medes. Astyages tried to summon Cyrus to meet with him when he heard about the advancing army. Cyrus replied that he would be seeing him sooner than he thought. Astyages was consumed with concern, and without giving his past dastardly conduct against Harpagus a thought, he appointed Harpagus commander of his forces.

When the armies met, all of those with whom Harpagus had colluded deserted the Median army to join the Persians. Most of the others fled. The small Median group that took up the fight was quickly overcome. Cyrus and his forces attacked Ecbatana, where Astyages was. He was captured and put in chains. Harpagus taunted him bitterly over his son's vile death and the cruel trick that had him eating his own son's flesh.

Uniting Conquerors and Conquered

Cyrus was already displaying his admirable and gracious style of dealing with his conquests. He took Astyages home with him and kept him there until he died. Cyrus was now king of the Medes and the Persians. According to some ancient sources, though, Astyages was killed after the battle in his capital city, Ecbatana, today's Hamadan in Iran.

This is where the different accounts really get confusing. According to some, Cambyses I was still alive and king of Persia. And in Ecbatana, the capital of Media, Cyaxares II, son of Astyages, now became king of the Medes, which became a vassal state of Persia. There was no bad blood between Cyrus and Cyaxares, who also happened to be Cyrus's uncle. In addition, Cyrus then supposedly married a daughter of Astyages, which would mean that he married his mother's sister. Surely, she would have been a bit too old for the able and vibrant Cyrus, who would go on to father several children.

This particular account has Cyrus going on campaigns against the Neo-Assyrian Empire and the Babylonian Empire on behalf of his uncle Cyaxares II.

Again, we must look to Herodotus, despite his embroidered version of many events, as it is generally accepted and corroborated by contemporary chronicles that the Babylonians and their allies had already conquered the Neo-Assyrians and took over their territories and vassal states before Cyrus was born.

Cyrus set out on his own after conquering Lydians to take on Elam and Babylon, with thoughts of taking over Egypt at a later stage. Egypt was eventually conquered by the Persians under Cyrus's son and heir, Cambyses II.

Pasargadae: The New Persian Capital City

After Cyrus conquered the Medes, he selected the plain where the two armies met for battle as the site for a new capital city of the Persian-Median Empire. The extensive plain on which it was built lies approximately ninety kilometers (fifty-six miles) northeast of the modern city of Shiraz. It was declared a World Heritage Site by UNESCO in 2004.

The name of the city was probably chosen by Cyrus in honor of the Persian Pasargadae tribe, to which his Achaemenid clan belonged. There are also opinions that its name was derived from the meaning of the word "Pasargadae," which could have been "throne of Pars" or "strong club."

The citadel was a large platform-like construction on a low hill that provided an unobstructed view across the plain to see any approach on the city. This may have been a crucial lookout point because the city was not enclosed by defensive walls. Below the citadel, there was apparently a magnificent garden.

Pasargadae was built in a unique style, which would become specific to the Achaemenid Empire. The large public buildings were positioned across the city as opposed to grouping them together in the city center. The large open site of Pasargadae now contains ruins of a *caravanserai* (an inn for travelers and their animals in the arid regions of Asia and North Africa) dating to the 14th century CE. The ruins of the ancient city include several garden features, decorated pillars, ruins of at least three palaces for different purposes, pavilions, water channels, and a high stone tower, the latter of which is considered to be the tomb of Cambyses II, the son and successor of Cyrus who only ruled for eight years.

Cyrus's tomb stands out in its simplicity. It resembles a small ziggurat with a chamber on top. According to ancient texts, Cyrus designed the tomb and selected its site between his private palace and the park-like garden. The garden was described by a companion of Alexander the Great, Aristobulus, as having all kinds of trees, running water features, and lawns. Aristobulus also said that, at that time, there was a Persian inscription on the tomb identifying it as the tomb of Cyrus:

"O man, I am Cyrus son of Cambyses, who founded the empire of Persia and ruled over Asia. Do not grudge me my monument." Aristobulus's writings are no longer extant, but the words are quoted by several later ancient writers, such as Arrian and Strabo, who credit Aristobulus as the source.

Cyrus the Great: Father and Husband

Cyrus was called the father of his people in several ancient sources. In his personal life, of which we know little, he was a father and a husband. At some point in his life, Cyrus married Cassandane, a fellow Achaemenid, so we can assume that it happened after his extended visit to his grandfather, Astyages, in Ecbatana. Cassandane is still celebrated today in Iran. She is said to have been the great love of Cyrus's life. Cassandane is thought to have died in 538 BCE.

Again, according to some later sources, Cassandane was just one of Cyrus's wives, but in other accounts, she was his only wife and the mother of his children, Crown Prince Cambyses II, Smerdis (Bardiya), Atossa, Artystone, and, according to some sources, Roxane. It is said that Cyrus mourned her passing for the rest of his life. The Achaemenid Empire, according to ancient contemporary records, officially mourned her passing for six days in 538 BCE. Cassandane was buried at Cyrus's new capital city, Pasargadae; some sources say she was buried next to the place planned for Cyrus's tomb.

Xenophon complicates matters of Cyrus's wife or wives and sons even further. He has Cyrus giving a long speech on his deathbed. In the end, he asks his sons to say goodbye to their mother for him. The sons here are called Cambyses and Tanyoxarces, and they are his chief heirs, with Cambyses inheriting the empire and Tanyoxarces several satrapies (provinces). Thus, his wife—or his first wife, the mother of Cyrus's eldest son Cambyses—was still alive.

If we use Xenophon's account of Cyrus's death, Cyrus could not have mourned her as some other ancient historians claimed because he sent her greetings from his deathbed! Here again, we come across one of the problems with different names between various sources, as Herodotus and others call the second son Bardiya or Smerdis, and here he is called Tanyoxarces. It must be mentioned that the name differences were often because of translations from Old Persian to the writer's language.

And then there is the question of Amytis as a wife of Cyrus. It appears from some sources that after overthrowing the king of the Medes, Cyrus may have married his mother's sister, and thus another daughter of Astyages, to legitimize his claim to the throne of the Median Empire. This does sound a little unnecessary because he already had the support of the Median elite and, by all accounts, was popular amongst the people. His armies had routed the small Median force that did not join the generals who fought with the Persians. Cyrus already had a close tie with the Median ruling family because Astyages was his grandfather. Astyages did not have a son to inherit the throne. So, why did Cyrus have to marry his aunt?

This Amytis could have been much younger than her sister, Cyrus's mother, Mandane. She is mentioned by Ctesias as demanding retribution for the death of Tanyoxarces (Tanaoxarces), who is called Bardiya and Smerdis by other authors, after his brother, Cambyses II, murdered him. When this did not happen, she killed herself by drinking poison.

The Children of Cyrus the Great

If you thought the royal houses in the Middle Ages were atrociously inbred, have a glance at some of the ancient ruling families.

Cyrus's eldest son, Cambyses, succeeded him. Atossa, the daughter of Cyrus and Cassandane, married her brother, Cambyses. Another daughter, Roxane, also married Cambyses II. She apparently died in Nubia during Cambyses II's Egyptian campaign. Atossa married their other brother, Smerdis, afterward. But this Smerdis was, in reality, a Mede usurper posing as Smerdis, the son of Cyrus. The real Smerdis had been murdered by Cambyses II out of jealousy before he embarked on his Egyptian campaign. After Darius I, who came from another branch of the Achaemenid family, and his co-conspirators reclaimed the throne for the Achaemenid dynasty, Darius married Atossa. Darius also married Atossa's full sister, Artystone, and their cousin, Parmys!

Darius and Atossa had four sons, of which one—Xerxes—would succeed him. Artystone and Darius had three children. She was said to have been Darius's favorite wife. He even had a golden statue of her in their garden.

Xenophon left us Cyrus's beautifully worded final speech that was addressed to his sons when he was on his deathbed. If only they had followed his advice, history might have turned out differently. But then, when did children ever follow the wise council of a parent?

"Consider again that there is nothing in the world more nearly akin to death than is sleep; and the soul of man at just such times is revealed in its most divine aspect and at such times, too, it looks forward into the future; for then, it seems, it is most untrammeled by the bonds of the flesh.

"Now if this is true, as I think it is, and if the soul does leave the body, then do what I request of you and show reverence for my soul. But if it is not so, and if the soul remains in the body and dies with it, then at least fear the gods, eternal, all-seeing, omnipotent, who keep this ordered universe together, unimpaired, ageless, unerring, indescribable in its beauty and its grandeur; and never allow yourselves to do or purpose anything wicked or unholy."

Chapter 4: The Conquest of the Lydian Empire

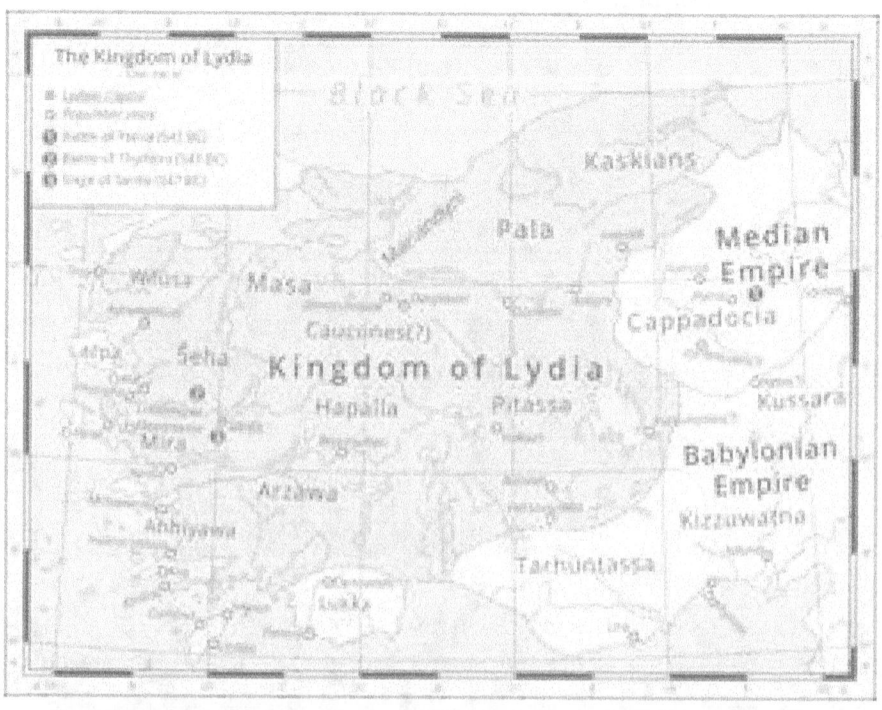

Lydian Kingdom under King Croesus, which was conquered by Cyrus in 547 BCE.
Cattette, CC BY 4.0 <https://creativecommons.org/licenses/by/4.0>, via Wikimedia Commons;
https://commons.wikimedia.org/wiki/File:Map_of_the_Kingdom_of_Lydia.png

After the Medes

Whichever ancient historian we believe, at least they seem to agree that Cyrus's next war was fought against Lydia. Lydia was the kingdom of the famous Croesus, to whom the idiomatic expression "as rich as Croesus" refers, at least in the English language. Lydia was situated in Asia Minor, thus to the north of the Levant or ancient Near East in modern Turkey. Croesus had a large army of mostly mercenaries. Many of the surrounding nations paid tribute to Lydia since they were afraid of angering King Croesus.

The Lydians had made several incursions into Media and vice versa over the years before this war. When Croesus's father, Alyattes, was still king of Lydia, Media and Lydia were engaged in bloody battles and skirmishes for five continuous years. This war stopped in its sixth year because of the paranormal fears of both nations when a solar eclipse happened one early afternoon during heavy fighting. It was recorded this particular eclipse had been predicted by one of the Seven Wise Men of Greece, Thales, from the Greek Ionian island of Milesia (today's Miletus). To seal their peace treaty, which was brokered objectively by two outside sources, Croesus's father was obliged to give his daughter, Aryenis, to Astyages of the Medes in marriage.

After Cyrus had thrown off the Median yoke and captured Astyages, Croesus felt compelled to avenge his brother-in-law. He had two other objectives up his sleeve as well. This rich king's land was crossed by a river with a seemingly endless supply of alluvial gold, but like many of the super-rich, Croesus wanted more—in this case, land! So, he attacked some of the states that had previously been vassals of the Medes but were now under Cyrus. Croesus destroyed the settlements and captured the people as slaves. Croesus also thought it prudent to show his strength and stop the young Cyrus before he became too powerful.

Now, Croesus, like most of his contemporaries, consulted an oracle or two before he committed to war. He did his due diligence and found the Oracle of Delphi, also known as Pythia, at the Temple of Apollo, was the most respected. So, Croesus gathered together a massive gift of treasures and sent his representatives to Delphi to ask the oracle if he should go to war against Cyrus and if he should gather allies to join him.

Pythia replied in her usual obscure manner that could be interpreted in several ways by an unwary listener, especially after the fact. The answer was that Croesus would destroy a great empire if he went to war against

Cyrus. The second question was answered in a separate reply, and she advised Croesus to ally himself with the strongest Greek states.

Croesus assumed Pythia predicted he would destroy Cyrus and the forces of Media and Persia, but he had to get a strong Greek ally. Croesus made a pact of mutual defense with the Spartans and prepared for war with Cyrus. Lydia's vassal state in Phrygia made overtures to Cyrus and became a Persian vassal state instead. Croesus used this as an excuse to go to war with Cyrus.

His forces encamped at an ideal spot in Cappadocia and proceeded to attack this newly acquired vassal state of the Persians. They destroyed everything in their path, from the fields to the settlements, and took the people as slaves. Their booty included the nearby city of Pteria, which was the capital city of the province.

Meanwhile, Cyrus, who had heard of Croesus's escapades, gathered his forces and prepared to meet Croesus. On his way, his armies gathered more and more soldiers, as many were eager to join this new charismatic leader. They met in a province of Cappadocia, and a battle commenced in which many soldiers from both sides perished. The battle was still undecided by evening when the troops retired to their respective encampments.

Croesus's Miscalculations

The next day, Cyrus's troops did not turn up on the battlefield. Croesus assumed the Medes and Persians had gone home since the fighting season was over. He was convinced that he did not win the battle outright only because his army was outnumbered by Cyrus's men.

At this time in history, the Lydian soldiers had everything going for them. They were known to be brave, strong, and battle-hardened. Moreover, they were well equipped, and their greatest strength lay in their cavalry. They were skilled riders and fought from their horses with long, deadly spears that they wielded with great precision. The only obvious reason they did not gain an outright victory must have been as Croesus determined: the Persians' superiority in numbers. However, if one takes into account Xenophon's remarks about the hero worship and desire to please Cyrus that all his men felt toward him, you might wonder if there was perhaps a psychological difference in the driving force behind the armies on this battlefield. Most of Croesus's soldiers were mercenaries driven by payment for their services.

As Croesus set out to return to Sardis, the magnificent Lydian capital, he resolved to call in reinforcements from all his previous allies to remedy the matter of sheer numbers before the battle season resumed in spring.

From his palace on the fortified hilltop in Sardis, he sent the mercenary troops home and dispatched messengers to his allies to join him or send reinforcements in spring. He also sent messengers to Sparta, Babylonia, and Egypt, with whom he had previously concluded defense treaties, to come to his aid when the war resumed. He speculated this would be in around five months when spring started.

Cyrus, meanwhile, had discussed matters with his officers and advisors, and they decided the time was ideal for attacking the unsuspecting Croesus.

Croesus was very surprised and unprepared when Cyrus turned up on the plains outside his capital. He gathered his forces and marched out to meet him. Once the forces were set up in battle formations facing each other, Cyrus could not help but be concerned over his enemy's magnificent cavalry display. One of his commanders, the Mede Harpagus, suggested they should use the camels of the baggage trains and mount them with soldiers as the first line of attack. Horses, he said, were sorely spooked by camels. It would sow confusion amongst Croesus's cavalry when the horses reared and threw their riders off to flee the battlefield.

Cyrus followed this excellent advice and sent the camels to the front. When the two armies met, the pride and strength of Croesus's army—the cavalry—were thrown into disarray. But Croesus's men still fought valiantly until they had to retreat into their city.

Sardis Besieged

Cyrus laid siege to the city. Each side watched and waited, one from the open plain, the other from the city walls. Who would give up first? Winter was coming, so the Lydians in the city were adequately provisioned for many months. Croesus and the Lydians assumed it would be a long siege, but they knew they could hold out as long as they needed to. On the other hand, the army on the unprotected plain had only their tents to protect them against the chilly winter winds of the treeless plain. They had only the food they carried with them.

Siege of Sardis, engraving by Jacob Abbott, 1803-1879.
https://commons.wikimedia.org/wiki/File:The_Siege_of_Sardis.jpg

The Lydians were laughing and taunting the Medes and Persians down below. They felt safe and cozy in their well-fortified city. The messengers that Croesus had sent to his allies before the siege would by now have arrived at their destinations. Reinforcements would be arriving in five months, just as Croesus had requested of them. The mercenaries whom he had sent to their homes would also be back in five months when spring started.

Croesus felt safe and comfortable in his palace, where he could indulge in every luxury. Life could go on as usual. He was, after all, the richest man in the world and could wallow in lavishness since his city was safe and secure. According to legend, the city walls had been blessed never to be breached because the previous king, Meles, had carried a sacred lion around the walls. The legend was that this lion was born from one of his concubines. Meles carried the miracle lion cub around every nook and cranny, every inch of the surrounding wall, for this sacred protection—except where the wall was an extension on top of a sheer cliff face. But nobody could climb up there anyway.

Below the walls, out of reach of missiles and arrows from the city guards, Cyrus and his men were scanning the walls with sharp-eyed attention to find any vulnerabilities. The officers and men were considering any feasible way to enter, but no Lydian ever entered or left the city. Cyrus promised great rewards to the man who would be the first to climb the walls because that seemed the only way in.

One day, after two weeks of watching and waiting, one of Cyrus's men noticed a man from the city climb down the wall and the sheer cliff face to retrieve a helmet. He climbed skillfully back up the cliff and the wall. Furtively, the Persian crept closer when the man was gone. He tried to copy the Lydian's actions and managed to climb the same route. Other soldiers followed him, and soon, they were inside Sardis! The city was taken. By Cyrus's order, Croesus, who was hiding inside his palace, was not to be hurt in any way. He was brought unharmed to King Cyrus.

Cyrus built a large funeral pyre, and he set Croesus and fourteen young Lydians on top of this. As their captors were kindling the wood, Croesus, who had not spoken at all since he was captured, suddenly sighed and cried out the name of Solon three times. Solon (630 BCE–560 BCE) was one of the Seven Wise Men of Greece. Croesus had remembered the words of Solon that no living man was blessed. He obviously thought of his own multitude of blessings that he had taken for granted while always considering himself to be a blessed man.

Upon hearing all this, Cyrus was contrite, thinking of how he was in the process of putting another to death while thinking himself blessed, just as Croesus had. He realized that people could not count on any kind of security in life; one's circumstances could change in an instant. Cyrus ordered the fire to be put out. But by this time, the flames had taken hold, and try as they might, they could not extinguish it.

From the pyre, Croesus saw what was about to happen. Thinking of all the offerings, gifts, and riches he had bestowed on the Temple of Apollo at Delphi every time he consulted the oracle there, he called on Apollo. As if in answer to his plea, a sudden rainstorm quenched the flames, and the Lydian youths and Croesus were saved.

Treatment of Croesus after Defeat

Croesus standing in front of King Cyrus.
https://commons.wikimedia.org/wiki/File:Croesus_and_Cyrus.jpg

Afterward, Cyrus wanted to know why Croesus had, without being provoked in any way, attacked and destroyed Persian lands. Croesus fully admitted he was the only one to blame, for no man should desire war over peace. He added that sons buried their fathers during peacetime, but in war, fathers buried their sons. Croesus's reply and his actions on the stake made Cyrus aware that he was saved just in time from committing a cruel deed. According to both Herodotus and Xenophon, Cyrus resolved to keep Croesus by his side for his valuable counsel. And so, Croesus became a part of the advisory group that Cyrus always kept near when he wanted to hear other points of view while considering options and actions.

The usual controversies arise when other sources are consulted on the demise or, rather, subjugation of the Lydians by Cyrus. Bacchylides, a Greek lyrical poet, says that Croesus did not want to be enslaved by Cyrus after his victory of Sardis. He, therefore, built his and his family's funeral pyre and had a slave set it alight. Zeus put the fire out with a thunderstorm. Apollo then saved Croesus from the flames by carrying him off to the land of the Hyperboreans—a mythical kingdom beyond the northern edge of the known world. Hyperborea is thought to be a land of perpetual spring, a place that is beautiful and plentiful. It was generally interpreted as the land of the afterlife.

Cyrus Grows the Persian Empire Once More

Cyrus the Great, painting by Jean Fouquet, c. 1470.
https://www.wikiart.org/en/jean-fouquet/emperor-cyrus-the-great-of-persia-who-permitted-the-hebrews-to-return-to-the-holy-land-and

After the defeat of Lydia, several of Lydia's vassal states stopped paying the required tribute. They were unaware that Croesus and Cyrus had reached an agreement that the Persians would not ransack Sardis if the Lydians freely shared their riches. Croesus also bequeathed all his income from the Lydian tributary kingdoms to Cyrus and the Persians. However, the kingdoms over which Croesus was overlord thought it expedient to take the chance of becoming independent. Cyrus soon crushed these revolts.

One of these other kingdoms, that of the Ionians, had been invited by Cyrus before his incursion into Lydia to join forces with him. They refused because they fully expected that Croesus would be the victor. The Ionians now quickly requested that Cyrus take over their overlordship under the same terms as they had before with Lydia. The Ionians lived in the cities and islands in the southeast of modern Turkey, in and around the Ionian Sea, most of which are today well-known archaeological and tourist sites, such as Ephesus and Priene.

Cyrus shrewdly messaged back the story of a flutist who expected the fishes, which he saw swimming in the clear waters, to join him on the beach to listen to the beautiful music he was making. The fish did not do so. The flutist then caught them in a net. Watching them jumping and flapping about in the net, he told them to stop dancing. It was too late now, as when he played for them before, they did not come to him. The Ionians understood his message.

The Ionians expected war. They fortified their cities and called the Ionian League to their sacred meeting place, a temple dedicated to Poseidon. They decided to send a delegation to Sparta to ask for assistance. The Spartans refused to join them. However, the Spartans sent a warning to Cyrus that he must stay away from the Greek territories, or they would punish him. Cyrus replied that he was not afraid of men who had a sanctuary in which to hold their meetings in a secret conclave. He implied that in that kind of council, deceit and lies reigned supreme. He added the Spartans would be better off forgetting about the Ionians and looking after their own people.

Cyrus left Sardis under the charge of one of his Persians. A Lydian was put in charge of Croesus's treasures, which he was supposed to deliver to Pasargadae's treasury. Cyrus was on his way back to Persia to plan further campaigns, with Elam and Babylon heading his list. A messenger arrived to inform him the Lydians, under the leadership of the Lydian left in charge of the treasury, had revolted against the Persian governor.

With Croesus's treasure in hand, the rebels under the Lydian had fled Sardis and were hiring mercenaries to help them drive the Persians out of Lydia. It seems the rebel leader had dreams of becoming king of Lydia. Cyrus sent one of his Median generals to quell the revolt. Croesus successfully talked him out of enslaving the Lydians as punishment. He advised Cyrus to forbid the Lydians from making or carrying weapons. He said Cyrus should order them to change their lifestyle so they could pursue peace and harmony instead of war.

Once this Median general subdued the Lydian rebellion, he set about conquering the rest of Anatolia and then pursued the Ionians. When he died of an illness during these campaigns, he was replaced by Harpagus, the same Mede who had helped Cyrus conquer the Median Empire. Harpagus was successful in conquering the nations to the north and east of Iran.

Chapter 5: The Fall of Babylon

Neo-Assyrians: Enough Is Enough

Before the time of Cyrus, the Medes and Babylonians had, at times, stood together against the mighty Neo-Assyrian Empire. The Neo-Assyrian Empire was a harsh overlord. After bloody and brutal battles, the Assyrians took conquered peoples, or at least huge numbers of them, as prisoners and resettled them elsewhere in exile. A good example of this would be the ten tribes of Israel in the 8th century BCE. They were deported by Tiglath Pileser III in 722 BCE from northern Israel and replaced with exiles from other countries.

The replacements were mostly Mesopotamian peoples. In this way, the Assyrians kept revolts of conquered peoples in their vast empire under control and to a minimum. They removed the rulers, the elite, and craftsmen from other conquered countries, leaving mostly just peasants behind. These exiled peoples were then spread amongst other conquered folks to be assimilated and lose their national identity.

There are magnificent reliefs of sieges and various deportations that were recovered from the Neo-Assyrian period at the palace of Nineveh; they are now displayed in the British Museum. At the settlement sites of these forced immigrants in Israel, clay tablets, pottery, and other cultural objects confirm that fairly large Babylonian groups were among the resettled and exchanged populations.

The Chaldeans in the Arabian Gulf, meanwhile, had grown strong. Around 626 BCE, their king, Nabopolassar, rid them of their Assyrian overlords. He crowned himself king of Babylon and set about restoring the erstwhile glory of Babylon. He revamped the infrastructure of the capital city, Babylon, and added new public buildings, temples, and irrigation channels, there and elsewhere in Babylonia, while keeping the Assyrians at bay. By the time of Cyrus and the Achaemenid Empire, the city of Babylon was one of the largest and most prosperous cities in the known world. The Babylonians and their allies had taken advantage of civil strife and attacked the Neo-Assyrians in 612 BCE. Nineveh, the Assyrian capital at that time, was taken in 609 BCE. The Neo-Assyrian Empire would never rise again.

At Last, Going for the Prize: Babylon

Nabopolassar had trained and educated his son, Nebuchadnezzar II, well in state affairs and warfare to successfully inherit and expand the Neo-Babylonian Empire after his death. Nebuchadnezzar became the most successful ruler of the Chaldean dynasty of Babylonia, but he was followed by weaker rulers. Cyrus finally marched against the last king of the independent Chaldean dynasty in Babylon when a rather weak and very unpopular ruler, Nabonidus, was on the throne.

According to Xenophon, Cyrus was sidetracked several times in this endeavor and only reached his destination after many other adventures. Herodotus, in his usual style of describing the ins and outs of every significant person and geographical aspect along the way, eventually describes the incredibly strong fortifications of Babylon. A third extant source for Cyrus's conquest of Babylon is the very fragmented and damaged Chronicle of Nabonidus. Out of these several sources, which, in truth, are extremely difficult to compare due to the usage of different personal and country names, historians have managed to put together a reasonable scenario of Cyrus's conquest of Babylon.

Sieges and Battles

The first major clash between the Persians and the Babylonians happened at the Battle of Opis, located northeast of Babylon. Nabonidus had sent a certain commander, Belshazzar, to intercept the Persians, but his forces were decisively beaten by the Persians. According to some ancient sources, Belshazzar was the son and regent of Babylon when Nabonidus lived in Arabia for ten years. He was also the king or acting king whom Daniel of the Christian Bible had told that he had been weighed and found wanting and would be struck down that very night. Daniel, a Jew in exile, had been called by Belshazzar to explain text that suddenly appeared on the wall of his palace while he was having a party.

It seems Nabonidus was a bit of a coward, as he did not participate in the Battle of Opis. The remnants of his army fled back to Babylon. Nabonidus was hiding in Sippar and left the city to be attacked, fully expecting it not to be conquered and that he could return and remain king.

At last, the greater forces of the Persian armies arrived at Babylon and encamped a distance away from the city when Babylonian troops did not come out to meet them in battle. It must be kept in mind that several of Cyrus's armies, under the command of his trusted and loyal friends, were constantly busy in other regions of the Persian Empire, ensuring peace, nipping revolts in the bud, and conquering new territories.

At Babylon, Cyrus first planned to parade his troops right under the city walls. He was dissuaded by one of his companions and advisors, who suggested they march by at a fair distance. Cyrus wanted to gain knowledge and insight into Babylon's defenses and fortifications. He compromised by selecting a distance that was just far enough to be safe from enemy arrows and missiles from the city walls.

It was evident from Cyrus's own inspection that the tales of Babylon's unbreachable walls were true. Apart from the water-filled ditches that surrounded the outer walls of the city, the walls were thick and strong. Herodotus says they were built with baked clay bricks set together in tar and that the walls were up to fifty royal cubits deep (a royal cubit is about twenty-one inches or fifty-three centimeters). The soil dug from the trenches was used to make the bricks, and the tar came from another Babylonian city. Babylon was split in half by the Euphrates River, which was a ready supply of water. The city was also stocked with a good food supply in case of a siege.

On either side of the riverbanks were parallel walls with bronze gates that could be opened to give access to the streets. According to Herodotus, the city was filled with houses built three and four stories high. On one side of the city was the center, which was occupied by the royal palace, and on the other side was a sacred precinct with a temple for Marduk named the Esagila and a ziggurat. The ziggurat was topped with another temple for Marduk, the chief god of the Babylonians. This was known as Etemenanki (Home of the Foundation of Heaven and Earth), although Herodotus, being thoroughly Greek, called it the temple of Zeus.

Semiramis and Nitocris

An interesting tidbit about Babylon's defenses comes from Herodotus. Two queens in different eras are mentioned as contributing to the building and construction works of Babylon. Semiramis, whom ancient Greek writers mistakenly place as a ruler in Babylon (r. 811 BCE–806 BCE) instead of Ashur in Assyria, made drainage channels and canals across the wide open plain on which the city of Babylon was built. This stopped the Euphrates from regularly flooding the city and the plain.

The history of this woman is clouded in mystery. Ctesias describes her as half-goddess and half-human. According to myths, she was raised by doves. Other ancient writers attribute the famous Hanging Gardens of Babylon—one of the Seven Wonders of the Ancient World—to her. It is likely she was a Babylonian princess who married an Assyrian king, Shamshi-Adad V. After his death, she became regent over the Assyrian Empire until her son, Adad Nirari III, could take the throne. Her name was Sammu-ramat or Shammuramat, but the later Greek historians called her Semiramis. Most of what is written about her are legends, but she is clearly mentioned in Assyrian records and had her own obelisk in Ashur, Iraq.

The second queen mentioned by Herodotus is Nitocris (c. 550 BCE). Nitocris greatly strengthened the defenses of Babylon in numerous ways. She is said to have rerouted the mighty Euphrates River before it neared Babylon so that it flowed with several twists and turns, winding back and forth upon its previously straight course. This influenced the progress of any army approaching the city. Then she built reinforcements along the riverbanks to make them higher and sturdier. She also dug a basin deep enough to find the groundwater level so that water could seep into the basin and form marshland on the quickest route toward the country of the Medes, who, according to Herodotus, was her most dangerous enemy at the time.

In the city of Babylon, Nitocris bricked out the bed and banks of the Euphrates where it ran through the city. The boats previously used to cross from one side of the city to the other, but she built a bridge that was only open during the daytime. According to Herodotus, Nitocris had her tomb built on top of the main city gate with a luring inscription for some future ruler who really needed funds, saying they could open the tomb and take her burial goods. Somehow, nobody ever tried until Darius the Great came along. He found the tomb empty except for a note that said,

"Wert thou not insatiate of wealth and basely desirous of gain, thou hadst not opened the coffins of the dead."

Cyrus took the city in October 539 BCE, using the river to breach Babylon's defenses. One portion of his troops was left in readiness at the site where the river entered the city, while he took the rest miles away to divert the river. The Babylonians were taken completely by surprise because all the activities of digging large trenches to divert the mighty and swiftly flowing Euphrates happened out of sight. And the water was diverted during the night.

It was the night of a national feast day in Babylon. By the time the feasting citizens noticed, the Persians were already amongst them. They had entered through the shallow riverbed and found many of the inside city gates in the river wall had been carelessly left open.

Cyrus Welcomed

According to the fragmented Nabonidus Chronicle, Nabonidus was absent from Babylon for extended periods. For example, he once lived in Tayma, a large oasis in the Arabian Desert, for ten years, ostensibly to subject Arabia. It may have been that he was too afraid to handle the ever-present palace intrigue and was as uncomfortable in Babylon as the people there were with him. Eventually, he returned to Babylon and was captured in his palace. According to the Nabonidus Chronicle, there was much bloodshed, especially among private citizens throughout the city. This fact can be questioned, as Cyrus had instructed the troops to order the people back into their homes, with a warning that only those caught on the streets after the fact or who resisted would be killed.

Cyrus was a man who craved peace rather than war, as attested by inscriptions on clay tablets that were excavated from several sites across his empire. One example comes from an inscription on a baked clay brick found in Ur by the British archaeologist Sir Leonard Woolley. It is now on display at the British Museum. It is inscribed in Babylonian and has Cyrus's various names and titles, along with a statement that he established peace in the land. It is dated to the 6th century BCE and was probably one of many that were used throughout the empire.

In this scenario, it follows that most of the people of Babylon welcomed Cyrus into their city. In addition, there were lots of foreign exiles present in the city and the country because the Babylonians had, since the time of their greatest king, Nebuchadnezzar, displaced the conquered peoples, similar to what the Assyrians did. But the Assyrians had often switched their captives with those of other conquered countries, while the Babylonians had them in their own cities amongst their own people. Naturally, these groups were jubilant to be rid of the Babylonian yoke and celebrated the conquerors.

With the conquest of Babylon, as happened after the conquest of the Medes and then the Lydians, Cyrus automatically became the overlord of its vassal states. In the case of the large Babylonian Empire, this included countries bordering the Mediterranean Sea, like Syria and Palestine.

Elam at Last

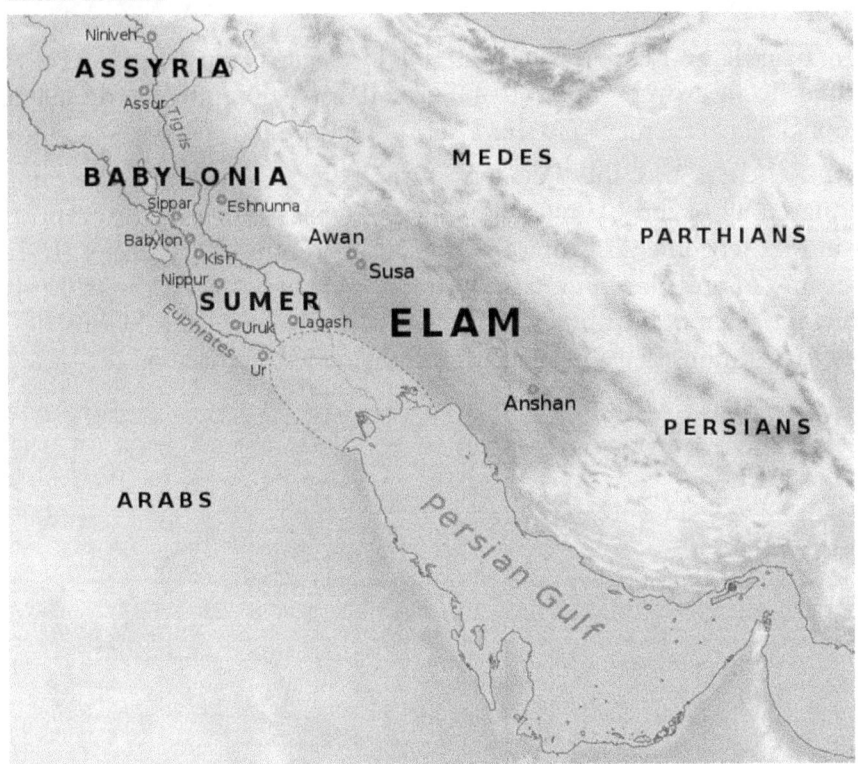

A map of Elam.
By File:Near East topographic map-blank.svg: SémhurFile:Elam-map-PL.svg: Wkotwicaderivative work: Morningstar1814 - File:Elam-map-PL.svg, CC BY-SA 3.0, https://commons.wikimedia.org/w/index.php?curid=61956849

Although Cyrus had his sights set on Elam as one of his next targets when he left Sardis, he only conquered their capital city, Susa, sometime between 540 and 538 BCE, just before or just after the conquest of Babylon. The Elamites had fluctuated between greatness, being conquered by stronger nations, being vassals to several overlords, and being independent for more than a millennium. They were frequent raiders of neighboring nations and vice versa since the time of the Sumerians and the Akkadians.

At times, the Elamites were allied with other foreign powers in attacks on their neighbors. In around 1000 BCE, their capital city was conquered by the Babylonians. Their fortunes waxed and waned as vassals of Babylon. They developed their own script, which remains largely undeciphered, despite several claims of breakthroughs. Part of the problem is the minimal number of extant texts or inscriptions available to scholars.

In 645 BCE, Elam was conquered by Ashurbanipal of Assyria. He completely destroyed the city of Susa. It was subsequently rebuilt and repopulated over a relatively short period of just one century.

And then it was the Persians' turn. After Cyrus the Great finally conquered all of the Elamites by 538 BCE, Susa remained an important city in the Achaemenid Empire, acting as an administrative center. In fact, it became one of the three administrative capitals of the Persian Empire during the reign of Cambyses II (the son of Cyrus) and later Darius I. The other two administrative capitals were Babylon and Ecbatana.

Chapter 6: Ruling the Empire

History of Empires: Tyrants Fall

Cyrus realized that throughout the history of the ancient world, empires fell because it was impossible for one person to control vast territories of conquered peoples. So, he employed various methods to counter the mistakes of past emperors. Xenophon's *Cyropaedia* is especially helpful due to his account of Cyrus's background and education and analysis of Cyrus's successful rule that laid the foundation of the Achaemenid Empire.

The education system of the Achaemenid tribe, and by implication the rest of the Persian tribes, reminds one of modern-day Montessori and Ad Astra approaches. Xenophon describes the male education system, but many accounts from this time indicate that women had the same education and rights as men.

Xenophon says the public square in Anshan was divided into four spaces: one for boys, one for youths, one for mature men, and one for elders. Although Cyrus spent his first ten years in Media as the son of a cowherd (at least according to Herodotus), his innate intelligence and abilities allowed him to learn from each experience. After Cyrus was recognized and returned to his own family, King Cambyses and his wife, Mandane of Media, he was educated in the Persian ways.

The main lessons of the boys' section in the Persian town square centered around justice and discipline. Self-discipline and self-control were valued above most other traits. Presiding over each of the spaces in the square were twelve officers—one from each of the twelve Persian tribes. They were selected for their skills and abilities. These officers provided judgment and punishment when the boys laid charges against each other. Apart from charges of theft, robbery, assault, cheating, and other offenses that our laws generally include today, the Persians saw crimes stemming from ingratitude as the most serious. In their view, ingratitude caused selfishness, and selfishness caused most offenses and neglect of duty.

Cyrus The Great's Central Philosophy

"Whenever you can, act as a liberator. Freedom, dignity, and wealth – these three together constitute the greatest happiness of humanity. If you bequeath all three to your people, their love for you will never die." – Cyrus the Great, according to Xenophon.

The above quote shows the philosophy Cyrus had about life in general, and this included the way in which he ruled.

This philosophy would become central to how Cyrus ruled his vast empire of 2.1 million square miles (5.5 million square kilometers). It informed the doctrine that made his rule over such an empire manageable and prosperous in terms of innovations, business, and societal frameworks.

How Did Cyrus Conquer and Manage This Vast Empire?

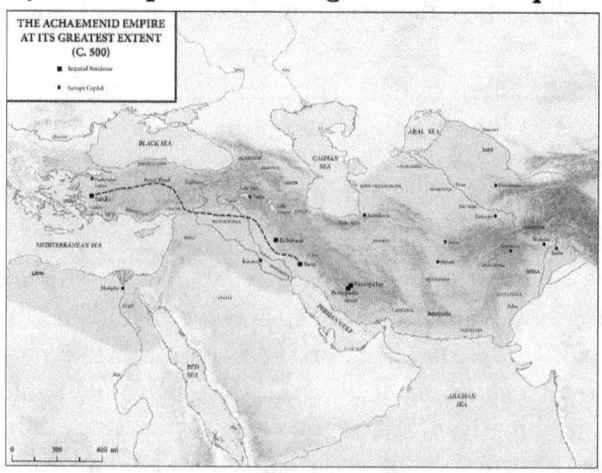

Achaemenid Empire.
Original creator: MossmapsCorrections according to Oxford Atlas of World History 2002, The Times Atlas of World History (1989), Philip's Atlas of World History (1999) by पाटलिपुत्र, *CC BY-SA 4.0 <https://creativecommons.org/licenses/by-sa/4.0>, via Wikimedia Commons; https://commons.wikimedia.org/wiki/File:Achaemenid_Empire_at_its_greatest_extent_according_t o_Oxford_Atlas_of_World_History_2002.jpg*

The empire that Cyrus created spanned from the Mediterranean Sea in the west to the Indus River in the east. The Persian Empire was, without a doubt, the largest empire up to that time. Following the death of Cyrus, his successors, Cambyses II and Darius the Great, continued to expand the empire until it reached the Balkans, southeastern Europe, and Egypt. Cyrus the Great left the administration framework of the territories he conquered in place, although he made some adjustments and left people there that reported to him and his administration centers. He set up an unequaled structure to administer and manage this vast empire, and since the infrastructure and logistics were already in place, his successors simply had to maintain and improve the existing methods of rule.

The First Victory

Other versions of Cyrus the Great differ in detail from what we have looked at so far, which has mostly been from Herodotus and Xenophon.

After the death of his father, Cambyses I, Cyrus became king of Anshan. However, since Anshan was a vassal state of Media, he was not an independent ruler. Cyrus's kingdom paid tribute to the king of Media, who happened to be his maternal grandfather, Astyages.

In the Nabonidus Chronicle, a clay tablet exhibited at the British Museum in London, a scribe details the attack on Cyrus by his grandfather Astyages. The cuneiform text specifically states that Astyages launched an attack on the "king of Anshan." There are various accounts of this battle and who initiated it.

In the Nabonidus Chronicle, Ecbatana's mutiny and Astyages's capture are confirmed. Historians Herodotus and Ctesias wrote that Cyrus married the daughter of Astyages, Amytis, to pacify the Median vassals, including Saka, Bactria, Parthia, and Hyrcania. Herodotus also notes that Cyrus integrated Sogdia into his Persian Empire during his military campaigns against the rebels who wanted their freedom after Media was conquered.

Further Unification: A Family Business

Since Cyrus became king of all the vassal states that were previously under Media's rule, Parsa, which was ruled by his uncle Arsames, peacefully became part of the new empire. Cyrus left the governing of this city-state in the hands of his uncle. Hystaspes, Cyrus's cousin and son of Arsames, was given charge of Parthia and Phrygia. Cyrus united the Achaemenid kingdoms, including Parsa and Anshan, and made the budding Persian Empire a well-run family business.

Expansion

The occupation and takeover of Media was only the beginning of what would become Cyrus's vast empire. According to some accounts, Cyrus did not want to take over any neighboring kingdoms at this point. He was satisfied with running the Persian Empire, which now included Media. He was managing state affairs and governing successfully, so there was no need to go to war after squashing rebellions that broke out in Media's vassal states.

As was customary, Croesus, King of Lydia, sent regular messengers to the Oracle of Delphi to request advice from Pythia before momentous decisions. As is noted by Pausanias, a Greek geographer and scholar (110–180 CE), the magnificent gifts from King Croesus to Apollo and the Oracle of Delphi were a regular testament to his wealth and trust in her prophecies.

During one of these deputations to the oracle, Croesus was told he would "destroy a great empire" if he attacked the Persians. Croesus took this to mean that he would destroy Cyrus's empire. Croesus decided to attack Pteria in 547 BCE. Although Pteria was previously a vassal state of Lydia, it had declared its loyalty to the Persian Empire and Cyrus the Great.

When King Cyrus heard of the siege of Pteria, he gathered his armies and moved to defend the city. However, on his arrival, he found that Pteria had already been conquered and the citizens enslaved by Croesus. Croesus had burned down the city so that Cyrus could not use it as a strategic location from which to fight.

Croesus retreated to Sardis, assuming Cyrus would not follow. Cyrus did the opposite and attacked Croesus and the Lydian army at Thymbra. Cyrus conquered Sardis and brought an end to the Lydian Empire and the Mermnad dynasty. Cyrus spared Croesus's life, and Croesus became a part of the team of military advisors that Cyrus relied on.

The approximate end of the Lydian Empire is generally accepted as being 547 or 546 BCE. After the fall of Lydia, its vassal states in Anatolia, Lycia, Ionia, Cilicia, and Phoenicia became part of the Persian Empire.

Blueprint for the Persian Empire

Cyrus became the ruler of Anshan, then conquered the Median Empire with the Median general Harpagus by his side. This was followed by his conquests of the Lydian Empire, the Elamites and their capital of Susa, the Babylonian Empire, and further military expansions into Central

Asia. These broad facts seem to be historically confirmed across most sources, both primary and secondary.

During Cyrus's thirty-year reign, he showed the qualities of being a great statesman and military leader, especially when it came to invading foreign territories. He would first approach the leader of the region with an option to negotiate the takeover in a non-violent manner. Only once his offer was declined would he declare war. Even in the event of war, Cyrus acted with humanity, as can be seen with King Croesus, who joined Cyrus's empire as part of a military advisory unit. Cyrus had the option of killing Croesus, as was customary at the time, but he did not.

A different version of the Babylonian conquest is that the ruler of Babylon, Nabonidus, fled to Sippar after Cyrus conquered Elam. Nabonidus left Ugbaru in charge of the army. Ugbaru, previously the governor of Gutium, changed allegiance. According to the Babylonian Chronicle, "Ugbaru, governor of the district of Gutium, and the army of Cyrus entered Babylon without a battle." Ugbaru is called Gobryas by the Greek historian Xenophon. He was appointed as the Babylonian governor by Cyrus after the Babylonian conquest.

Nabonidus was captured, but his life was spared, and he was sent into exile to live his life out in the region of Carmania. It is assumed that his co-ruler and son, Belshazzar, was killed during the taking of Babylon. Nabonidus was still living in exile during Darius the Great's rule.

Accounts of Cyrus and his military expansion campaigns were recorded as bringing "into subjection every nation without exception."

According to some historians, the Persian Empire always tried to negotiate with its enemies before engaging in battle, as battles were (and still are) costly in every respect, and Cyrus would rather attempt to get the enemy to surrender.

Sharing Power: How to Rule a Large Empire

Cyrus the Great was an ingenious statesman, charismatic leader, and military genius. This was because he was wise enough to surround himself with advisors who were specialists in their fields and knew the people and geographical areas they intended to enter.

After establishing his new capital, Pasargadae, in Fars Province of today's Iran, Cyrus refined the way of ruling and managing his vast Persian Empire. He showed great administrative prowess in the development of a socially acceptable and organized government.

By establishing a regional government system that reported to the central government, Cyrus managed to effectively administrate the Persian Empire. He divided it into twenty-six provinces called satrapies.

Satrapies

The Achaemenid Empire spread across most of West Asia and much of Central Asia, including areas of the Mediterranean and Hellespont (the Strait of Dardanelles in modern-day Turkey) in the west and stretching to the Indus River in the east.

Cyrus developed a system where each region became an autonomous province with a satrap or governor who represented him in each province. This system of provincial governments originated in the Median era around 648 BCE and became more formalized and effective under the rule of Cyrus the Great beginning in 547 BCE.

Throughout the centuries, lands were ruled by the kings or emperors who conquered those regions—until Cyrus the Great, that is. Cyrus adapted previous styles of ruling to suit his own requirements. He likely studied how previous empires failed and avoided known problems.

Cyrus divided his empire into twenty-six provinces under satraps who ruled in his name. Each satrap had to be a guardian of the well-being of his people and territory. A satrap was responsible for law and order, tax collection, civil administration, and the selection and training of an army for each province that the king could call upon when the need arose. Additionally, Cyrus understood the need to honor the social and cultural activities of each nation. Oversight was left in the capable hands of the satrap.

Although the satraps had autonomous and broad powers over their provinces, there were many checks and balances in place to ensure the satraps did not overstep the line.

Delving Deeper

Cyrus the Great earned his reputation not only because of his military conquests but also due to his natural communication skills and his understanding of the human psyche. The basic method of ruling via a governor or satrap might not initially have been his idea. However, the extent of local autonomy, understanding of the local people, accountability of the satraps, and the systems of checks and balances in the administration of these satraps were due to his ingenious methods.

Five-Layer System

By the time of Darius, a five-layer system of governance was used. It is assumed that it was started by Cyrus and later refined and adapted to a more centralized system by Darius I. Cyrus knew there had to be checks and balances at all levels, as he had to ensure he could rule successfully and with maximum efficiency. The different hierarchies would run independently yet be interwoven to form a system of checks and balances on the satraps.

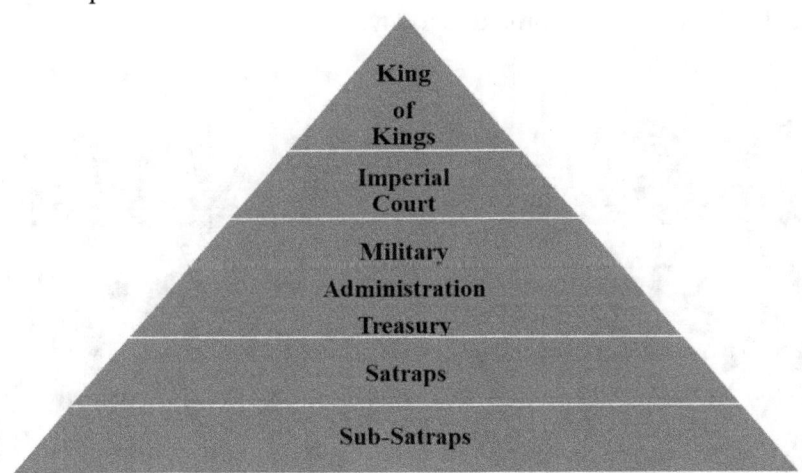

Five-layer system of rule of the Achaemenid Empire.

King of Kings

The monarch, in this instance, King Cyrus, was the supreme authority. He was seen to have no equal on earth, and his word was law. Theoretically, from this position of great power, the king could do as he pleased. However, for all practical purposes, he was supposed to be accountable to the imperial court.

Imperial Court

The imperial court was chosen from the nobility and elite citizens of the Persian Empire. These ministers played a key role in advising and counseling the king and kept a watchful eye on the satrapies. When selecting the members of his imperial court, King Cyrus again displayed his innovative ideas. He surrounded himself with the most loyal advisors selected from the Persians and from each conquered territory.

Military, Administration, and Treasury

The third tier of the hierarchy had immense responsibility and great power. They were the flexible yet permanent and immovable institutions that ran the day-to-day governance of the empire.

The famous army unit of the Achaemenid army, known as the Ten Thousand Immortals, was established by Cyrus the Great and formed the core security of the Persian Empire. Herodotus describes the Immortals as "heavy infantry," and the size was kept at a constant number of ten thousand soldiers. Beneath their robes, they wore scale armor. They used swords, large daggers, short spears, bows, and arrows, and for defense, they used wicker shields. These legendary Immortals are still a fascinating subject for Hollywood filmmakers today.

The Immortals, a photo of the 1971 celebration of the Achaemenid Empire in Iran.
https://commons.wikimedia.org/w/index.php?curid=7497892

The imperial administration's main objective eventually became profit and control. But, of course, over time, corruption and nepotism set in, obscuring Cyrus's high ideals of equality for all. Even Darius I, arguably one of the greatest rulers in history, appointed family members as satraps. Darius was also responsible for monetizing tributes and making it a compulsory fixed sum contribution, whereas Cyrus relied on willingly contributed "gifts" of goods and objects of value, often surplus production of what a country produced or precious metals and stones. Cyrus took a chance and trusted the loyalty of his subjects and their willingness to come to his aid whenever he needed them. In return, they looked up to him and called him their father.

Later, the reallocation of ownership of conquered lands from low-class citizens to the elite ensured the empire remained profitable for a while.

This reallocation and upliftment of the elite class would eventually contribute to the fall of the mighty Persian Empire. The luxurious lifestyles of the elite began to cripple the economy. At that time, Cyrus was a distant memory.

Satraps

The satraps were the governors in charge of the empire's provinces and its administration, finance, law and order, and social and cultural activities. The satrap wielded the same amount of power over their regions as the king had over the empire. This essentially meant the satraps were extremely powerful in their own right. At times, a specific satrap that had governed his region well would be given a neighboring province to rule over, naturally increasing his income and power.

To maintain law and order, the satrap acted as the supreme judge in civil and criminal cases and was responsible for exacting justice. According to Xenophon, a satrap was also responsible for the safety and security of the interprovincial roads and had the right to put down rebels and bands that tried to rob travelers and postal workers on the Royal Road.

Here again, Cyrus was wise and allowed governors of conquered regions to continue their rule but insisted they adhere to the five-layer system of governance. Since they were already rulers of their local regions, they knew the culture, administration, and financial requirements to run their provinces successfully.

Sub-Satraps

The final layer of the Persian government formed a part of the satraps' "royal" court and was chosen from the local citizens, who knew the customs and traditions of their people. Their role was to advise and assist the satraps in integrating new taxation or administrative practices into the provinces. They would also advise on various subjects, such as religious practices, dress codes, and local traditions.

Modus Operandi

Some historians suggest that Cyrus's method of ruling a multi-national empire that tolerated ethnoreligious and cultural diversities emerged from necessity. He understood that enforcing a singular identity across such a diverse and large geographical area would result in constant conflicts.

As a form of monarchial rule, the methods used by King Cyrus were complex, flexible, and strategic while exemplary in terms of humanity.

Later kings abused the central bureaucratic form of governance. All positions under the king had to obey the monarch's command implicitly, whereas Cyrus negotiated outcomes. His commands were more like requests. One can only imagine that the legendary Ten Thousand Immortals would have been enough to keep the peace and enforce the law if called upon. Satrapies obeyed the monarch in every aspect of local governance and knew the result of rebellion or theft: the Immortals!

During Cyrus the Great's rule, no rebellions were recorded, and the respect he earned can be seen in the way he was reportedly viewed as a father by his subjects. There can be no greater honor than to see your ruler as a father figure.

George W. F. Hegel, a German philosopher, in his book *Lectures on the Philosophy of History*, describes the Persian Empire as "the first to pass away" and the people as the "first historical people."

"The Persian Empire is an empire in the modern sense—like that which existed in Germany, and the great imperial realm under the sway of Napoleon; for we find it consisting of a number of states, which are indeed dependent, but which have retained their own individuality, their manners, and laws. The general enactments, binding upon all, did not infringe upon their political and social idiosyncrasies, but even protected and maintained them; so that each of the nations that constitute the whole, had its own form of constitution. As light illuminates everything—imparting to each object a peculiar vitality—so the Persian Empire extends over a multitude of nations and leaves to each one its particular character. Some have even kings of their own; each one its distinct language, arms, way of life, and customs. All this diversity coexists harmoniously under the impartial dominion of Light ... a combination of peoples—leaving each of them free. Thereby, a stop is put to that barbarism and ferocity with which the nations had been want to carry on their destructive feuds." (Hegel's *Philosophy of History*, Chapter III)

Cyrus's philosophy influenced great historical figures, such as Karl Marx, Friedrich Nietzsche, Friedrich Engels, Jean-Paul Sartre, and more.

Cyrus the Great mostly ruled from Ecbatana until Pasargadae was built, but the empire had four capital cities. Xenophon goes on to specify the monarch's annual schedule. We cannot be sure this schedule applied to Cyrus, but it was in place by the time of Darius I. Babylon had a warm and sunny climate, and the king ruled from there for seven months of the year. During spring, he would rule from Susa for around three months. During the heat of mid-summer, he would rule from Ecbatana in the Median Highlands, where the climate was tolerable and cooler. Pasargadae, the ceremonial capital, was a place of vision and comfort for Cyrus, where he had his famous gardens with trees and plants from all across the empire. Here, he spent time with his family in his private palace. Pasargadae remained a sacred place even after it was replaced with Persepolis in the time of Darius I. All the Achaemenid kings were crowned at Pasargadae.

Intelligence Services

To ensure each satrapy functioned in accordance with the rules and regulations of the empire, Cyrus created special positions for monitoring the provinces. These men were specialized agents of the "King of Kings." During the time of Darius I, they could make unannounced inspections in the provinces.

The "Eye of the King" served as an extension of the king's purview. They watched the satraps and were an almost covert extension of the monarch, as he wished to have knowledge of what happened behind his back. To put it more bluntly, they were the king's spies. Both Xenophon and Ctesias emphasized the power wielded by the Eye of the King. They enabled the king to have firsthand knowledge of his subjects. In Cyrus's time, it was done for justice and fairness, but afterward, it became corrupted. Xenophon, who was born long after Cyrus died, wrote about seeing people on the roads as he traveled through the Persian Empire who had lost their eyes due to committing a crime against the king. In Ctesias's *Persica*, he mentions Persians gouging out eyes as punishment for treason.

The "Ears of the King" would listen for any rumors and investigate and confirm findings before reporting directly to the king. This included corruption, mismanagement, theft, and satraps who had abused their power.

The king's secretaries held independent positions and were seen as the most important authorities besides the King of Kings. They had a direct line of communication with the king. Functioning as a monitor, the secretary's role included checking on the administration, tax collection, and law and order in their provinces. They were seen as the king's closest and most trusted confidants. The responsibility of reading the king's private letters to the satraps also fell to the king's secretaries.

An example of how this position functioned comes to us via Herodotus, who describes an instance of Darius the Great's use of a secretary; yet again, we do not know if it was the same in the time of Cyrus

II. Oroetes (also called Oroetus in some translations), the satrap in charge of Phrygia, Lydia, and Ionia during the rule of Darius I, had a personal army of one thousand soldiers. When the king's secretary read out instructions for the one thousand soldiers to cease protecting Oroetes and execute him, they immediately obeyed.

The Achaemenid Empire was advanced, successful, innovative, and ruled by a centralized bureaucratic government that built an unequaled infrastructure. According to some ancient accounts, the framework of what Cyrus initiated and Darius refined was so efficient that after Alexander the Great conquered Persia, he made very few changes, if any.

The road system called the Royal Road, which went from Susa to Sardis, led to the innovative postal service by the time of Darius that served the whole empire. It was called Chapar Khaneh ("courier house"). Each Chapar Khaneh was a resting and resupply station along the Royal Road. Here, the *chapars* or couriers could switch to a fresh horse and get supplies for their journey. It only took the *chapars* seven days to travel from Sardis to Susa, whereas an ordinary traveler would take ninety days or more, according to Herodotus. They were thought to have traveled "twenty-four seven" (night and day, every day) in safe areas and in emergencies.

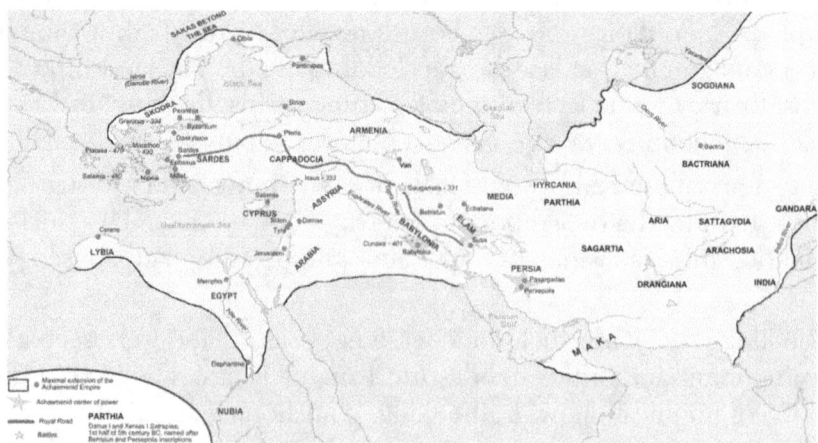

Map of the Achaemenid Empire with the Royal Road, which went from Susa in Elam to Sardis in Lydia.
Fabienkhan, CC BY-SA 2.5 <https://creativecommons.org/licenses/by-sa/2.5>, via Wikimedia Commons; https://commons.wikimedia.org/wiki/File:Map_achaemenid_empire_en.png

Excavations in the 1930s uncovered over ten thousand fragments of cuneiform tablets that detailed the daily administration and transactions of the Persian Empire. The language is mostly Elamite, which has not been deciphered. Only one tablet in Old Persian—the brainchild of Darius—has been read and understood thus far. Personal and governmental seals and impressions were also found in what is known as the Persepolis Administrative Archives.

After the subjection of the whole of Mesopotamia and Iran, all written communication between provinces was in Official Aramaic or Imperial Aramaic. According to historians, this contributed greatly to the successful control of the vast empire.

Herodotus complimented these bureaucratic systems and stated they were well maintained and excellently served.

Chapter 7: Religious Tolerance

Diplomat Par Excellence

Cyrus the Great, the charismatic monarch of Persia, had a way with words. He was an excellent diplomat, yet it appears that his wisdom came from a deeper origin. It was as if his words echoed the true feelings, beliefs, and emotions in his heart. He spoke from his heart to his subjects, his administrators, his military, and his advisors. He was a genuinely great man who became a great ruler and, in the process, created a great empire.

Of course, we are aware that much of his words and deeds are embroidered with myths and legends by those who wrote about him years after his reign, but there are signs in the annals of conquered nations that he was admired by his friends and enemies.

Xenophon's account of Cyrus's advice to his sons, friends, and magistrates when he was on his deathbed almost makes one wish that we had a contemporary record of his sayings and advice. Something similar to Confucius's or Solomon's proverbs would be ideal, but for now, scholars have to be content with what records and secondhand sources exist.

The Achaemenid Empire was once home to 44 percent of the world's population, according to guestimates by some scholars. This multiethnic civilization was comprised of nations and tribes that spoke different languages, practiced diverse religions, wore different clothing, and had different cultural and societal frameworks and worldviews.

When Cyrus conquered these foreign territories, he must have thought deeply and sought input from his councilors on ideas of how to rule an empire that stretched such a large geographic area. We know he mostly left each region's system in place at the beginning while he figured it all out.

Perhaps his thought process was influenced by his childhood years, which were spent as the son of a cowherd playing with the sons of the nobles or elites. At the age of ten, his social status changed completely when he was sent to fill his real role as the son of the king of Anshan. Cyrus experienced the world from both sides, first as the son of a servant and then as the crown prince of a kingdom. His experiences in life must have influenced his personality and his attitude toward people at all levels of society.

And then he became a powerful but benevolent king. His subjects were from all classes and came from many different societies, different ethnicities, and diverse cultures. He had to find a way to rule, and he undoubtedly realized that if he acknowledged, respected, tolerated, and managed the diversity, he would rule from a place of strength and peace since he would not be faced with religious, cultural, and societal rebellions.

In practical terms, tolerance was the best way to keep the peace and for Persia to become a prosperous, harmonious, multicultural empire. Cyrus was unconventional in his approach to ruling at that time in history. His policies of respect and acceptance of the traditions, beliefs, and customs of his subjects secured the unification of his empire. He was a king like none before him. He was honored as the father of his people, even when his power was sometimes feared by the people he ruled.

After conquering Babylon, he presented himself as a liberator and the legitimate successor to the vanquished king rather than a conqueror. His words were followed by actions that supported his policy statement.

The conquest of Babylon played a significant role during King Cyrus's reign. It gave him control of the trade routes on the Silk Road, the road that linked Babylon to Ecbatana, and the road that linked Susa in Elam to Sardis in Anatolia. Later, the road between Susa and Sardis was turned into the well-constructed Royal Road by Darius I. At that point, it was even more valuable because the new road had grooves for wagons. Imagine the impact on trade and travel!

Having control of such a vast empire inspired Cyrus to have his vision for the empire inscribed onto a clay cylinder and placed in the foundations of the temple of Marduk, known as Esagila, in the city of Babylon.

According to some sources, both Alexander the Great and Julius Caesar were inspired by Cyrus.

Historians and scholars today postulate the policies of Cyrus the Great were based on the teachings of Zoroaster. Zoroastrians emphasize the freedom of choice between dark and light or good and evil by the individual. This choice, when followed by honorable deeds, good thoughts, and good words of the individual, will increase the *aša* in the world and in the person. *Aša* refers to the "good working" or "good order" of the world.

Cyrus's ideology and the strategies he used to rule the empire formed the central thread through which he prevented rebellion and received cooperation from servants up to the highest of elite classes. His policies of respect and freedom when it came to religion, customs, and social structures ensured the smooth running of the administration. The government was efficient and functional on all levels while he was alive.

King Cyrus declared himself the guardian of temples and sanctuaries of all the religions across the empire. He allowed customs and traditions to continue without interruption after conquered nations became part of the Persian Empire. At times, he even participated in local ceremonies and rituals. The nobles and priests of new regions became a part of his framework, and he granted regions limited political autonomy. This was usually done as part of a larger strategy. So, for example, allowing the Jewish people to return to Judea helped him create a boundary between the Persian Empire and Egypt.

An interesting fact regarding the Persian Empire is that religious tolerance and the role of women in society were innovative and visionary. Clay tablets excavated in Persepolis, the ceremonial capital started by Darius, detail the position of women in society, business, and finance. Texts detail financial transactions between women who traveled for personal reasons or conducting business. These texts date back to the rule of Artaxerxes I (465-424 BCE) and record a considerable number of transactions.

Snapshot of Equality

To understand the extent of the equality of women in the Persian Empire, we must delve deeper into the exact role women played in business, culture, and society.

Ancient Persian women were basically considered equal in status to men. Owning land, running a business, traveling, and getting equal pay for work were basic rights for Persian women. Royal women were allowed to have their own council meetings to discuss policies, and their opinions mattered. Cyrus ensured women of different classes were treated with dignity and respect.

Women's rights fluctuated throughout the ages. Their independence drastically deteriorated much later, especially from the 1st millennium CE, often due to religious beliefs, including those of the Abrahamic faiths. Views that women are inherently sinful, incapable of deciding their own fate, and need to be controlled under the veil of protection are present in correspondence between Christian church fathers. This is essentially a lapse in civilizations' progress that has lasted up to the present day and is legally still entrenched in the policies of certain countries.

Although the Achaemenid Empire was a patriarchal system, women had rights. A female hierarchy later formed an essential framework within the Persian Empire.

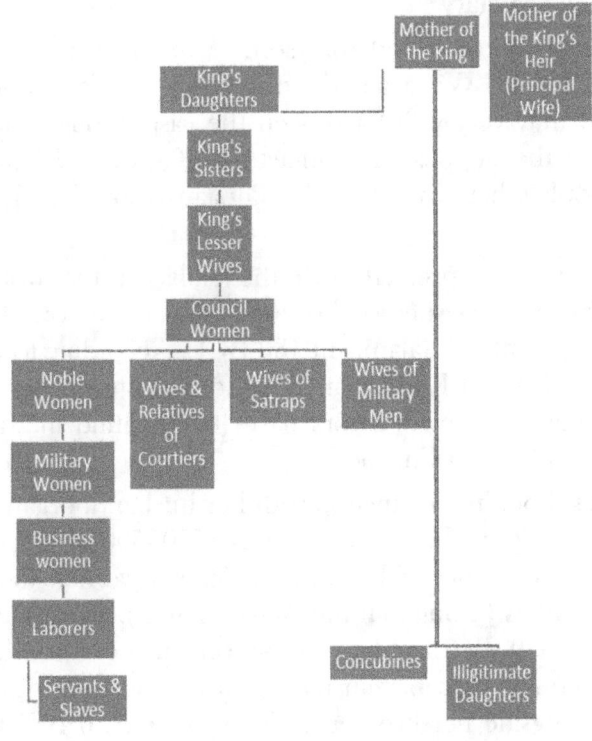

Hierarchy of women.

Key Roles of Women

Mother of the King and the Principal Wife

The king's mother and the principal wife, also called Shahbanu or "King's Lady," traveled with the king on military campaigns, like Cambyses II's wife, Roxane, who was killed in Nubia while traveling with him on a military campaign. They were accompanied by their own attendants, had places of honor at banquets, held their own courts, signed treaties and agreements with their own seals, and had unlimited access to the king. We know from the Book of Esther in the Christian Bible that this had changed by the time of Esther, who replaced Vashti as the wife of the Persian king, Xerxes I or Ahasuerus in the Torah.

Women could choose whom they wanted to marry, although treaties, alliances, and business transactions were secured with marriages to the king's daughters and sisters.

Women in the Military

Excavations have confirmed that some women were warriors in the Achaemenid Empire. We again do not know if this happened during Cyrus's rule. It may very well have been the case, though, as the women warrior tribes of the steppes had contact with Cyrus in the past and were part of his people's heritage when the Persians moved to Iran centuries before Cyrus.

Xerxes I was so impressed with the skills of the woman warrior Artemisia I of Caria that she was honored by being escorted to safety by his sons after the Battle of Salamis in 480 BCE. According to reports from a scholar by the name of Kaveh Farrokh, "tombs attesting to the existence of Iranian-speaking women warriors have [been found in Iran and] also been excavated in Eastern Europe."

Pantea Arteshbod, in conjunction with her husband, organized the elite Immortals under Cyrus the Great. Artunis (540–500 BCE) was a skilled lieutenant commander of the Immortals. Persian women warriors fought in the Persian armies throughout the Achaemenid period, such as Youtab Aryobarzan (d. 330 BCE), who was among those who defended the Persian Gate. Youtab Aryobarzan had great courage and skill and is said to have died alongside her brother, Ariobarzanes (330 BCE), during the Battle of the Persian Gate during Alexander the Great's conquest of the Persian Empire.

Women in Business

Women conducted business, as can be seen in texts excavated in Persepolis. Irdabama was a businesswoman, probably during the reign of Darius, who personally managed trade and production in Iran, Babylonia, Egypt, Media, and Syria. She oversaw around 480 laborers, excluding her extensive number of personal attendants.

Laborers, Servants, and Slaves

Women and men worked side by side, and women were often supervisors and managers. Female supervisors were known as *arashshara*. They were well paid and given a larger amount of grain and wine as overseers of a large number of subordinates.

Wages were based on skill, experience, and the type of job. There was no difference in wages based on gender. Pregnant women were actually paid higher wages. New mothers received higher wages for the first month after the birth of their child. The physician, mother, and midwife received an additional amount if the child was a boy.

Slaves throughout Persia were treated more like servants and earned a wage. Laws under Darius I stated that no slave could be mistreated or killed. A slaveowner who disobeyed this law would be judged according to the crime, and a slave would be viewed in the same light as a free citizen.

Religions in Cyrus's Empire

Depiction of the chief god of Babylon, Marduk, on a cylinder seal from the 9th century BCE.
https://commons.wikimedia.org/wiki/File:Marduk_and_pet.jpg

Proto-Indo-Iranian Pantheons

The nomadic tribes that inhabited the area around the Zagros Mountains and the Elamites worshiped a pantheon of gods. These nomadic tribes were also referred to as Proto-Indo-Europeans and wandered the steppes of the region. The Proto-Indo-Iranians were an offshoot of these Indo-European nomads, and they mixed with Semitic and other people groups as they moved. They may even be linked to an extinct Anatolian branch of civilization and appear to date to around 1900 BCE.

The pantheon of gods may have matured in the Cradle of Civilization (Mesopotamia), but we are aware of many earlier gods, such as the mother goddess represented in almost every ancient culture. When we compare the pantheons of Greek, Roman, Celtic, and Scandinavian peoples, there are similarities in the myths and powers of the gods. The religious concepts were essentially the same or similar, but the names were different. For example, the Sky Father morphed into Zeus in Greek mythology and was called Jupiter in the Roman pantheon.

According to Xenophon, Cyrus made vows to the god Mithra. Mithra was associated with light, the sun, justice, oaths, and covenants. Mithra was the all-seeing god that protected the harvest, guarded livestock, and reigned over the waters. Texts that have been deciphered have led scholars to believe Cyrus followed a polytheistic belief system; however, other scholars and historians are certain that he was a Zoroastrian.

Nevertheless, we can be certain there was a plethora of deities across his empire. Cyrus certainly must have done his homework because, by all accounts, he made offerings to each town's patron deities when he visited there.

The ancient pantheons from the earliest records and excavations had gods that ruled all aspects of life and origins. However, we do not fully know or can interpret all of the gods yet. A case in point is the new findings in Anatolia over the past few decades, such as Göbekli Tepe. Most pantheons usually included a god of the sky, a dawn deity, a fertility or mother earth goddess, a weather or thunder god, and a water god.

Sky Father

The Sky Father was the supreme deity of the Proto-Indo-European pantheon, according to verbal accounts. Dyeus, the Sky Father, has similar powers as Zeus (Greek) and Jupiter (Roman). Tiwaz, a Germanic god (Tyr in Old Norse), wielded the same power and influence over the elements. When translated directly, Dyeus means "daylight-sky god." Dyeus was noted as having a relationship with the Earth Mother.

The Dawn Goddess

Mallory and Adams, who edited the *Encyclopedia of Indo-European Culture* in 1997, reconstructed the name of the Dawn Goddess to *hausos*, meaning "dawn," and other texts refer to her as *dhughtēr diwos*, meaning "daughter of the sky god." The evidence supporting their work can be found in the Vedas and a poem by Homer. Mallory is an expert in archaeology, and Adams is a distinguished linguist.

The Dawn Goddess drove the night away and was revered as an important deity, as can be seen in preserved texts from ancient Indo-European languages.

Mother Earth

Information about the Mother Earth deity remains controversial to this day, as some evidence refers to Mother Earth not as a goddess but as the earth itself. The translated meaning of her name is "broad earth." According to other uncovered evidence, she is revered as the wife of the sky god. In Greek, Gaia is the personification of the earth as a goddess, and in the Roman pantheon, this goddess is called Tellus Mater.

Regardless of the controversies, the Mother Earth goddess illustrates the ancient thought processes. People wondered about the things around them that were inexplicable, like the process of childbirth. Childbirth is similar to the earth sprouting new life in the spring.

The Thunderer

When directly translated, the name Perkwunos or *perk'unos* means "The Striker" or "The Lord of Oaks." This deity rules over the weather, and his name is invoked during times of drought. In Indo-European mythology, the god of thunder battles a multi-headed water serpent so the serpent will release the water it has been holding. Perkwunos's weapon is referred to as meld-n, which linguists interpret as being either a hammer or a lightning bolt.

The Nephew of Waters

The name of this god appears to be Apąm Napāt in Zoroastrianism, which has been translated as son, grandson, or nephew by various scholars of Indo-Iranian cultures. Evidence of this god is only found in Indo-Iranian accounts, and he does not have a Roman or Greek counterpart. Neptune is the Roman god of freshwater and seawater, and the Greek god

Poseidon would be the equivalent god to Neptune. However, there is no "nephew" god, at least according to linguists who have examined Greek, Roman, Old Irish, and Latin texts.

There is little or no evidence left of the other gods or goddesses of the Proto-Indo-European pantheon. Even the creation story of the Proto-Indo-European civilization is fragmented, as written accounts are scarce or nonexistent. Excavations in Turkey during this century have pushed back the timeline of religious ceremonial centers to the centuries following the last ice age. Scholars do not yet understand how to interpret and understand the magnificent etchings and carvings discovered at these centers, but they are fairly certain that most were done in honor of one or more deities.

Zoroastrianism

Xenophon's *Cyropaedia* is filled with accounts regarding the beliefs, life, and religious tolerance of Cyrus the Great. He goes further by saying the policies of king Cyrus were "based on a respect for individual people, ethnic groups, other religions, and ancient kingdoms."

The *Cyropaedia* extols the virtues of an ideal ruler, which Xenophon sees personified in Cyrus the Great. "What other man but Cyrus, after having overturned an empire, ever died with the title of their father from the people whom he had brought under his power? For it is plain that this is a name for one that bestows, rather than for one that takes away."

There are plenty of indications that Cyrus followed the teachings of Zoroastrianism, although there is no conclusive proof of that. In addition, he called on Mithra instead of Ahura Mazda in an account by Xenophon. In the *Histories* by Herodotus, he stresses that Cyrus was referred to as father by his subjects. He was a fair, kind, uncorrupt, and charismatic ruler.

Cyrus and the Jews

The Hebrew Bible mentions the Persian king as the "anointed one" who liberated the Jewish people from slavery in Babylon. The Old Testament of the Bible mentions King Cyrus over twenty-three times in the books of Ezra, Chronicles, Daniel, and Isaiah.

King Nebuchadnezzar II invaded Judea and conquered Jerusalem in 597 BCE. He enslaved some of the Jewish people and exiled the king of Judah and the people he captured to Babylon.

The next attack on Jerusalem in 586 BCE is described in the Old Testament:

"He burned the house of the Lord, the king's house, and all the houses of Jerusalem; every great house he burned down. All the army of the Chaldeans who were with the captain of the guard broke down the walls around Jerusalem. Nebuzaradan the captain of the guard carried into exile the rest of the people who were left in the city and the deserters who had defected to the king of Babylon – all the rest of the population. But the captain of the guard left some of the poorest people of the land to be vinedressers and tillers of the soil." (2 Kings 25:9-12)

These events resulted in what is called the Babylonian captivity. What was almost worse for the Jewish people was that Nebuchadnezzar destroyed Solomon's Temple and took everything in it, including the sacred objects that validated their faith, to Babylon's treasury.

While enslaved in Babylon, the Jewish people were persecuted by their masters and the rest of the Babylonian citizens. Initially, they tried to continue to worship God, but this resulted in severe beatings and punishment, at times even death. The priests redacted, changed, and transcribed ancient texts to influence and keep Judaism alive. For instance, Abraham came from "Ur of the Chaldeans" because the Chaldeans and their lands would be understood by the Jewish people. The ancient inhabitants of that land in Abraham's time, including the Sumerians of Ur and other Mesopotamian peoples, were long gone by the time of the Babylonian captivity.

Cyrus is mentioned in the Christian Old Testament in the Book of Isaiah, Chapter 45, where he is referred to as the Lord's "anointed" one. "He is my shepherd, and he shall carry out all my purpose, and who says of Jerusalem, it shall be rebuilt, and of the temple, your foundation shall be laid. Thus says the Lord to his anointed, to Cyrus, whose right hand I have grasped to subdue nations before him and strip kings of their robes, to open doors before him and the gates shall not be closed."

After Cyrus conquered Babylon in 539 BCE, the Jewish people who were enslaved in the city welcomed King Cyrus as their liberator. Cyrus decreed the Jewish people were free to return to their homeland. In the Old Testament Book of Ezra, it is recorded that 42,360 Jews returned to Jerusalem and Judah, excluding their servants and handmaids.

Cyrus the Great also instructed the Jews to rebuild the Temple in Jerusalem and provided finances for this project. The project was completed during the reign of King Darius I, who also provided funds for the Temple's reconstruction. King Cyrus also issued orders that all items of value that had been taken by the Babylonians were to be returned to them and the Temple.

Some of the Jewish people remained in Babylon, where, over the decades, they started businesses and had families that often included Babylonians. The Jews who remained in Babylon were given the freedom to practice their religion and were left unhindered during times of worship or religious festivals.

Reliable Proof of the Babylonian Invasion

Recent archaeological discoveries prove, without a doubt, that the Babylonians invaded Judah and destroyed their cities. Jewish chronicles and prophets also recorded the events that happened.

Geomagnetic fields throughout Israel have enabled researchers from Tel Aviv University (TAU) and the Hebrew University of Jerusalem (HU) to form a clearer understanding and provide physical evidence of the Babylonian attacks and conquests of Israel and Judah.

In 2020, researchers reconstructed the magnetic field on the day the First Temple and the city of Jerusalem were invaded by Nebuchadnezzar and the mighty Babylonian army. The date was the ninth of Av, 586 BCE. This date has become a traditional day of mourning for the Jewish people, during which they remember the destruction of the First Temple in Jerusalem, which was built by King Solomon. Av is a month in the Jewish calendar. According to the Gregorian calendar, Av takes place in July and August. The start and end dates of Av vary, but the days always fall across both months.

Using items recovered at archaeological sites across the region, geophysicists have tracked magnetic minerals that recorded the magnetic field at the time of the conflagration. They tested the new dating method at several ancient sites where the results could be compared to already confirmed dates. The destruction of Jerusalem by Nebuchadnezzar II was confirmed to have happened on the ninth of Av. They also proved archaeologists' theories that the Babylonians did not destroy all the Judean cities and towns during this invasion.

Scientific Breakthrough of the Century

This new method of dating will help archaeologists determine the age of findings at excavation sites by using geomagnetic data.

Twenty researchers from different countries and disciplines accurately dated twenty-one layers of destruction that occurred in seventeen archaeological sites in Israel. The destruction of the Kingdom of Judah was one of the most interesting date confirmations exposed by this new method of dating.

Chapter 8: The Cyrus Cylinder

What Is the Cyrus Cylinder?

The Cyrus Cylinder is made of clay. It resembles a small barrel. The clay was applied and baked in stages around a core of large grey stones. The cylinder was thus built up in layers and baked numerous times until its final shape and size were achieved. Once this was done, a fine slip of clay was added to be used as the surface for the inscription.

The Cyrus Cylinder was used to describe King Cyrus, his exploits, his conquests, his building projects, and his magnanimity toward the people and places he conquered.

The inscription praises Cyrus and details his lineage, stating that he was a descendant of an age-old line of kings and that he had defeated the common-born king of Babylon, Nabonidus, who was an oppressor of the people. According to the text, the chief Babylonian god, Marduk, had chosen Cyrus to restore peace and prosperity to the Babylonians. The text also asks for blessings from the god Marduk for Cyrus and his son Cambyses. The cylinder refers to King Ashurbanipal, who restored the walls previously during the Assyrian occupation and who left a similar inscription, which was found while restoring the city wall of Babylon. It continues by praising Cyrus as being a generous king to the citizens of Babylon and for rebuilding temples and cult sanctuaries across Mesopotamia and the empire. The text concludes by describing the restoration of Babylon's city wall.

The Cyrus Cylinder.
Prioryman, CC BY-SA 3.0 <https://creativecommons.org/licenses/by-sa/3.0>, via Wikimedia Commons; https://commons.wikimedia.org/wiki/File:Cyrus_Cylinder_front.jpg

During the original excavations in 1879 under the auspices of the British Museum, the cylinder broke into fragments. The section known as Fragment A was sent to the British Museum in London.

Fragment B was acquired by James B. Nies from Yale University from an antiquities dealer. Nies published the inscription in 1920. Fragment B could have been among the rubble left behind by the archaeologists, or it could have been removed during the original excavation. Fragment B was not identified as being part of the original Cyrus Cylinder until 1970 when Paul-Richard Berger of the University of Munster definitively confirmed its origin.

The script used on the baked cylinder is cuneiform, and the language of the text is Akkadian. It can be dated to around 539 BCE.

What Was Its Use

The Cyrus Cylinder was used as part of the foundational deposit of the temple of Marduk, known as the Esagila, in ancient Babylon. Foundation deposits are lined pits or holes under specific points of important buildings. These pits were filled with ceremonial objects and often included a clay tablet that chronicled the story of the person or building or why the tablet was placed there. These ceremonial objects were believed to ensure the building's divine protection and prevent it from falling into ruin.

These foundation deposits also typically described a ruler's legacy and provided future rulers with an account of the conquests and virtues of the builders of the temple or other important buildings.

However, the Cyrus Cylinder has proved to be much more important than the usual foundation deposit. Modern-day Iran adopted the cylinder as the national symbol of Iran by Shah Mohammad Reza of the Pahlavi family. In 1971, the Cyrus Cylinder went on display in Tehran to commemorate the 2,500-year celebration of the Persian Empire; it was on loan from the British Museum.

A replica of the Cyrus Cylinder was presented to the United Nations Secretary General at the time, U Thant, by Princess Ashraf Pahlavi. According to Princess Ashraf, "the heritage of Cyrus was the heritage of human understanding, tolerance, courage, compassion, and, above all, human liberty." She added that her brother, the shah of Persia (now Iran), Mohammad Reza Pahlavi, saw the Cyrus Cylinder as a "charter of human rights."

There are scholars who suggest the wording on the cylinder follows the usual pattern of a declaration, something most ancient rulers did at the beginning of their rule. In their eyes, the cylinder is propaganda. But in the case of Cyrus, there is proof from contemporary sources that his deeds matched his words. The best example here is the Jewish people who were allowed to return to their homeland. Cyrus was also respected and admired by his enemies, which would indicate that the words on the cylinder had at least some truth to them.

Why Is It Important

Neil MacGregor, former director of the British Museum, occasionally said the importance of the Cyrus Cylinder is that it represents "the first attempt we know about running a society, a state, with different nationalities and faiths—a new kind of statecraft." He is seen as the foremost expert on the subject of the Cyrus Cylinder.

Biblical scholars have traditionally seen the inscriptions on the cylinder as proof of biblical authenticity regarding the Jews' return to Jerusalem to rebuild the temple that Nebuchadnezzar had destroyed. The edict of Cyrus that allowed the Jewish people and other exiles to return home after being held captive in Babylon was issued after he captured the city of Babylon. This is told in the Book of Ezra, which states, "Then the family heads of Judah and Benjamin, and the priests and Levites—everyone whose heart God had moved—prepared to go up and build the house of the Lord in Jerusalem. All their neighbors assisted them with articles of silver and gold, with goods and livestock, and with valuable gifts, in addition to all the freewill offerings" (Ezra 1:6-11).

The biblical interpretation has been refuted by numerous other academics, as the text in some translations only refers to people from Mesopotamia and does not specify any one people group in particular.

In Shah Mohammad Reza Pahlavi's book, published in 1967, titled *The White Revolution*, he refers to the Cyrus Cylinder as the "first declaration of human rights." The shah describes Cyrus the Great as an advocate for humane principles, justice, and liberty, things that are all stated on the Cyrus Cylinder. He continues by saying that Cyrus was the first ruler to allow his subjects "freedom of opinion and other basic rights."

In 1968, the United Nations held a human rights conference in Tehran, which was opened by the shah, the last ruler of Iran before it became a strictly Muslim country. In his opening address, the shah said the text as written on the Cyrus Cylinder was the predecessor of what we refer to as the Universal Declaration of Human Rights.

It is interesting to note that several of the Founding Fathers and signatories of the Declaration of Independence of the United States of America are known to have had copies of Xenophon's *Cyropaedia*, which they treasured. It is said Thomas Jefferson had three copies! The Declaration of Independence is echoed in the UN Charter of Human Rights and seeks to guarantee basic and equal human rights for all people in the world, something that is astonishingly similar to Cyrus the Great's vision as stated in the cuneiform text on the Cyrus Cylinder.

Shah Mohammad Reza Pahlavi stated in a Nowruz (New Year) address that 1971 would become known as the Cyrus the Great Year. The year would be dedicated to the celebration of the anniversary of the Achaemenid Empire and Cyrus the Great. The shah hoped civilization would recognize the Persian Empire's contributions to society, business, and humanity. He stated in speeches that the Achaemenid era was a moment from Iran's national past that would serve as a model for the modern imperial society he hoped to create.

During that year, the Cyrus Cylinder and the official crest of Iran became a worldwide symbol. Magazines and journals published articles about the ancient Persian Empire. The British Museum loaned the original Cyrus Cylinder to Iran for the duration of the festivities. The cylinder was displayed at the Shahyad Tower, now renamed the Azadi

Tower, in Tehran.

The official celebrations began on October 12th, 1971, and ended a week later in a spectacular ceremony at the tomb of Cyrus in Pasargadae. The date of October 12th coincides with the day Cyrus is believed to have entered Babylon in 539 BCE.

Where Is It Today?

The excavations of the temple of Marduk in Babylon, where the cylinder was found, were done on behalf of the trustees of the British Museum and with a decree from the Ottoman Sultan, Abdul Hamid I, which stated that antiquities found at the site could be removed, packed, and sent to England, provided there were no duplicates. To ensure these instructions were followed, a representative of the sultan was on hand to examine all objects as they were uncovered.

The Cyrus Cylinder was dispatched to the British Museum in London after its excavation in March 1879 by Assyriologist and archaeologist Hormuzd Rassam, who had taken over from the original excavator, Austen Henry Layard, who also taught and trained him. Rassam was trained further in London to become the first-known Middle Eastern archaeologist.

Fragment A and Fragment B were reunited in 1972 after Yale gave Fragment B to the British Museum on a permanent loan in return for the loan of a similar clay tablet. The Cyrus Cylinder remains in the British Museum in London to this day and has only been loaned out for exhibitions four times.

This ancient declaration of human rights is continuously used as a symbol by the United Nations. A replica of the Cyrus Cylinder can be seen at the United Nations Headquarters in New York City.

Archaeological Value

The archaeological information that can be gathered from the Cyrus Cylinder is invaluable, as it gives details on the cities and towns invaded by King Cyrus and the timelines of these conquests. Additionally, the information on the cylinder also corresponds with the information in the Bible, specifically in the books of Isaiah, Ezra, and Chronicles. It basically confirms that in 539 BCE, the Persian conqueror Cyrus the Great allowed the Jewish people to be freed from captivity in Babylon.

Information from the Cyrus Cylinder tells us exactly how the city was conquered. On October 12th on the Julian Calendar (October 7th on the

Gregorian Calendar) in 539 BCE, the Achaemenid army entered the gates of Babylon without any resistance from the inhabitants, including the army. Cyrus the Great entered the city on October 29th. He was welcomed by the citizens as a liberator and proclaimed himself "king of Babylon, king of Sumer and Akkad, king of the four corners (or quarters) of the world."

An important text on the Cyrus Cylinder describes the conquest of Babylon and that his army peacefully marched into the city as liberators. This claim is supported by a statement inscribed in the Chronicle of Nabonidus. Nabonidus was the last king of Babylon. He was considered an evil tyrant who offended the city god Marduk and forced his foreign religious ideas upon his subjects by honoring the moon god Sin. Myth has it that his disrespect for the patron deity of Babylon caused Marduk to intervene and summon Cyrus to rectify the abominations in Babylon. Cyrus is considered to be chosen by the supreme god.

The Cyrus Cylinder remained under the walls of the Esagila, the temple of the patron god Marduk, until it was rediscovered in 1879. Placing this cylinder as a foundation deposit continued a centuries-long Mesopotamian tradition. Cyrus honored this tradition, as he did the sacred customs of every society that he conquered.

The archaeological value of the Cyrus Cylinder is based on its three main decrees:

1. A formally stated political declaration of racial, religious, and linguistic equality, which includes formerly displaced, enslaved, and deported peoples. They were allowed to return home and restore their destroyed temples.

2. Further text detailing the respect Cyrus had for humanity, freedom, and the humane treatment of all people, regardless of their origins or religious beliefs.

3. Cyrus the Great's commitment, which was to turn the empire into a prosperous, peaceful, innovative, and harmonious empire of nations that traded and shared with each other and the rest of the world.

Chapter 9: Death and Burial

Unless we believe that Cyrus's tomb is empty or contains his headless remains, we have to consider Xenophon's version of his death. Xenophon states that Cyrus died at a ripe old age in his bed in his palace in Pasargadae. As a righteous man who always honored Ahura Mazda and the other gods of his subjects when in their regions, Cyrus was warned by the gods that his end was near. He was tired and happy to face death because, as a Zoroastrian, he believed that only the body died; the soul went on. He had time to put his affairs in order.

Cyrus called his two sons, who had accompanied him to Pasargadae from Babylon, and his friends and some magistrates to his bedside, where he was resting. He appointed his son Cambyses in his place as king of kings and his son Tanyoxarces as ruler of the satraps of Media, Armenia, and Cadusia. He advised them to always honor and support each other and to have each other's backs at all times against conspiracies. He said the key to successfully ruling over such a large empire was to make others your fellow guardians of territories. After what seemed an enormously long speech for such a tired old man, passing out instructions and advice to all present, Cyrus pulled the covers over his head and passed away.

According to Ctesias, Cyrus was mortally wounded in a battle against the Derbices, a familial clan of the Massagetae nomadic tribe in the northeast of Iran. He lingered for three days, during which time he put his affairs in order before dying. His troops brought his body home to Pasargadae. According to Strabo, the Greek geographer, philosopher, and historian (63 BCE-23 CE), Cyrus died in a battle against the Scythians.

According to Berossus, a Babylonian scribe and astrologer who wrote a history of Babylonia (c. 310 BCE), Cyrus died in battle against the Dahae, another Scythian-linked tribe.

It is clear that many different legends were repeated by many ancient scribes and would-be historians. Folktales and the passing of time, along with migrations and replacements of tribes and peoples, further confused the issue. Despite Herodotus's embroidered histories, his version of Cyrus's death remains perhaps the most popular and is well worth repeating.

Herodotus's *Histories* Version

Herodotus believed the Caucasus Mountains to be the highest of all the mountain ranges. To the east of the mountains lay the Caspian Sea. Bordering the Caspian Sea and stretching far to the east from there lay a very large plain. The strongest tribe dwelling there was the Massagetae.

Again, according to Herodotus, the Massagetae were akin to the Scythians in dress, except for their distinctive pointed caps. They also shared many other similar customs. Unlike the Scythians, though, Herodotus says there were stories that the Massagetae ate their men folk once they got old. Only those who died from an illness were buried. Maybe that is why Herodotus did not visit this region in his travels. Herodotus also mentions they had a strange custom where women could sleep around after marriage but not the men.

The Massagetae were often confused with the Scythians. They are still referred to as one of the Scythian tribes, the Saka, or at least as relatives of the Saka. Recent studies have indicated the tribal links across the Eurasian steppe, from the Balkans eastward, were often intertwined and genetically linked with Indo-European and Indo-Iranian peoples.

One of the outstanding qualities of the Massagetae was their horsemanship. They may even have had a cult centered around horses since they sacrificed horses to their gods. These nomadic warrior people may have had settlements at cult centers. Scholars hypothesize this due to their extensive use of metals and bronzemaking, which means they surely must have had permanent facilities for the process of smelting and making metal alloys.

Herodotus says they only worshiped one deity, their sun god. Mounted on fleet horses, the Massagetae often raided towns and cities of neighboring kingdoms and states and got away with it. In 530 BCE, Cyrus wanted to safeguard his eastern borders against the incursions by the nomadic peoples of the steppe. The king of the Massagetae had died, and his wife, Queen Tomyris, inherited the throne. In other versions, Tomyris was the only child of the overlord of several tribes. She was raised to take over. She married a king from another tribe but was already queen over all the tribes when this happened.

Cyrus thought the change in leadership was an excellent opportunity to gain control of the steppes and their gold and bronze. The Massagetae used gold and bronze in everything, including armor and weapons. Even horse bits contained portions of bronze and gold.

Queen Tomyris was a warrior princess who then became a warrior queen. Legends couple the Massagetae with the famous Amazon warrior women described by the ancient Greek authors. It is likely that, instead of the tribes consisting of only women, they were tribes with equal standing, joint duties, and the training of both men and women from an early age.

An interesting tomb containing four women was discovered in 2019 on the River Don in Russia, which seems to confirm the Greek legends of these fighting women. They were of different ages; there was a teenager, two young women, and a forty-five to fifty-year-old woman. They were buried at the same time. This burial confirmed the warrior status of women. It contained various types of weapons, such as spears, knives, and arrowheads, as well as jewelry. The crowning glory of the find was arguably the magnificent headdress, called a calathus, on the head of the older woman—the first to be found in situ.

Testing the Waters

Cyrus sent a delegation to Tomyris with gifts and a letter asking for her hand in marriage. The astute Tomyris knew that he was after her kingdom rather than her. She refused to accept his proposal. Cyrus realized his ploy was not going to work and that he would have to engage in battle with the Massagetae if his heart was set on conquering the steppes. This led to Cyrus himself leading the Persians in his quest.

When Cyrus and his vast army arrived at the Araxes River bordering his empire, he tasked his engineers and troops with building a bridge to safely cross the river with their cavalry and carts loaded with their equipment, tools, tents, food, and weapons. Tomyris sent him a message suggesting in no uncertain terms that he should stay in his empire and leave her and her people in peace. She added that if he insisted on testing the strength of the Massagetae, there were two options. Either Cyrus should let her ride back from the border to give him time to cross into her territory, or he could withdraw the same distance and leave her army to invade his territory.

As was his habit, Cyrus called together his advisors. Most agreed that it was better for them to withdraw and allow the Massagetae to cross since they could choose a battlefield and set up their troops in ideal formations. Wise old Croesus, though, disagreed. He reminded Cyrus that he and his men were not immortal. If the Massagetae should enter his realm and win a battle, they would not stop there but go on to conquer his provinces. Cyrus could lose his empire. If, on the other hand, Cyrus should attack the Massagetae in their own territory, he could lay an ambush to trap them and gain victory.

Croesus's plan was that they should cross the river, then set up their camp with a scrumptious feast laid out with all sorts of foods and lots of wine. The main Persian forces would withdraw to the river, leaving only a small force of decrepit soldiers at the feast. The Massagetae would attack the camp, easily overcome these men, and then undoubtedly be tempted to celebrate their victory by carrying on with the feasting and drinking. Once they were drunk and incapacitated, the main Persian force could attack and capture them.

Croesus's plan sounded solid, and Cyrus went with it. Everything happened as Croesus had predicted. When the Massagetae were thoroughly drunk, the main Persian army attacked. Amongst their captives was Tomyris's son. Tomyris was livid. She sent a message to Cyrus saying there would be no retribution if he gave her son back unharmed, even though he was the victim of deceit and not beaten in an open and honest battle. However, if her son was harmed and Cyrus was set on continuing the war, she would drench him in more blood than he could ever want.

Meanwhile, Tomyris's son had revived from his drunken stupor. He begged Cyrus to set him free. The moment he was freed, he committed suicide because of his shame. There was no going back for Cyrus. The war would have to continue. The battle was fought with cavalry and foot soldiers, and this time, the Massagetae were the victors. Cyrus was among the casualties.

Queen Tomyris receiving the head of Cyrus.
https://commons.wikimedia.org/wiki/File:Queen_Tomyris_and_the_head_of_Cyrus_the_Great.jpg

Herodotus tells us that Tomyris collected a sack of human blood. She searched for Cyrus's body among the dead and stuck his head in the bag full of blood, just as she had threatened in her final message. In another version, her soldiers chopped off Cyrus's head after the battle and brought it to her. She then dunked it in blood.

The Tomb in Pasargadae

Cyrus's body was brought back to Pasargadae to the tomb that he had designed. There are no extant records of the trip or the burial ceremony. We can only imagine when and how the body of the beloved King of Kings was transported back to his city and laid to rest in his tomb. What we do know from Xenophon's descriptions of Cyrus's lifestyle is that he likely did not desire a grand ceremony. We can assume there were lots of mourning and burial rituals that had to be adhered to. Cyrus believed, at least according to Xenophon, that the body was merely a vessel for the soul, which carried on in the afterlife with intelligence while being unencumbered by the trappings of earthly life.

Alexander the Great, who greatly admired Cyrus's history and is said to have been inspired by him, entered the tomb when he and his troops conquered the Persians two centuries later. The ancient author known as Arrian (born c. 90 CE), in his work *The Anabasis of Alexander*, quotes a description from Aristobulus, a companion of Alexander, that they found the tomb damaged and broken into. Alexander was upset and gave Aristobulus instructions to restore the tomb.

Tomb of King Cyrus in Pasargadae.
Truth Seeker, CC BY-SA 3.0 <https://creativecommons.org/licenses/by-sa/3.0>, via Wikimedia Commons; https://commons.wikimedia.org/w/index.php?curid=14482534

The inside of the tomb had been greatly damaged and robbed. The lid of Cyrus's coffin had been broken, and pieces had been chopped off to remove it from the tomb, but the robbers were unable to get it out since the door was too small. At the time of Alexander, the burial chamber contained a divan and a table with Cyrus's gold-covered coffin. The divan had feet of gold, and on it was an array of richly colored clothes, jewelry, and weapons. The robbers had made off with anything else the tomb may have held. The remains of the skeleton were in disarray on the floor.

Chapter 10: The Legacy of Cyrus the Great

The Last Shah Commemorated Persia's Legacy in 1971

King Cyrus the Great's legacy has worldwide credence and is reinforced by the *Cyropaedia*, written by Xenophon in the 4th century BCE. Xenophon writes an idealized account of the Persian king and extolls his creation of the largest empire in the known world at the time, as well as his central theme of governance that included freedom of religion, freedom of speech, equality of sexes, and respect for other cultures and their traditions.

The somewhat fictionalized *Cyropaedia* is based on firsthand knowledge of the Persian Empire during Xenophon's travels across Persia. He used his personal knowledge and listened to accounts from people who were direct descendants of people who had lived during the reign of Cyrus the Great.

The *Cyropaedia* presents King Cyrus as a virtuous leader, an excellent politician and military strategist, and a man of the people. Based on the writings of Xenophon, Alexander the Great and Julius Caesar both drew on Cyrus's experiences and methods of ruling a vast empire.

The 16th-century depictions of King Cyrus in art show him as one of four great rulers. The other rulers are Ninus of Nineveh (the mythical founder of Nineveh), Alexander, and Julius Caesar. Thomas Jefferson was a great admirer of Cyrus the Great, and three well-read and marked copies of the *Cyropaedia* were found in his belongings after his death. Benjamin

Franklin was another US Founding Father who believed in the principles of Cyrus the Great, as stated in the *Cyropaedia*. Both Jefferson and Franklin saw value and honor in King Cyrus's statecraft, as explained by Xenophon.

King Cyrus is valued as a liberator and benefactor of the Jewish people, especially since he was paramount in the reconstruction of the Temple of Solomon in Jerusalem. The fall of Babylon and setting the Jewish people free made Cyrus a revered figure in Jewish history.

The discovery of the Cyrus Cylinder in 1879 gave the world physical proof that the proclamations of King Cyrus were, in fact, true and not merely biblical or Jewish accounts of stories.

In 1971, the Cyrus Cylinder became an iconic symbol of Iran and was claimed to be the first "charter of human rights" by the last shah of Iran, Mohammad Reza Pahlavi. This modern-day commemoration of the long-ago Persian Empire brought new focus to Cyrus the Great's legacy. It is interesting to note that Reza Shah, the father of Mohammad Reza Pahlavi, requested the name of Persia be changed to Iran in 1941.

The last shah's hopes of resurrecting the Achaemenid era came to an end, as the monarchy was replaced by the Islamic Republic of Iran. Mohammad Reza Pahlavi fled into exile. Many scholars state the shah's rule would not have ended if he had earned the respect of the people and had worked with religious leaders. Iranians wanted greater democracy and less monarchial rule. This might have been possible since the religious leaders wielded great power over the people and could have managed to mediate between the shah and the people.

Shah Mohammad Reza Pahlavi was a Muslim himself but had lost the backing of the clergy of Iran, the Shi'a Muslims, due to his policies of modernization and his relationship with the Israelis. Confrontations with the religious community and an increase in support from the Soviet Union ushered in a time of political unrest.

In August 1953, the streets of Teheran were filled with violence and angry citizens. Fights between rival groups broke out in squares across the city and at the city's major radio station. The home of the prime minister, Mohammad Mossadegh, was protected by armored vehicles and machine guns. Crowds chanted "Zendebad Shah" ("Long live the Shah"), and Mossadegh's government fell. The new government was led by General Fazlollah Zahedi and Shah Mohammed Reza Pahlavi.

Following this coup, the shah spent his time ruling from Iran and maintaining a good relationship with the US until his fall during the Islamic Revolution, which lasted from 1978 to 1979. After ruling for thirty-seven years, the shah and his family fled the country, and the new government converted the country into an Islamic republic.

Islamic Inspiration

In 1978, Shah Mohammed Reza Pahlavi revived the humanitarian legacy of Cyrus the Great by presenting a duplicate of the Cyrus Cylinder to the United Nations to commemorate Cyrus's reign and policies. Unfortunately, the Islamic Revolution was gaining momentum during this time, and in 1979, the Pahlavi rule was overthrown.

After a successful revolution, the Islamic regime wanted the Islamic religion and way of thinking to be accepted by all the Iranian people. In an attempt to mediate, they allowed some pre-Islamic traditions to remain, especially after the death of Ruhollah Khomeini, the first Supreme Leader of the Islamic Republic, in June 1989. Old Persian traditions, such as Noruz or New Year and Chaharshanbeh Suri or the New Year's festival for expelling the Evil Eye from the people, remained.

During the last decade, the Iranian people have started protests at unofficial gatherings to remember Cyrus the Great on October 29th each year. This day was added to the official Iranian calendar in 1977. The protests are aimed against the current government's ideals for religious identity.

On October 29th, 2016, Cyrus the Great Day violence broke out between the Iranian security forces and thousands of civilians who came to celebrate at the tomb of King Cyrus at Pasargadae.

Thousands of citizens rallied together and shouted anti-government slogans. The Iranian regime announced in 2017 that there would be no further festivals at the tomb of Cyrus the Great. Since then, they have had armed forces staffing roadblocks on all major roads leading to the Pasargadae tomb. The situation has been escalating over the years, with over one thousand protesters arrested in the weeks leading up to Cyrus the Great Day in 2022 in various places across the country.

The Fars Province commander of the Revolutionary Guards issued a statement warning that security forces and the judiciary laws would not allow anti-revolutionary forces to gather in the area in celebration of Cyrus the Great Day. He said this would threaten the stability of the region and that measures would be taken to prevent any such gatherings.

Iranian citizens retaliated by starting a social media campaign, inspiring the people of Iran to protest against the autocratic Muslim authorities and continue to celebrate Cyrus the Great Day. This major social media campaign reinforced the historical importance of Cyrus the Great as a national symbol for freedom of religion and freedom of speech. They further denounced the Islamic regime's actions against the celebrations. Social media showed footage of the roadblocks on the main routes. Photographs of civilians crossing the mountains on foot in order to reach the site of the tomb at Pasargadae without using the roads were posted on social media to encourage others to follow.

Further social media comments compared the regime's actions of preventing celebrations on Cyrus the Great Day with the costly efforts used by the regime to encourage pilgrimages to the Muslim holy sites in Iraq. One social media post claimed the regime provided free taxis to the holy sites of Shi'a Muslims during Arba'een, a festival held forty days after Ashura.

The social media campaign provided a platform for people to voice their disagreement with the regime. Opposing forces of the regime used this time to protest the regime. Another post on the social media platform stated, "Today it has been clearly shown that the Islamic Republic and Iran are not the same."

Supporters of the Islamic regime and government policies stated that Cyrus the Great Day was a Western-Zionist plot to undermine the Iranian government and cause harm to Islam.

Ayatollah Ka'abi, a conservative cleric and member of the Assembly of Experts, denounced Cyrus the Great Day in his Friday sermon in Shiraz near the ancient site of Pasargadae and said enemies of Iran and Iranian monarchists created a fake event. The celebration, according to Ayatollah Ka'abi, has no historical proof. In his opinion, the origin was biblical (Jewish) and Israeli and aimed to sow discontent amongst the Iranian people. He continued by saying that Cyrus the Great would convert to Islam if he rose from his grave and saw the power of Iran under Islamic rule.

Mehran Solati, a prominent sociologist, stated that the prevention of celebrations on Cyrus the Great Day is comparable to the shah's efforts to erase Islam, which failed. Solati further said the constant social media discussions reinforced the pre-Islamic culture and identity, even though the regime is trying to Islamize the population.

According to Tabnak, a Persian news website, there is an increased interest in the celebrations of Cyrus the Great Day amongst the people of Iran. People believe the steps taken by the regime are ineffective. An alternative view on this is that the regime should view the respect the people have for the founder of the Persian Empire, Cyrus the Great, as an opportunity to strengthen national solidarity and sentiment instead of seeing it as a threat to national security.

Iranian police barred people from visiting the mausoleum in October 2021, and although Cyrus the Great Day remains an unofficial celebration on the calendar, we are not sure what will happen to it in the future.

Conclusion

The Fascinating Conundrums of Reconstructing Ancient Histories

The accounts of ancient civilizations passed down to us by ancient historians vary greatly. It is understandably influenced by the time and space between the actual occurrences and their recording.

The so-called father of history, Herodotus, relied on accounts of descendants, but even then, he admits that he is recording what he heard and not what he had seen. He often interweaves the mythology and belief systems of the subject matter with his own Greek cultural interpretations. He was fascinated with the Persians, especially the wars of the Persians against the Greeks, and obtained much of his information from second-generation accounts. Thus, he was much closer in time to the actual wars than the later accounts of Xenophon and others.

On the other hand, Xenophon was directly involved with the Persians, as he became the commander of the most elite Persian military unit, The Immortals, which, if you don't recall, were ten thousand crack troops. At this time (c. 401 BCE), the unit was largely made up of Greek mercenaries. Xenophon was gifted and accomplished as a military leader, philosopher, and historian. His account of Cyrus in the *Cyropaedia* is, however, an attempt at biographical fiction akin to hero worship, which is not surprising if we remember that the King of Kings, Cyrus himself, was born nearly two centuries before Xenophon.

Another ancient writer of the history of the Persians was Ctesias. He was a physician at the Achaemenid court around 400 BCE, acting as the personal doctor of the king and his family. He wrote twenty-three books called the *Persica* on the history of Persia up to that time. Despite it being relatively close to the era of Cyrus and his direct descendants, his accounts differ greatly from those of Herodotus and Xenophon. This may be due to the fact that the line of kings that he served was from a different branch of the Achaemenid dynasty, which started with Darius I.

Ctesias's original work did not survive, but several ancient writers refer to and quote directly from it. Of the twenty-three books, five were apparently devoted to Cyrus the Great. But even the ancient authors criticize Ctesias heavily, as he was more interested in court intrigues, harem scandals, and romances at court than in facts of historical importance.

One significant aspect where Ctesias differs greatly from Herodotus is the lineage of Cyrus. Ctesias states Cyrus was the son of a female shepherd or goatherd named Argoste and a male bandit named Artadates. Cyrus became Astyages's cupbearer, then conspired with the Persians, overthrew Astyages, and became king in his stead. What is fascinating about Ctesias's version of Cyrus's story is the obvious similarities to the birth, youth, and rise to kingship of Sargon the Great, the founder of the Akkadian Empire, which fell more than a thousand years before Cyrus's birth. However, the future empire builder Sargon was raised by the king's gardener instead of a goatherd! Incidentally, this kind of legend was spun more than once in the case of hero figures in ancient times.

It, therefore, remains an intricate endeavor for any modern scholar to extract and balance fact from fiction when it comes to these ancient written documents, the records of other contemporary nations, and archaeological, linguistic, and even genetic data. In the case of the Medes, for example, the meager knowledge of their existence has been enhanced by more archaeological excavations and discoveries during the past few years. We have to bear in mind that the climatic conditions of most of the geographical areas in which Cyrus and the Achaemenids held sway often prevented the preservation of written documents—both the ink and the vellum or other materials on which it was written—unlike those inscribed with a stylus on wet clay or inscriptions on monuments or stelae.

Admired by Enemies

The Nabonidus Chronicle is the primary source of information for this period and gives a good account of Cyrus's rise to power and his conquest of the Medes. It describes his destruction and plunder of Ecbatana, which had been the capital and home of Astyages. Here, we get a glimpse into

Cyrus's mind as he dethrones Astyages; according to Herodotus, Astyages lives at the court of Cyrus until his death. Ctesias, however, states that Astyages was given a province to rule in the region of Parthia but died when a neighboring province invaded.

Capturing King Croesus of Lydia was the foremost in Cyrus's mind when it came to conquest. After capturing Croesus, the former Lydian king asked Cyrus to allow him to live. Cyrus, always the forward thinker, considered what would happen to him if he was in the same position as Croesus. This made him reconsider lighting the pyre Croesus was on, and subsequently, Croesus became one of his major advisors in military conquests.

Wise and Charismatic but Not Infallible

Throughout his reign, Cyrus the Great displayed charisma and skill on all levels, social and political. A great example is when he wanted to expand his empire into the steppes. He considered a more diplomatic approach and asked Queen Tomyris to marry him.

Tomyris was also a skilled and clever ruler in her own right. She was also a skilled warrior on horseback. She knew the proposal from Cyrus only meant he wanted her land. In the end, King Cyrus, who was initially quite content with what he had already achieved, was enticed into battle by his ambition for more land, despite his abhorrence and lifelong abstinence from greed. It cost him his life.

It Is a Wrap

Of all the rulers in the ancient and current world, King Cyrus deserves the title "Great" attached to his name due to his success and skill. He pursued a policy of ruling by generosity and tolerance. During King Cyrus's rule, there were no rebellions of satrapies or regions since Cyrus managed his empire like a good CEO would manage a large company in modern times. He had advisory boards, imperial courts, and governments and allowed them to function as part of the empire with responsibilities for their own regions. This gave them the autonomy they needed to feel in control. Cyrus knew on an instinctual level that rulers needed to feel empowered and act as guardians of their own territories. By fulfilling this basic need, he could be assured of their loyalty. His assumptions proved true.

Professor Richard Frye, Professor Emeritus of Iranian Studies at Harvard University, had this to say about Cyrus the Great and his legacy:

"In short, the figure of Cyrus has survived throughout history as more than a great man who founded an empire. He became the epitome of the great qualities expected of a ruler in antiquity, and he assumed heroic features as a conqueror who was tolerant and magnanimous as well as brave and daring. His personality as seen by the Greeks, influenced them and Alexander the Great, and, as the tradition was transmitted by the Romans, may be considered to influence our thinking even now." ("Cyrus the Great and Religious Tolerance in Achaemenid Persia")

Continuing to extol his virtues would be unnecessary. We have seen through our journey back in time that this man was unique. He was indeed worthy of his title Cyrus the Great!

Here's another book by Enthralling History that you might like

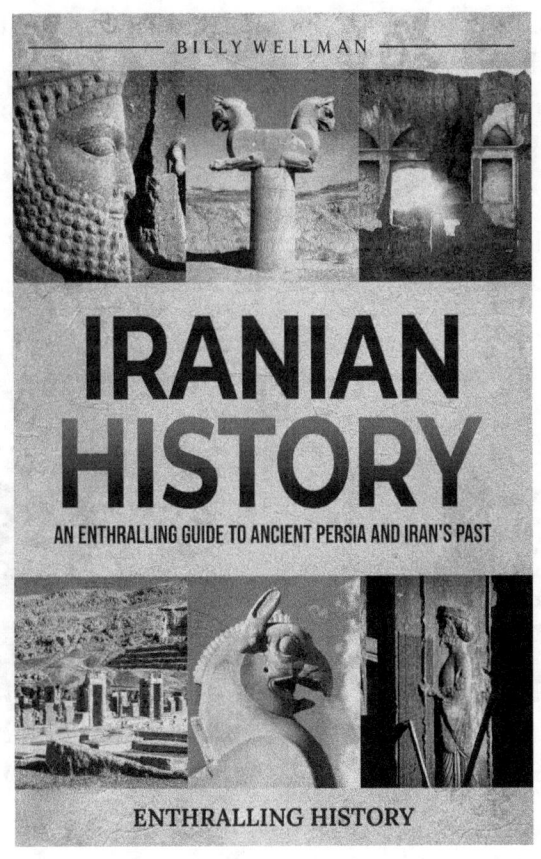

Free limited time bonus

Stop for a moment. We have a free bonus set up for you. The problem is this: we forget 90% of everything that we read after 7 days. Crazy fact, right? Here's the solution: we've created a printable, 1-page pdf summary for this book that you're reading now. All you have to do to get your free pdf summary is to go to the following website:

https://livetolearn.lpages.co/enthrallinghistory/

Once you do, it will be intuitive. Enjoy, and thank you!

Bibliography

Al Atrash, Sami. "The Rise and Fall of the Scythians in Western Asia." TheCollector, 14 July 2022, https://www.thecollector.com/rise-of-the-scythians/.

Arteshe Iran. "Siege of Pasargadae Hill." Arteshe Iran - Persian Military History, 2009, http://arteshe-iran.blogspot.com/2009/01/siege-of-pasargadae-hill.html

Badian, E. "Darius III." Harvard Studies in Classical Philology, vol. 1000, 2000, pp. 241-267. JSTOR, https://doi.org/10.2307/3185218.

Baldwin, Tanya. "Cyrus the Great Facts & Achievements | Who was King Cyrus the Great? - Video & Lesson Transcript." Study.com, 26 April 2022, https://study.com/learn/lesson/cyrus-the-great-facts-achievements.html.

Bawden, Charles R. "Darius III | king of Persia | Britannica." Encyclopedia Britannica, 1 January 2023, https://www.britannica.com/biography/Darius-III.

Behroozi, Mehrnaaz, and Leila Kochaki Kia. "The Administrative Structure of Achaemenid and Seleucid Empires in Observing Civil Rights." International Journal of Culture and History, vol. 3, no. 1, 2017, http://www.ijch.net/vol3/077-SD0018.pdf.

BlueBox Creighton. "Art and Architecture of the Achaemenid Empire." BlueBox Creighton, 2016, https://bluebox.creighton.edu/demo/modules/en-boundless-old/www.boundless.com/art-history/textbooks/boundless-art-history-textbook/art-of-the-ancient-near-east-3/persia-863/art-and-architecture-of-the-achaemenid-empire-292-1911/.

Bosanquet, I. W. "Chronology of the Medes, from the Reign of Deioces to the Reign of Darius, the Son of Hystaspes, or Darius the Mede." Journal of the Royal Asiatic Society of Great Britain and Ireland, vol. 17, 1860, pp. 39-69. JSTOR, https://www.jstor.org/stable/25581223?seq=6.

Bowman, Alan K., et al. "Ancient Egypt | History, Government, Culture, Map, & Facts." Encyclopedia Britannica, 3 January 2023, https://www.britannica.com/place/ancient-Egypt.

Briant, Pierre. "Darius II." Oxford Classical Dictionary, 10 August 2022, https://oxfordre.com/classics/display/10.1093/acrefore/9780199381135.001.0001/acrefore-9780199381135-e-2030;jsessionid=B1D1E132F1430380405FB5B68CE2294D.

Briant, Pierre. From Cyrus to Alexander: A History of the Persian Empire. Pennsylvania State University Press, 2002.

Britannica, The Editors of Encyclopedia. "Ancient Iran | History, Map, Cities, Religion, Art, Language, & Facts." Encyclopedia Britannica, 2022, https://www.britannica.com/place/ancient-Iran.

Britannica, The Editors of Encyclopedia. "Battle of Issus." Encyclopedia Britannica, 4 January 2023, https://www.britannica.com/event/Battle-of-Issus-Persian-history

Britannica, The Editors of Encyclopedia. "Deioces | king of Media | Britannica." Encyclopedia Britannica, 2016, https://www.britannica.com/biography/Deioces.

Britannica, The Editors of Encyclopedia. "Greco-Persian Wars | Definition, Battles, Summary, Facts, Effects, & History." Encyclopedia Britannica, 2022, https://www.britannica.com/event/Greco-Persian-Wars.

Britannica, The Editors of Encyclopedia. "Greco-Persian Wars | Definition, Battles, Summary, Facts, Effects, & History." Encyclopedia Britannica, 2022, https://www.britannica.com/event/Greco-Persian-Wars.

Britannica, The Editors of Encyclopedia. "Magus | Persian priesthood | Britannica." Encyclopedia Britannica, 2022, https://www.britannica.com/topic/Magus.

Britannica, The Editors of Encyclopedia. "Media | ancient region, Iran | Britannica." Encyclopedia Britannica, 2020, https://www.britannica.com/place/Media-ancient-region-Iran.

Britannica, The Editors of Encyclopedia. "Battle of Cnidus | Persian history | Britannica." Encyclopedia Britannica, 2022, https://www.britannica.com/topic/Battle-of-Cnidus.

Cartwright, Mark. "Lydia." World History Encyclopedia, 3 April 2016, https://www.worldhistory.org/lydia/.

Charles, Michael. "TWO NOTES ON DARIUS III." The Cambridge Classical Journal, vol. 62, 2016, pp. 52-64, https://doi.org/10.1017/S1750270516000063.

Chua, Michelle. "The Strength and Structure of the Ancient Persian Army." Brewminate, 21 June 2019, https://brewminate.com/the-strength-and-structure-of-the-ancient-persian-army/.

The Columbia Encyclopedia. "Artaxerxes II." Encyclopedia.com, 2023, https://www.encyclopedia.com/reference/encyclopedias-almanacs-transcripts-and-maps/artaxerxes-ii.

The Columbia Encyclopedia. "Darius II." Encyclopedia.com, The Columbia Encyclopedia, 2023, https://www.encyclopedia.com/reference/encyclopedias-almanacs-transcripts-and-maps/darius-ii.

Course Hero. "Histories Book 5 The Persian Conquest of Thrace Summary." Course Hero, 2019, https://www.coursehero.com/lit/Histories/book-5-the-persian-conquest-of-thrace-summary/.

Criss, Megan. "Achaemenid Art & Architecture: Definition & Characteristics." Study.com, 2016, https://study.com/academy/lesson/achaemenid-art-architecture-definition-characteristics.html.

Cristian, Radu, and Osama Shukir. "Darius I." World History Encyclopedia, 10 April 2017, https://www.worldhistory.org/Darius_I/.

Crystalinks. "Median Empire." Crystalinks, 2023, https://www.crystalinks.com/media.html.

Cyrus, Emperor, and Reza Abbasi. "Persian Art - A History of Ancient Persian Paintings and Iranian Art." Art in Context, 28 June 2022, https://artincontext.org/persian-art/.

Dandamayev, M. A. "ARTABAZUS – Encyclopedia Iranica." Encyclopedia Iranica, 1986, https://iranicaonline.org/articles/artabazus-gk.

Dandamayev, Muhammad A. "CAMBYSES – Encyclopedia Iranica." Encyclopedia Iranica, 1990, https://www.iranicaonline.org/articles/cambyses-opers.

Dandamayev, Muhammad A. "MAGI – Encyclopedia Iranica." Encyclopedia Iranica, 30 May 2000, https://www.iranicaonline.org/articles/magi.

Deering, Mary. "Persian Empire Timeline & Culture | When Did the Persian Empire Start? - Video & Lesson Transcript." Study.com, 20 January 2022, https://study.com/academy/lesson/persian-empire-history-culture-timeline.html.

Department of Ancient Near Eastern Art. "Assyria, 1365–609 B.C. | Essay." The Metropolitan Museum of Art, 2004, https://www.metmuseum.org/toah/hd/assy/hd_assy.htm.

Ducksters. "Iran History and Timeline Overview." Ducksters, Technological Solutions, 2023, https://www.ducksters.com/geography/country/iran_history_timeline.php.

Dunn, Jimmy. "Egypt: Cambyses II, the First Persian Ruler of Egypt and His Lost Army." Tour Egypt, 12 June 2011, http://www.touregypt.net/featurestories/cambyses2.htm.

Encyclopedia Iranica. "ARTAXERXES I – Encyclopedia Iranica." Encyclopedia Iranica, 2011, https://www.iranicaonline.org/articles/artaxerxes-i.

Encyclopedia Judaica. "Medes and Media." Jewish Virtual Library, 2008, https://www.jewishvirtuallibrary.org/medes-and-media.

Encyclopedia of Ancient Art. "Ancient Persian Art & Culture." Visual Arts Cork, 2022, http://www.visual-arts-cork.com/ancient-art/persian.htm.

The Famous People. "Artaxerxes I Of Persia Biography - Facts, Childhood, Family Life & Achievements." The Famous People, 2020, https://www.thefamouspeople.com/profiles/artaxerxes-i-of-persia-37603.php.

"From Artaxerxes III to Alexander III, 342–332." Trouble in the West: Egypt and the Persian Empire, 525-332 BC, by Stephen Ruzicka, Oxford University Press, USA, 2012, pp. 199-209.

Frye, Richard N., and Matthew Smith. "Cyrus the Great | Biography & Facts | Britannica." Encyclopedia Britannica, 6 January 2023, https://www.britannica.com/biography/Cyrus-the-Great.

Garlinghouse, Tom. "Who were the ancient Persians?" Live Science, 14 July 2022, https://www.livescience.com/who-were-the-persians.

Gill, NS. "Ancient Persian Rulers Timeline (Modern Iran)." ThoughtCo, 30 May 2019, https://www.thoughtco.com/timeline-of-the-ancient-rulers-of-persia-120250.

Gill, NS. "The Battle at Issus." ThoughtCo, 6 September 2018, https://www.thoughtco.com/overview-battle-issus-november-333-bc-116810.

Giotto, M. "The Peloponnesian Wars ("The Great War" 431-404 BC)." Penfield Edu, 2013, https://www.penfield.edu/webpages/jgiotto/onlinetextbook.cfm?subpage=1649849.

GotQuestions. "Who was Artaxerxes in the Bible?" GotQuestions.org, 25 February 2022, https://www.gotquestions.org/Artaxerxes-in-the-Bible.html.

Gottheil, Richard, and Eduard Meyer. "ARTAXERXES III. - JewishEncyclopedia.com." Jewish Encyclopedia, 2023, https://www.jewishencyclopedia.com/articles/1829-artaxerxes-iii.

Gottheil, Richard, and Eduard Meyer. "ARTAXERXES II - JewishEncyclopedia.com." Jewish Encyclopedia, 2022, https://www.jewishencyclopedia.com/articles/1828-artaxerxes-ii.

Gottheil, Richard, and Eduard Meyer. "ARTAXERXES I - JewishEncyclopedia.com." Jewish Encyclopedia, 2023, https://www.jewishencyclopedia.com/articles/1827-artaxerxes-i.

Harding, Robert. "The Battle of Gaugamela, 1 October 331 BC." The Past, 8 September 2021, https://the-past.com/feature/the-battle-of-gaugamela-1-october-331-bc/.

Heritage History. "Persian Wars of Conquest." Heritage History, 2022, https://www.heritage-history.com/index.php?c=resources&s=war-dir&f=wars_persianconquest.

Hirschy, Noah Calvin. Artaxerxes III Ochus and His Reign: With Special Consideration of the Old Testament Sources Bearing Upon the Period; An Inaugural Dissertation (Classic Reprint). Fb&c Limited, 2016.

History.com Editors. "Peloponnesian War." History, 22 August 2019, https://www.history.com/topics/ancient-greece/peloponnesian-war.

HIstory.com Editors. "Zoroastrianism." History.com, 13 February 2018, https://www.history.com/topics/religion/zoroastrianism. Accessed 19 February 2023.

History World. "History of Iran (Persia)." HistoryWorld, 2023, http://www.historyworld.net/wrldhis/PlainTextHistories.asp?ParagraphID=azt.

Hodsdon, Edd. "Darius the Great: 9 Facts About the King of Kings." TheCollector, 5 February 2021, https://www.thecollector.com/darius-the-great-king-of-kings/.

Hodsdon, Edd. "King Xerxes I: 9 Facts About His Life and Rule." TheCollector, 26 February 2021, https://www.thecollector.com/king-xerxes-i/.

Holmes, Robert CL. "Kings of Persia: These 12 Achaemenid Rulers Led an Empire." TheCollector, 18 July 2020, https://www.thecollector.com/kings-of-persia/.

Homepages. "Artaxerxes II King of Persia." Homepages, 2003, https://homepages.rpi.edu/~holmes/Hobbies/Genealogy2/ps22/ps22_441.htm.

Homepages. "Xerxes I 'The Great' King of Persia." Homepages, 2003, https://homepages.rpi.edu/~holmes/Hobbies/Genealogy2/ps22/ps22_444.htm.

Horne, Charles F. "Ancient Mesopotamia: Biography of Cyrus the Great." Ducksters, 2023, https://www.ducksters.com/history/mesopotamia/cyrus_the_great.php.

Hyland, John O., and Stephen Ruzicka. "Persian Interventions | Hopkins Press." JHU Press, 2017, https://www.press.jhu.edu/books/title/11954/persian-interventions.

Iran Chamber Society. "Historic Personalities of Iran: Median Empire." Iran Chamber Society, 2023, https://www.iranchamber.com/history/median/median.php.

Iran Chamber Society. "History of Iran: Cyrus the Great." Iran Chamber Society, 2023, https://www.iranchamber.com/history/cyrus/cyrus.php.

Iran Chamber Society. "History of Iran: Darius the Great." Iran Chamber Society, 2023, https://www.iranchamber.com/history/darius/darius.php.

Jameson, Zachary, and Stephanie Przybylek. "Persian Empire Architecture & Art | What was the Persian Empire? - Video & Lesson Transcript." Study.com, 28

July 2022, https://study.com/learn/lesson/persian-empire-architecture-art.html.

Joe, Jimmy. "Darius III: The Last King of the Great Persian Empire." Timeless Myths, 2022, https://www.timelessmyths.com/characters/darius-iii/.

Joe, Jimmy. "Darius II: The Authentic Legacy of This Persian King of Kings." Timeless Myths, 2022, https://www.timelessmyths.com/characters/darius-ii/.

Kennedy, Stetson. "Cyrus the Great and Religious Tolerance | Tolerance." Tolerance: Tavaana, 2022, https://tolerance.tavaana.org/en/content/cyrus-great-and-religious-tolerance.

Kerrigan, Michael. "Battle of Nineveh | Summary | Britannica." Encyclopedia Britannica, 2017, https://www.britannica.com/event/Battle-of-Nineveh.

Khan Academy. "The Rise of Persia (article)." Khan Academy, 2017, https://www.khanacademy.org/humanities/world-history/ancient-medieval/ancient-persia/a/the-rise-of-persia.

Kidd, Fiona. "Ideas of Empire: The "Royal Garden" at Pasargadae." Metropolitan Museum of Art, 29 July 2013, https://www.metmuseum.org/blogs/now-at-the-met/features/2013/pasargadae.

Klein, Christopher. "How Cyrus the Great Turned Ancient Persia into a Superpower." How Cyrus the Great Turned Ancient Persia into a Superpower, 14 July 2022, https://www.history.com/news/cyrus-the-great-persian-empire-iran.

Klein, Christopher. "How Cyrus the Great Turned Ancient Persia into a Superpower." How Cyrus the Great Turned Ancient Persia into a Superpower, 14 July 2022, https://www.history.com/news/cyrus-the-great-persian-empire-iran.

Kohansal, Hassan. "The Function of Non- Iranian Languages in the Persian Achaemenid Empire | PalArch's Journal of Archaeology of Egypt / Egyptology." PalArch's Journals, 30 December 2020, https://archives.palarch.nl/index.php/jae/article/view/8871.

Kovalev, R. K. "Scythians." Encyclopedia.com, 2018, https://www.encyclopedia.com/history/modern-europe/russian-soviet-and-cis-history/scythians.

Landious Travel. "Artaxerxes III." Landious Travel, 2023, https://landioustravel.com/egypt/pharaohs-egypt/artaxerxes-iii/.

The Latin Library. "The Persian Empire." The Latin Library, 2023, http://www.thelatinlibrary.com/imperialism/notes/persia.html.

Lendering, Jona. "Amyrtaeus." Livius.org, 30 April 2020, https://www.livius.org/articles/person/amyrtaeus/.

Lendering, Jona. "Artabazus (2)." Livius.org, 4 August 2020, https://www.livius.org/articles/person/artabazus-2/.

Lendering, Jona. "Cambyses II." Livius.org, 30 April 2020, https://www.livius.org/articles/person/cambyses-ii/.

Lendering, Jona. "Cambyses II." Livius.org, 30 April 2020, https://www.livius.org/articles/person/cambyses-ii/.

Lendering, Jona. "Cambyses II (2)." Livius.org, 23 June 2020, https://www.livius.org/articles/person/cambyses-ii/cambyses-ii-2/.

Lendering, Jona. "Cyaxares." Livius.org, 9 May 2019, https://www.livius.org/articles/person/cyaxares/.

Lendering, Jona. "Cyrus the Great." Livius.org, 12 October 2020, https://www.livius.org/articles/person/cyrus-the-great/.

Lendering, Jona. "Darius II Nothus." Livius.org, 12 October 2020, https://www.livius.org/articles/person/darius-ii-nothus/.

Lendering, Jona. "Darius the Great: Death." Livius.org, 21 April 2020, https://www.livius.org/articles/person/darius-the-great/9-death/.

Lendering, Jona. "Medes." Livius.org, 12 October 2020, https://www.livius.org/articles/people/medes/.

Lendering, Jona. "Mycale (479 BCE)." Livius.org, 10 August 2020, https://www.livius.org/articles/battle/mycale-479-bce/.

Lendering, Jona. "Persepolis, Hall of 100 Columns." Livius.org, 23 April 2020, https://www.livius.org/articles/place/persepolis/persepolis-photos/persepolis-hall-of-100-columns/.

Library of Congress. "Religion - A Thousand Years of the Persian Book | Exhibitions." Library of Congress, 2022, https://www.loc.gov/exhibits/thousand-years-of-the-persian-book/religion.html.

Livius. "The treaties between Persia and Sparta." Livius.org, 15 October 2020, https://www.livius.org/sources/content/thucydides-historian/the-treaties-between-persia-and-sparta/.

Lloyd, H. F. "Iranian art and architecture | ancient art | Britannica." Encyclopedia Britannica, 2018, https://www.britannica.com/art/Iranian-art.

Lohnes, Kate, and Donald Sommerville. "Battle of Thermopylae | Date, Location, and Facts." Encyclopedia Britannica, 12 February 2023, https://www.britannica.com/event/Battle-of-Thermopylae-Greek-history-480-BC.

Lorenzi, Rossella. "Vanished Persian army said found in desert." NBC News, 9 November 2009, https://www.nbcnews.com/id/wbna33791672.

Lumen Learning. "Government and Trade in the Achaemenid Empire | World Civilization." Lumen Learning, 2022, https://courses.lumenlearning.com/suny-hccc-worldcivilization/chapter/government-and-trade-in-the-achaemenid-empire/.

Mark, Joshua J. "The Battle of Pelusium: A Victory Decided by Cats." World History Encyclopedia, 13 June 2017, https://www.worldhistory.org/article/43/the-battle-of-pelusium-a-victory-decided-by-cats/.

Mark, Joshua J., et al. "Ancient Persian Art and Architecture." World History Encyclopedia, 22 January 2020, https://www.worldhistory.org/Ancient_Persian_Art_and_Architecture/.

Mark, Joshua J., et al. "Ancient Persian Government." World History Encyclopedia, 14 November 2019, https://www.worldhistory.org/Persian_Government/.

Mark, Joshua J., et al. "Ancient Persian Warfare." World History Encyclopedia, 25 November 2019, https://www.worldhistory.org/Persian_Warfare/.

Mark, Joshua J., et al. "Artaxerxes II." World History Encyclopedia, 6 March 2020, https://www.worldhistory.org/Artaxerxes_II/.

Mark, Joshua J., et al. "Battle of Thymbra." World History Encyclopedia, 3 November 2022, https://www.worldhistory.org/Battle_of_Thymbra/.

Mark, Joshua J., et al. "Xerxes I." World History Encyclopedia, 2018, https://www.worldhistory.org/Xerxes_I/.

Mark, Joshua J., and Bruce Allardice. "Artaxerxes II." World History Encyclopedia, 6 March 2020, https://www.worldhistory.org/Artaxerxes_II/.

Mark, Joshua J., and Mark Cartwright. "Artaxerxes I." World History Encyclopedia, 3 March 2020, https://www.worldhistory.org/Artaxerxes_I/.

Mark, Joshua J., and Marc De Mieroop. "Behistun Inscription." World History Encyclopedia, 28 November 2019, https://www.worldhistory.org/Behistun_Inscription/.

Mark, Joshua J., and Katarina Maruskinova. "Elam." World History Encyclopedia, 27 August 2020, https://www.worldhistory.org/elam/.

Mark, Joshua J., and Osama Shukir. "Ancient Persian Religion." World History Encyclopedia, 11 December 2019, https://www.worldhistory.org/Ancient_Persian_Religion/.

Mark, Joshua J., and Osama Shukir. "Assyria." World History Encyclopedia, 2018, https://www.worldhistory.org/assyria/.

Matthews, Rupert. "Battle of Gaugamela." Encyclopedia Britannica, 4 January 2023, https://www.britannica.com/event/Battle-of-Gaugamela.

Matthews, Rupert. "Battle of Granicus | Summary | Britannica." Encyclopedia Britannica, 2017, https://www.britannica.com/event/Battle-of-the-Granicus-334BCE.

Maurino, M. "Battle of Opis - The Great Battles of History." Ars Bellica, 2014, http://www.arsbellica.it/pagine/battaglie_in_sintesi/Opis_eng.html. Accessed 16 February 2023.

McCollum, Daniel. "The Persian Empire: Government & Army - Video & Lesson Transcript." Study.com, 28 December 2021, https://study.com/academy/lesson/the-persian-empire-government-army.html.

McGill. "Cyrus the Great." Cyrus the Great, 2023, https://www.cs.mcgill.ca/~rwest/wikispeedia/wpcd/wp/c/Cyrus_the_Great.htm.

The Met Museum. "Relief: figure in a procession." MetMuseum, 2017.

Mildenberg, Leo. "Artaxerxes III Ochus (358 – 338 B.C.). A Note on the Maligned King." Zeitschrift Des Deutschen Palästina-Vereins, vol. 115, no. 2, 1999, pp. 201-227. JSTOR, http://www.jstor.org/stable/27931620.

Military History. "Artaxerxes III." Military Wiki, 2022, https://military-history.fandom.com/wiki/Artaxerxes_III.

Military History. "Battle of Pasargadae | Military Wiki | Fandom." Military Wiki, 2023, https://military-history.fandom.com/wiki/Battle_of_Pasargadae.

Ministry. "Research: The Seventh Year of Artaxerxes I." Ministry Magazine, 1953, https://www.ministrymagazine.org/archive/1953/06/research-the-seventh-year-of-artaxerxes-i.

Munn, JM. "Darius I | Biography, Accomplishments, & Facts | Britannica." Encyclopedia Britannica, 2022, https://www.britannica.com/biography/Darius-I.

Muscarella, O. W. "IRON AGE." Encyclopedia Iranica, 15 December 2006, https://www.iranicaonline.org/articles/iron-age.

Muscato, Christopher. "Persian Empire: Religion & Social Structure | History & Significance - Video & Lesson Transcript." Study.com, 19 April 2022, https://study.com/academy/lesson/the-persian-empire-religion-social-structure.html.

National Geographic Society. "The Peloponnesian War." National Geographic Society, 19 May 2022, https://education.nationalgeographic.org/resource/peloponnesian-war.

New World Encyclopedia. "Cyrus the Great." New World Encyclopedia, 23 June 2022, https://www.newworldencyclopedia.org/entry/Cyrus_the_Great.

Nijssen, Daan, and Larry Hedrick. "Cyrus the Great." World History Encyclopedia, 21 February 2018, https://www.worldhistory.org/Cyrus_the_Great/.

Nijssen, Daan, and Simon Seitz. "Cambyses II." World History Encyclopedia, 18 May 2018, https://www.worldhistory.org/Cambyses_II/.

Nikiforov, Leonid Alekseyevich. "Phraortes | king of Media | Britannica." Encyclopedia Britannica, 4 February 2023, https://www.britannica.com/biography/Phraortes.

"Pasargadae | For UNESCO World Heritage Travellers." World Heritage Site, 2022, https://www.worldheritagesite.org/list/Pasargadae.

Peel, Mike. "Cyrus the Great Biography - The Great King of Persia." Totally History, 2013, https://totallyhistory.com/cyrus-the-great/.

Penner, Jay. "The Story of the Lost Army of Cambyses." Jay Penner Books, 2020, https://jaypenner.com/blog/the-story-of-the-lost-army-of-cambyses/.

The Persians. "Iran, the world's first superpower." The Persians, 2018, https://www.the-persians.co.uk/medes.htm.

The Persians. "IRAN: The world's first superpower." The Persians, 10 August 2022, https://www.the-persians.co.uk/.well-known/captcha/?r=%2FartaxerxesII.1.htm.

The Persians. "IRAN The world's first superpower." The Persians, 10 August 2022, https://www.the-persians.co.uk/.well-known/captcha/?r=%2FartaxerxesII.1.htm.

Persians Are Not Arabs. "Persian Architecture • Evolution of modern art (& famous buildings) | PANA." Persians Are Not Arabs, 2019, https://www.persiansarenotarabs.com/persian-architecture/.

PressBooks. "Persian Art – Art and Visual Culture: Prehistory to Renaissance." PressBooks, 2023, https://pressbooks.bccampus.ca/cavestocathedrals/chapter/persian/.

Przybylek, Stephanie. "The Persian Empire: Art & Architecture - Video & Lesson Transcript." Study.com, 31 December 2022, https://study.com/academy/lesson/the-persian-empire-art-architecture.html.

Public Broadcasting Service. "The Greeks - Sparta and Persia strike up an alliance in 413." PBS, 2023, http://www.pbs.org/empires/thegreeks/keyevents/412_c.html.

Radpour, Ardeshir, and Andre Castaigne. "Achaemenid Military Equipments | CAIS©." The Circle of Ancient Iranian Studies, 2022, https://www.cais-soas.com/CAIS/History/hakhamaneshian/AchaemenidMilitaryEquip.htm.

Rahnamoon, Fariborz. "History of Persian or Parsi Language." Iran Chamber Society, 2023, https://www.iranchamber.com/literature/articles/persian_parsi_language_history.php.

Rattini, Kristin Baird. "Darius I—facts and information." National Geographic, 11 February 2019, https://www.nationalgeographic.com/culture/article/darius-i-persia.

Rattini, Kristin Baird. "Who was Cyrus the Great?" National Geographic, 6 May 2019, https://www.nationalgeographic.com/culture/article/cyrus-the-great.

"The Religion of Xerxes." Xerxes: A Persian Life, by Richard Stoneman, Yale University Press, 2015, pp. 88-108.

Rensselaer Polytechnic Institute. "Cyaxares King of the Medes." Rensselaer Polytechnic Institute, https://homepages.rpi.edu/~holmes/Hobbies/Genealogy2/ps22/ps22_460.htm.

Rezakhani, Khodad. "Medes, the First (Western) Iranian Kingdom - (The Circle of Ancient Iranian Studies - CAIS)©." CAIS @ SOAS, 2023, https://www.cais-soas.com/CAIS/History/madha/medes_first_iranian_kingdom.htm.

Rickard, J. "Artaxerxes III, r.359-338 BC." History of War, 14 September 2016, http://www.historyofwar.org/articles/people_artaxerxes_III.html.

Rickard, J. "Artaxerxes II (r.404-359 BC)." History of War, 14 September 2016, http://www.historyofwar.org/articles/people_artaxerxes_II.html.

Rickard, J. "Darius II, r.423-404 BC." History of War, 6 April 2017, http://www.historyofwar.org/articles/people_darius_II.html.

Rickard, J. "Persian Conquest of Egypt, 525 BC." History of War, 24 March 2015, http://www.historyofwar.org/articles/wars_persian_egypt_525.html.

Ronan, Mark. "The Rise and Fall of Nimrud." History Today, 6 June 2015, https://www.historytoday.com/archive/history-matters/rise-and-fall-nimrud.

Ryder, T. T.B. "Spartan Relations with Persia after the King's Peace: A Strange Story in Diodorus 15.9." The Classical Quarterly, vol. 13, no. 1, 1963, pp. 105-109. JSTOR, https://www.jstor.org/stable/637943.

Sancisi-Weerdenburg, Heleen. "DARIUS iv. Darius II – Encyclopedia Iranica." Encyclopedia Iranica, 1994, https://iranicaonline.org/articles/darius-iv.

Savoia, Gianpaolo. "The Median Dynastic Empire; The Coming of the Aryans & Creation of the First Iranian Dynastic Empire | CAIS©." CAIS @ SOAS, 2004, https://www.cais-soas.com/CAIS/History/madha/medes.htm.

Schmitt, R. "ARTAXERXES II – Encyclopedia Iranica." Encyclopedia Iranica, 1986, https://www.iranicaonline.org/articles/artaxerxes-ii-achaemenid-king.

Schmitt, R. "ARTAXERXES III – Encyclopedia Iranica." Encyclopedia Iranica, 1986, https://www.iranicaonline.org/articles/artaxerxes-iii-throne-name-of-ochus-gk.

Schmitt, R. "ASTYAGES – Encyclopedia Iranica." Encyclopedia Iranica, 1987, https://iranicaonline.org/articles/astyages-the-last-median-king.

Schmitt, Rüdiger. "DEIOCES." Encyclopedia Iranica, 17 January 2022, https://www.iranicaonline.org/articles/deioces.

Scmitt, R. "ASTYAGES – Encyclopedia Iranica." Encyclopedia Iranica, 2011, https://iranicaonline.org/articles/astyages-the-last-median-king.

Seymour, Michael. "The Later Legacy of Cyrus the Great." The Metropolitan Museum of Art, 24 June 2013, https://www.metmuseum.org/blogs/now-at-the-met/features/2013/cyrus-the-great.

Shahbazi, A. S. "History of Iran: Achaemenid Army." Iran Chamber Society, 2023, https://www.iranchamber.com/history/achaemenids/achaemenid_army.php.

Shannahan, John. "Artaxerxes II." Macquarie University, 28 March 2022, https://figshare.mq.edu.au/articles/thesis/Artaxerxes_II/19443077/1.

Shapur Shahbazi, A. "DARIUS iii. Darius I the Great – Encyclopedia Iranica." Encyclopedia Iranica, 1994, https://iranicaonline.org/articles/darius-iii.

Smith, Matthew. "Artaxerxes I | king of Persia | Britannica." Encyclopedia Britannica, 20 January 2023, https://www.britannica.com/biography/Artaxerxes-I.

Smith, Matthew. "Astyages | king of Media | Britannica." Encyclopedia Britannica, 20 January 2023, https://www.britannica.com/biography/Astyages.

Smith, Matthew. "Cambyses II | king of Persia | Britannica." Encyclopedia Britannica, 20 January 2023, https://www.britannica.com/biography/Cambyses-II.

Smith, Matthew. "Croesus | king of Lydia | Britannica." Encyclopedia Britannica, 20 January 2023, https://www.britannica.com/biography/Croesus.

Smith, Matthew. "Cyaxares | king of Media | Britannica." Encyclopedia Britannica, 20 January 2023, https://www.britannica.com/biography/Cyaxares.

Smith, Matthew. "Darius II Ochus | king of Persia | Britannica." Encyclopedia Britannica, 20 January 2023, https://www.britannica.com/biography/Darius-II-Ochus.

Smith, Scott, and Adrienne Mayor. "Scythian Warfare." World History Encyclopedia, 21 February 2022, https://www.worldhistory.org/Scythian_Warfare/.

Sommerville, Donald. "Battle of Plataea | Summary | Britannica." Encyclopedia Britannica, 2017, https://www.britannica.com/event/Battle-of-Plataea.

Stewart, M. "People, Places, & Things: Medes." Greek Mythology: From the Iliad to the Fall of the Last Tyrant, 2023, http://messagenetcommresearch.com/myths/ppt/Medes_1.html.

Sullivan, Richard E. "Artaxerxes III | king of Persia | Britannica." Encyclopedia Britannica, 31 January 2023, https://www.britannica.com/biography/Artaxerxes-III.

Sullivan, Richard E. "Artaxerxes II | king of Persia | Britannica." Encyclopedia Britannica, 31 January 2023, https://www.britannica.com/biography/Artaxerxes-II.

TAPPersia. "A History of Persian Art and Architecture." TAP Persia, 12 November 2022, https://www.tappersia.com/a-history-of-persian-art-and-architecture/.

"10. The Mythical Origins of the Medes and the Persians." Myth, Truth, and Narrative in Herodotus, edited by Emily Baragwanath and Mathieu de Bakker, OUP Oxford, 2012.

ThenAgain. "Darius III: 336-330 BC." thenagain.info, 2022, http://www.thenagain.info/WebChron/MiddleEast/DariusIII.html.

Time Graphics. "Artaxerxes I (Longimanus) King of Persia 475 - 423 B.C.E. (Nov 3, 475 BC – Feb 19, 423 BC) (Timeline)." Time Graphics, 2018, https://time.graphics/period/219447.

TimeMaps. "The Persian Empire: Government and State in Ancient Persia." TimeMaps, 2022, https://timemaps.com/encyclopedia/persian-empire-state/.

Truitt, Benjamin. "King Cyrus the Great: Biography & Accomplishments - Video & Lesson Transcript." Study.com, 14 September 2021, https://study.com/academy/lesson/cyrus-the-great-facts-accomplishments-quiz.html.

Twinkl. "What is Persian Religion? - Answered." Twinkl, 2022, https://www.twinkl.com.pk/teaching-wiki/persian-religion.

UC Santa Barbara. "History of Persian Language." Persian Languages and Literature at UCSB, 2017, https://persian.religion.ucsb.edu/home/history-of-persian/.

U*X*L Encyclopedia of World Mythology. "Persian Mythology." Encyclopedia.com, 2023, https://www.encyclopedia.com/history/encyclopedias-almanacs-transcripts-and-maps/persian-mythology.

Walvoord, John F. "6. The Medes and The Persians." Bible.org, 1 January 2008, https://bible.org/seriespage/6-medes-and-persians.

Wasson, Donald L., and Ruth Sheppard. "Battle of the Granicus." World History Encyclopedia, 20 December 2011, https://www.worldhistory.org/Battle_of_the_Granicus/.

Waterfield, Robin. "Darius the Great Conquers the Indus Valley." WikiSummaries, 11 November 2022, https://wikisummaries.org/darius-the-great-conquers-the-indus-valley/.

Waters, Matt, and Simeon Netchev. "Cyrus the Great's Conquests." World History Encyclopedia, 15 August 2022, https://www.worldhistory.org/article/2022/cyrus-the-greats-conquests/.

Waters, Matt, and Simeon Netchev. "Cyrus the Great's Conquests." World History Encyclopedia, 15 August 2022, https://www.worldhistory.org/article/2022/cyrus-the-greats-conquests/.

Wijnsma, Uzume Z. "And in the fourth year Egypt rebelled…" The Chronology of and Sources for Egypt's Second Revolt (ca. 487–484 BC." Journal of Ancient History, vol. 7, no. 1, 2016, pp. 32-61. https://doi.org/10.1515/jah-2018-0023.

World History Edu. "Cambyses II of Persia: History, Reign, Accomplishments, & Legacy." World History Edu, 15 November 2022, https://www.worldhistoryedu.com/cambyses-ii-of-persia-history-reign-accomplishments-legacy/.

World History Encyclopedia. "Persia Timeline." World History Encyclopedia, 2021, https://www.worldhistory.org/timeline/Persia/.

World History Encyclopedia. "Xerxes I Timeline." World History Encyclopedia, 2021, https://www.worldhistory.org/timeline/Xerxes_I/.

Young, T. C., and A. D.H. Bivar. "Ancient Iran | History, Map, Cities, Religion, Art, Language, & Facts." Encyclopedia Britannica, 2022, https://www.britannica.com/place/ancient-Iran.

Young, Jr, T. C. The Cambridge Ancient History. vol. 4, Cambridge University Press, 1988, https://doi.org/10.1017/CHOL9780521228046.002.

The Project Gutenberg eBook of Cyrus the Great, Makers Of History, by Jacob Abbott.

"Who was Cyrus the Great? - Culture." 06 May. 2019, https://www.nationalgeographic.com/culture/article/cyrus-the-great.

"Cyrus the Great | Biography & Facts | Britannica." 20 Oct. 2022, https://www.britannica.com/biography/Cyrus-the-Great.

"Cyrus the Great — M. Rahim Shayegan | Harvard University Press." 02 Apr. 2019, https://www.hup.harvard.edu/catalog.php?isbn=9780674987388.

"Cyrus The Great." https://cyrusthegreat.net/index.html.

"HOME | Cyrus the Great." https://www.cyrusthegreatstory.com/.

"History of Iran: Cyropaedia of Xenophon; The Life of Cyrus the Great." 19 Oct. 2022, https://www.iranchamber.com/history/xenophon/cyropaedia_xenophon_book1.php.

"Xenophon's Cyrus the Great: the arts of leadership and war." 25 Jan. 2022, https://archive.org/details/xenophonscyrusgr0000xeno.

"Leadership and 'The Art of War' - Ivey Business School." 03 Mar. 2022, https://www.ivey.uwo.ca/leadership/for-leaders/leadership-blogs/2022/03/leadership-and-the-art-of-war/.

"CYRUS ACCORDING TO HERODOTUS – Encyclopedia Iranica." 15 Dec. 2003, https://www.iranicaonline.org/articles/herodotus-iv.

"Herodotus on Cyrus' capture of Babylon - Livius." https://www.livius.org/sources/content/herodotus/cyrus-takes-babylon/.

"Herodotus and Xenophon. - Bible Hub." https://biblehub.com/library/abbott/cyrus_the_great/chapter_i_herodotus_and_xenophon.htm.

"Histories | Book 1, The Rise of Cyrus the Great | Summary." https://www.coursehero.com/lit/Histories/book-1-the-rise-of-cyrus-the-great-summary/.

"HERODOTUS BOOK 1: CYRUS THE GREAT AND RISE OF PERSIA." http://www.christophergennari.com/uploads/2/3/9/9/2399857/herodotus_on_early_cyrus.pdf.

"Herodotus, bk 1, logos 2 - Livius."
https://www.livius.org/sources/about/herodotus/herodotos-bk-1-logos-2/.

"Herodotus (5) - Livius." 16 Apr. 2020,
https://www.livius.org/articles/person/herodotus/herodotus-5/.

"THE EKTHESIS OF CYRUS THE GREAT: A CASE STUDY OF HEROICITY VERSUS." 27 Feb. 2017,
https://www.cambridge.org/core/journals/cambridge-classical-journal/article/ekthesis-of-cyrus-the-great-a-case-study-of-heroicity-versus-bastardy-in-classical-athens/9809094BB9FAC1DC67F7CB32C3D02890.

"Cyrus the Great - Livius." 12 Oct. 2020,
https://www.livius.org/articles/person/cyrus-the-great/.

"Herodotus: The defeat of the Persians under Cyrus the Great by Queen."
https://www.cais-soas.com/CAIS/History/hakhamaneshian/herod_tomyr.htm.

"Cyrus the Great's Accomplishments & Major Achievements - Totally History."
https://totallyhistory.com/cyrus-the-greats-accomplishments/.

"CYROPAEDIA – Encyclopedia Iranica."
https://iranicaonline.org/articles/cyropaedia-gr.

Cyrus the Great and Religious Tolerance,
https://tolerance.tavaana.org/en/content/cyrus-great-and-religious-tolerance.

"Cyropaedia | work by Xenophon | Britannica."
https://www.britannica.com/topic/Cyropaedia.

"Cyropaedia, by Xenophon - Project Gutenberg." 18 Jul. 2009,
https://gutenberg.org/files/2085/2085-h/2085-h.htm.

"Cyropaedia: Xenophon: Free Download, Borrow, and Streaming: Internet."
https://archive.org/details/cyropaediavolum00millgoog.

"Cyropaedia (The Education of Cyrus) Background | GradeSaver."
https://www.gradesaver.com/cyropaedia-the-education-of-cyrus.

"Cyrus' Paradise | The World's First Online Collaborative Commentary."
http://cyropaedia.online/.

"Cyropaedia Summary - eNotes.com." 06 May. 2015,
https://www.enotes.com/topics/cyropaedia.

"Achaemenid Empire - Wikipedia."
https://en.wikipedia.org/wiki/Achaemenid_Empire.

"Achaemenid Empire Timeline - World History Encyclopedia."
https://www.worldhistory.org/timeline/Achaemenid_Empire/.

"The Achaemenid Empire | World Civilization - Lumen Learning."
https://courses.lumenlearning.com/suny-hccc-worldcivilization/chapter/the-achaemenid-empire/.

"History of Iran: Achaemenid Empire - Iran Chamber." https://www.iranchamber.com/history/achaemenids/achaemenids.php."The Achaemenid Persian Empire (550–330 B.C.) - The Met's Heilbrunn." https://www.metmuseum.org/toah/hd/acha/hd_acha.htm.

"Achaemenid Empire - World History Maps." https://www.worldhistorymaps.info/civilizations/achaemenid-empire/.

"Persian Empire | History of the Achaemenid Persian Empire." https://persianempire.org/.

"Achaemenid Empire | Ancient Persia Wiki | Fandom." https://ancientpersia.fandom.com/wiki/Achaemenid_Empire.

"Persian Empire | National Geographic Society." 20 May. 2022, https://education.nationalgeographic.org/resource/persian-empire/.

"The Culture, People & Daily Life of Ancient Persia - Study.com." 13 Mar. 2022, https://study.com/learn/lesson/ancient-persia-clothing-people-daily-life.html.

"Ancient Persian Culture - World History Encyclopedia." 27 Nov. 2019, https://www.worldhistory.org/Ancient_Persian_Culture/.

"Ancient Persia - World History Encyclopedia." 12 Nov. 2019, https://www.worldhistory.org/Persia/.

"Persian Empire - HISTORY." 25 Jan. 2018, https://www.history.com/topics/ancient-middle-east/persian-empire.

"Ancient Persia: 12 Major Events - World History Edu." 02 Nov. 2021, https://www.worldhistoryedu.com/ancient-persia-12-major-events/.

"Who were the ancient Persians? | Live Science." 02 Mar. 2022, https://www.livescience.com/who-were-the-persians.

"Ancient Persia: The Achaemenid Empire to the History of Iran." 02 Feb. 2019, https://historycooperative.org/history-of-iran/.

"42 Astounding Facts About Life in Ancient Persia - Factinate." https://www.factinate.com/things/42-astounding-facts-life-ancient-persia/.

"Persians - Wikipedia." https://en.wikipedia.org/wiki/Persians.

"Persia: Ancient Iran and the Classical World - Getty Museum." https://www.getty.edu/art/exhibitions/persia/explore.html.

"Persian Empire | National Geographic Society." 20 May. 2022, https://www.nationalgeographic.org/encyclopedia/persian-empire/.

"Ancient Iran | History, Map, Cities, Religion, Art, Language, & Facts." https://www.britannica.com/place/ancient-Iran.

"Ancient Persia - ancient.com." https://ancient.com/category/articles/ancient-countries/ancient-persia/.

"Satrap - Wikipedia." https://en.wikipedia.org/wiki/Satrap.

"Satrap Definition & Meaning - Merriam-Webster." https://www.merriam-webster.com/dictionary/satrap.

"satrap | Persian provincial governor | Britannica." https://www.britannica.com/topic/satrap.

"Satrap - Encyclopedia of The Bible - Bible Gateway." https://www.biblegateway.com/resources/encyclopedia-of-the-bible/Satrap.

"Satrap | Encyclopedia.com." https://www.encyclopedia.com/history/asia-and-africa/ancient-history-middle-east/satrap.

"Who were the satraps in the book of Daniel? | GotQuestions.org." 04 Jan. 2022, https://www.gotquestions.org/satraps-Daniel.html.

"Satrap — Watchtower ONLINE LIBRARY - JW.ORG." https://wol.jw.org/en/wol/d/r1/lp-e/1200003846.

"Twelve Great Women of Ancient Persia - World History Encyclopedia." 31 Jan. 2020, https://www.worldhistory.org/article/1493/twelve-great-women-of-ancient-persia/.

"Women in Ancient Persia - World History Encyclopedia." 30 Jan. 2020, https://www.worldhistory.org/article/1492/women-in-ancient-persia/.

"Women in Ancient Persia - World History Encyclopedia." 30 Jan. 2020, https://www.worldhistory.org/article/1492/women-in-ancient-persia/.

"Women Warriors: The Ancient Female Fighters That Ruled Persia." 04 Aug. 2020, https://historythings.com/women-warriors-ancient-female-fighters-ruled-persia/.

"What Life Was Like for Women in Ancient Persia - Grunge.com." 19 Jul. 2020, https://www.grunge.com/227986/what-life-was-like-for-women-in-ancient-persia/.

"Women in Ancient Persia - Brewminate: A Bold Blend of News and Ideas." 02 Feb. 2020, https://brewminate.com/women-in-ancient-persia/.

"PERSIA WOMEN WARRIORS - ROOTSHUNT." https://rootshunt.com/aryans/bharatpersiawomenwarriors/persiawomenwarriors/persiawomenwarriors.htm.

"Warrior Women of the Ancient World - ThoughtCo." 11 Jul. 2019, https://www.thoughtco.com/ancient-women-warriors-121482.

"MASSAGETAE – Encyclopedia Iranica." https://www.iranicaonline.org/articles/massagetae.

"Massagetae Tribe And Its Queen Tomyris." 18 Nov. 2019, https://www.ancientpages.com/2019/11/18/massagetae-warlike-and-brave-nomadic-tribe-of-central-asia/.

"The Massagetae (Tomyris) - Civilization V Customisation Wiki." 27 Feb. 2015, https://civilization-v-customisation.fandom.com/wiki/The_Massagetae_(Tomyris).

"Tomyris: The cut-throat warrior queen of Massagetae."

"Massagetae — Google Arts & Culture."

"Achaemenid Persian Empire | Massagetae - Arcadian Venture LLC." https://persianempire.org/cultures/massagetae.

"Massagetes - Livius." https://www.livius.org/articles/people/massagetes/.

The Legend of Tomiris (2019). Movie.

"Tomyris, The Female Warrior and Ruler Who May Have Killed Cyrus the Great." 26 Feb. 2016, https://www.ancient-origins.net/history-famous-people/tomyris-female-warrior-and-ruler-who-may-have-killed-cyrus-great-005423.

"Tomyris - Wikipedia." https://en.wikipedia.org/wiki/Tomyris.

"Civilization VI: Leader Spotlight - Tomyris - YouTube." https://www.youtube.com/watch?v=zCGNMBi0O3c.

"Cyrus the Great and Persian control of the Middle East." 16 Jan. 2020, https://www.deseret.com/2020/1/16/21065608/daniel-peterson-cyrus-the-great-and-persian-control-of-the-middle-east.

"Cyrus the Great Day: Between Iranian and Islamic Identities." 28 Nov. 2017, https://dayan.org/content/cyrus-great-day-between-iranian-and-islamic-identities.

"Cyrus the Great Captures Babylon | History on This Day." 16 Dec. 2019, https://historyonthisday.com/events/middle-east/cyrus-the-great-captures-babylon/.

"Iranians arrested after celebrating ancient Persian king Cyrus the Great." 31 Oct. 2016, https://www.jpost.com/Middle-East/Iranians-arrested-after-celebrating-ancient-Persian-king-Cyrus-the-Great-471309.

"Pasargadae - Wikipedia." https://en.wikipedia.org/wiki/Pasargadae"

Darius the Great - Wikipedia." https://en.wikipedia.org/wiki/Darius_the_Great.

"Darius the Great - Wikipedia." https://en.wikipedia.org/wiki/Darius_the_Great.

"Darius I of Persia – Amazing Bible Timeline with World History." 25 Nov. 2012, https://amazingbibletimeline.com/blog/darius-i-of-persia/.

org/wiki/Pasargadae.

"Pasargadae - UNESCO World Heritage Centre." https://whc.unesco.org/en/list/1106.

"PASARGADAE - Encyclopedia Iranica." https://www.iranicaonline.org/articles/pasargadae.

"Pasargadae | ancient city, Iran | Britannica." https://www.britannica.com/place/Pasargadae-ancient-city-Iran.

"Pasargadae - History and Facts | History Hit." 18 Jun. 2021, https://www.historyhit.com/locations/pasargadae/.

"Home [https://www.pasargadae.info/fa/]." https://www.pasargadae.info/en/.

"Pasargadae - Amazing Facts, History, Site Map - Iran Safar." 13 Nov. 2021, https://www.iransafar.co/pasargadae-ultimate-guide/.

"Pasargadae - BiblePlaces.com." https://www.bibleplaces.com/pasargadae/.

"Darius (c.-550 - -486) - Genealogy - geni family tree." 18 Jun. 2004, https://www.geni.com/people/Darius-I-the-Great-King-of-Persia/6000000006131567298.

"Pasargadae - World Archaeology." 20 Sept. 2019, https://www.world-archaeology.com/features/pasargadae/.

"Pasargadae | Visit Iran." https://www.visitiran.ir/attraction/pasargadae.

"Pasargadae - UNESCO World Heritage Site | Iran Destination | Iran Tour." https://www.irandestination.com/pasargadae/.

"Pasargadae, Fars Province | Ultimate Guide | Photos - Iran Tourismer." 01 May. 2019, https://irantourismer.com/pasargadae-tomb-of-cyrus/.

"Pasargadae | The Tomb of Cyrus, the Great | Shiraz Attraction - Apochi." https://apochi.com/attractions/shiraz/pasargadae/.

"Pasargadae – Welcome to Iran." https://welcometoiran.com/pasargadae/.

"Cyrus Cylinder - Livius." 12 Oct. 2020, https://www.livius.org/sources/content/cyrus-cylinder/.

"Cyrus Cylinder - Wikipedia." https://en.wikipedia.org/wiki/Cyrus_Cylinder.

"The Cyrus Cylinder - World History Encyclopedia." 18 Jan. 2012, https://www.worldhistory.org/article/166/the-cyrus-cylinder/.

"10 Facts About the Cyrus Cylinder | Asia Society." https://asiasociety.org/northern-california/10-facts-about-cyrus-cylinder.

"What is the Cyrus Cylinder and why does it matter? – BibleMesh." 26 Jul. 2019, https://biblemesh.com/blog/what-is-the-cyrus-cylinder-and-why-does-it-matter/.

"What is the Cyrus Cylinder? - CYRUS CYLINDER FOR PEACE & HUMAN RIGHTS." 20 Apr. 2021, https://cyruscylinderforpeace.org/what-is-the-cyrus-cylinder/.

"CYRUS CYLINDER FOR PEACE & HUMAN RIGHTS." https://cyruscylinderforpeace.org/.

"Cyrus Cylinder - Bible History." https://bible-history.com/archaeology/cyrus-cylinder.

"cylinder | British Museum." https://www.britishmuseum.org/collection/object/W_1880-0617-1941.

"The Cyrus Cylinder - Tyndale House." https://academic.tyndalehouse.com/explore/articles/the-cyrus-cylinder/.

"The Cyrus Cylinder - Tyndale House." https://tyndalehouse.com/explore/articles/the-cyrus-cylinder/.

"History of Iran: Cyrus the Great - Iran Chamber."
https://www.iranchamber.com/history/cyrus/cyrus.php.

"History of Iran: The Cyrus the Great Cylinder - Iran Chamber." 22 Oct. 2022, https://www.iranchamber.com/history/cyrus/cyrus_charter.php.

"History of Iran: Cyropaedia of Xenophon, The Life of Cyrus the Great." https://mail.iranchamber.com/history/xenophon/cyropaedia_xenophon_book2.php.

"Cyrus the Great - The History Files."
https://www.historyfiles.co.uk/FeaturesMiddEast/EasternPersiaKings.htm.

"The Importance of Cyrus the Great in Iranian History - Destination Iran." 04 Mar. 2015, https://www.destinationiran.com/importance-of-cyrus-the-great-in-iranian-history.htm.

"History of Iran: Cyrus the Great: The decree of return for the Jews."
https://www.iranchamber.com/history/cyrus/cyrus_decree_jews.php.

"Iran Regime's Panic and Fear From the Ceremony of Cyrus the Great." 28 Oct. 2017, https://www.ncr-iran.org/en/news/society/iran-regime-s-panic-and-fear-from-the-ceremony-of-cyrus-the-great/.

"The Persian Empire: Culture and Society | TimeMaps."
https://www.timemaps.com/encyclopedia/persian-empire-culture-society/.

"Persepolis - Wikipedia." https://en.wikipedia.org/wiki/Persepolis.

"Persepolis - UNESCO World Heritage Centre."
https://whc.unesco.org/en/list/114.

"PERSEPOLIS – Encyclopedia Iranica."
https://www.iranicaonline.org/articles/persepolis.

"The Conquest of Babylon. - Bible Hub."
https://biblehub.com/library/abbott/cyrus_the_great/chapter_viii_the_conquest_of.htm.

"Fall of Babylon - Wikipedia." https://en.wikipedia.org/wiki/Fall_of_Babylon.

"How Cyrus Conquered Babylon: God's Kingdom Ministries." 01 Jun. 2015, https://godskingdom.org/studies/ffi-newsletter/2015/how-cyrus-conquered-babylon.

"Babylonian captivity - Wikipedia."
https://en.wikipedia.org/wiki/Babylonian_captivity.

"History of Babylon in the Bible - Learn Religions." 04 Dec. 2019, https://www.learnreligions.com/history-of-babylon-3867031.

"The Bible Journey | Assyria is conquered by the Babylonians." 26 Jul. 2015, https://www.thebiblejourney.org/biblejourney2/33-judah-after-the-fall-of-israel/assyria-is-conquered-by-the-babylonians/.

"Babylonia and the Conquest of Judah." 13 Apr. 2021, https://www.churchofjesuschrist.org/study/manual/old-testament-student-manual-kings-malachi/enrichment-g?lang=eng.

"Nabonidus - Wikipedia." https://en.wikipedia.org/wiki/Nabonidus.

"Archaeologists Find Inscribed Stone Honoring Babylonian King Nabonidus." 22 Jul. 2021, https://www.ancient-origins.net/news-history-archaeology/nabonidus-0015607.

"The Last King of Babylon - Archaeology Magazine." https://www.archaeology.org/issues/458-2203/features/10334-babylon-nabonidus-last-king.

"NABONIDUS, BELSHAZZAR, AND THE BOOK OF DANIEL: AN UPDATE." https://www.biblia.work/sermons/nabonidusbelshazzar-and-the-book-of-daniel-an-update/.

"The Babylonian King Nabonidus - World History Encyclopedia." 22 Mar. 2018, https://www.worldhistory.org/image/8412/the-babylonian-king-nabonidus/.

"Nabonidus Cylinder, Text | Mesopotamian Gods & Kings." 01 May. 2018, http://www.mesopotamiangods.com/nabonidus-cylinder-text/.

"Cambyses II | king of Persia | Britannica." https://www.britannica.com/biography/Cambyses-II.

"Cambyses II - Wikipedia." https://en.wikipedia.org/wiki/Cambyses_II.

"Cambyses - Encyclopedia of The Bible - Bible Gateway." https://www.biblegateway.com/resources/encyclopedia-of-the-bible/Cambyses.

"The Story of the Lost Army of Cambyses - Jay Penner." 21 Oct. 2019, https://www.jaypenner.com/blog/the-story-of-the-lost-army-of-cambyses.

"Lost Army of Cambyses - Wikipedia." https://en.wikipedia.org/wiki/Lost_Army_of_Cambyses.

"Mysterious Death Of Cambyses II - Ancient Pages." 21 Apr. 2021, https://www.ancientpages.com/2021/04/21/mysterious-death-of-cambyses-ii-natural-suicide-or-assassination-by-darius-i-the-great/.

"Cambyses II - Livius." https://www.livius.org/articles/person/cambyses-ii/.

"CAMBYSES – Encyclopedia Iranica." 15 Dec. 1990, https://www.iranicaonline.org/articles/cambyses-opers.

"Persian Emperors List & Timeline | Cyrus, Cambyses II & Darius - Study.com." 11 Apr. 2022, https://study.com/academy/lesson/kings-of-the-persian-empire-cyrus-cambyses-ii-darius-i.html.

"Ezra on Cyrus - Livius." https://www.livius.org/sources/content/bible/ezra-on-cyrus/.

"Ezra 1 NIV - Cyrus Helps the Exiles to Return - Bible Gateway." https://www.biblegateway.com/passage/?search=Ezra%201&version=NIV.

"Ezra 1:1-11 – Cyrus's Decree - Enter the Bible." https://enterthebible.org/passage/ezra-11-11-cyruss-decree.

"Ezra in the Bible - Who Was He and What Did He Do - Crosswalk.com." 21 Sept. 2021, https://www.crosswalk.com/faith/bible-study/important-things-we-can-learn-from-the-book-of-ezra.html.

"Ezra 1 - In the first year of Cyrus king of Persia..." https://www.esv.org/Ezra+1/.

"Enduring Word Bible Commentary Ezra Chapter 1." https://enduringword.com/bible-commentary/ezra-1/.

"Daniel and King Cyrus - Biblical Hermeneutics Stack Exchange." 30 Sept. 2021, https://hermeneutics.stackexchange.com/questions/69453/daniel-and-king-cyrus.

"Who was Cyrus in the Bible? | GotQuestions.org." 04 Jan. 2022, https://www.gotquestions.org/Cyrus-Bible.html.

"Daniel (biblical figure) - Wikipedia." https://en.wikipedia.org/wiki/Daniel_(biblical_figure).

"Daniel 10:1 In the third year of Cyrus king of Persia..." https://biblehub.com/daniel/10-1.htm.

"Daniel and Darius – Israel My Glory." https://israelmyglory.org/article/daniel-and-darius/.

"Daniel and Cyrus Before the Idol Bel - Google Arts & Culture." https://artsandculture.google.com/asset/daniel-and-cyrus-before-the-idol-bel-rembrandt-harmensz-van-rijn/bQEZf5tgp8ZerQ?hl=en.